The Wolfh

CW00687741

The Wolfhounds of Irish–American Nationalism

A History of Clan na Gael, 1867–Present

Seán Creagh

Peter Lang

Oxford · Bern · Berlin · Bruxelles · New York · Wien

Bibliographic information published by Die Deutsche Nationalbibliothek
Die Deutsche Nationalbibliothek lists this publication in the Deutsche
Nationalbibliografie; detailed bibliographic data is available on the Internet at
http://dnb.d-nb.de.

A catalogue record for this book is available from the British Library.

A CIP catalog record for this book has been applied for at the Library of Congress.

Cover design by Brian Melville for Peter Lang.

ISBN   978-1-80079-996-7 (print)
ISBN   978-1-80374-028-7 (ePDF)
ISBN   978-1-80374-029-4 (ePub)

© Peter Lang Group AG 2023

Published by Peter Lang Ltd, International Academic Publishers,
Oxford, United Kingdom
oxford@peterlang.com, www.peterlang.com

Seán Creagh has asserted his right under the Copyright, Designs and Patents Act, 1988,
to be identified as Author of this Work.

This publication has been peer reviewed.

I dedicate this book to my wife Karry, my daughter Katie and to my lifelong friend and mentor, Sean Oliver.

Contents

Figures

Introduction

While on a fundraising tour of the United States in 1878 Michael Davitt, the leading figure of the Land League movement in Ireland, described the Irish American nationalist community of the time as "the avenging wolfhounds of Irish nationalism". The "avenging wolfhounds" that Davitt was referring to was the dominant Irish nationalist organization in the U.S. during this time period, Clan na Gael. The image of an Irish hunting dog stalking a larger prey over long distances and periods of time was certainly a fitting image for the movement.

Clan na Gael were the inheritors of the Fenian revolutionary tradition which collapsed in the aftermath of the failed military raids into Canada in the early 1870s. From the 1870s up until the early 1920s Clan na Gael evolved into not only the most successful Irish American revolutionary organization ever but also one of the most successful transatlantic revolutionary movements in history. Not only was the Clan instrumental in instigating the 1916 Easter Rising in Dublin but was also vital in providing the financial lifeblood and international propaganda necessary for the Irish revolution from 1919–21. Clan na Gael's role in inspiring revolution in Ireland also inspired and motivated other social and political movements in the U.S. as well as foreign movements outside of America which has also been a long-neglected area of study.

The Clan and its sister organization in Ireland, the Irish Republican Brotherhood, proved to be a very lopsided relationship for most of its history up until 1916. While the IRB in Ireland was largely ineffective and borderline irrelevant pre-1916, it was Clan na Gael that kept Irish Republican ideology as part of the broader political discussion in Ireland when Home Rule looked like it would completely dominate. The Clan's role as the dominant partner in the Republican movement was highlighted in the New Departure when against the wishes of the IRB the Clan joined in political alliance with the Home Rule Party and Land League to achieve short term political goals that fell short of full independence. The IRB's

very existence often relied on the financial support from the Clan as well
as political pressure levied to be more pro- active.

The successful revolutionary model provided by Clan na Gael did not
go unnoticed by those outside of Irish American circles. The early American
Zionist movement, Indian nationalists in the U.S. and African American
nationalists were among the most prominent groups to have taken notice
of and been deeply influenced by Clan na Gael revolutionary activities.
Domestic social movements such as the Suffragettes were also quick to see
the successful model provided by Clan na Gael. The Clan's organizational
structure, fundraising abilities and forms of protest proved a model which
a number of transatlantic revolutionary and domestic social movements
aspired to and copied elements of.

In the end Clan na Gael was to become a victim of its own success.
After failed attempts by the Home Rule movement in Ireland to take over
the financial wing of Clan na Gael it would be the reborn and revitalized
Republican movement in Ireland that the Clan played such a massive role
in creating in the first place that would prove its eventual demise. The new
movement in Ireland, under the leadership of Eamon De Valera, saw as
an absolute necessity to control the financial aspects of the revolutionary
struggle that would become known as the Irish War of Independence. The
major split that came about in 1920 was one from which the Clan never fully
recovered. The last meaningful contribution made by the Clan in order
to expel the British from the north of Ireland was the development of
what became known as the S-plan which was the orchestration of an IRA
bombing campaign in Britain from 1939-40 which ended in futile failure.
Despite the long decline experienced after the failed bombing campaign in
Britain the Clan did play an important role in the early formation and success of the newly formed Provisional IRA after the split in the Republican
movement in Ireland in 1969.

The Clan would linger on to the present day as a mere rump of an
organization becoming increasingly ineffective as the result of internal
disagreement and splits over the years. It's disconnection from political
events and reality in Ireland left the Clan as one of the most militant and
uncompromising Irish American organizations. The very fact the Clan even
exists today is a remarkable statement on its ability to endure numerous

setbacks and splits over many decades. With the advent of the Good Friday Agreement and the IRA ceasefire in 1998 Clan na Gael has gravitated more toward militant splinter groups which in turn have found themselves marginalized in a war weary Irish society. The future looks bleak indeed for any increase in the political prospects for the Clan. With the Brexit debacle a united Ireland seems closer than ever through peaceful constitutional means. The long history of violent revolutionary Irish American Republicanism seems overwhelmingly to have entered its final phase.

In terms of Irish History Clan na Gael is the least studied of the Irish revolutionary organizations and its role in the struggle for Irish independence the most underappreciated. In many studies the Clan is little more than a footnote, being dismissed merely as a fundraising arm of the Irish Republican movement and having little or no voice or political contribution in the overall struggle. While books have been written that cover certain time periods in the Clan's history such as "War in the Shadows" by Shane Kenna, "Blood Runs Green" by Gillian O'Brien and "Transatlantic Defiance" by Gavin Wilke there has been no single volume detailing the history of the movement in its entirety. Only by looking at the entire history of the Clan can one truly understand and appreciate its contribution not just to Irish nationalism but to international transatlantic nationalism and global anti-imperialism more broadly.

There can also be an argument made as to an academic bias in Ireland against the study and recognition of groups like Clan na Gael in the overall struggle for Irish independence. This may be the result of a negative view of Irish American nationalism as being of an overly romanticized and therefore a shallower version of its Irish counterpart. The geographic distance of Clan na Gael was also viewed as representing a deep ideological and political chasm which meant that the movement never had to deal with the realities in Ireland of political repression and the deeply complicated problem of Northern Ireland loyalism. The fact that so much of the Clan's funding and political pressure went toward pushing for armed conflict and violence in Ireland without itself having to face the harsh reality and consequences of its actions may also have left a bitter taste for many in Ireland who had to face the full consequences and who may have been of an anti-Republican position or at least seeing political violence as deeply problematic. Historical revisionism by such academics and writers as Conor Cruise O'Brien and Ruth Dudley Edwards, who were well known for their hostility toward militant Irish Republicanism, would have viewed Irish American nationalism as little more than a financial enabler of political violence and not actually view Clan na Gael as a wing of the broader Republican movement worth much more academic attention and which contained many unique features and struggles not seen with its counterparts in Ireland.

This academic bias is not always of an overt or even conscious in nature. In Tim Pat Coogan's definitive history of the Irish Republican Army he discusses Clan na Gael in less than 30 pages out of a total of 669. In Robert Kee's acclaimed "The Green Flag – A History of Irish Nationalism" Clan na Gael is discussed in an even more diminished role with just 5 pages dedicated to the organization out of a total of 752. Such a lack of attention in these cases is more to do with an underappreciation of the role of Irish American nationalism, particularly in the aftermath of the collapse of the Fenian movement in late 1860s.

Revolutionary Origins

When looking for a starting point to the centuries long Anglo-Irish conflict there is perhaps no better starting point than the year 1169. In this year the deposed king of Leinster, Diarmait mac Murchada, invited an Anglo-Norman army under the leadership of Richard "Strongbow" de Clare to help him regain his throne. In return mac Murchada offered his daughter in marriage and his throne after his death. The Norman invasion was at first rapid and successful in the face of militarily inferior and divided opposition. Unlike the developing strong centralized state in England Ireland still existed on a basis of local clan loyalty and small kingdoms who were more often than not warring with each other. As Strongbow was a vassal of Henry II of England the newly conquered territory fell under the initially loose rule of the English monarchy. As the decades and centuries passed this rule would become ever tighter.

Despite the initial Norman successes their expansion slowed and stalled in the generations following due primarily to inter-feuding among the Normans themselves, lack of interest from the government in England and stubborn resistance by Irish Chieftains who still clung fiercely to their independence. As well as this intermarriage and alliances became a common feature between the newly arrived Anglo-Norman Lords and local Chieftains. This became so common that a saying developed of the Anglo-Norman invaders becoming "more Irish then the Irish themselves". By the end of the Middle Ages what now became known as "the Old English" became indistinguishable in customs and looks to their native Irish counterparts. As a result the Anglo-Normans never came close to fully conquering Ireland and this task would be left to later generations of English monarchs.

Despite this assimilation of the Anglo-Normans the concept of Ireland as a nation still had not developed as local Chieftains and Clans continued to wage war amongst themselves and carry out cattle raids as their forefathers had done for centuries prior. The last High King of Ireland, Ruaidri Ua Conchobair had died in 1198 and so too the last vestiges of any remaining concept of a unified Irish kingdom. Everything was to change with the ascension of Henry VIII to the throne of England in 1509 and the Reformation which followed. Henry VIII dedicated himself to the total conquest of the remaining independent Irish clans and the assimilation of Ireland into his kingdom. It would be under Henry that religion would be brought into the ferment of Anglo-Irish antagonism. With Ireland remaining strongly Catholic Henry began to view the island as a vulnerability in the growing religious wars on the continent and the conflict with Rome.

Although Henry started the process it would be left up to his successors, Elizabeth I and James I to complete what would be a bloody and violent process of conquest. Elizabeth would face the Desmond Rebellions of 1569-73 and the most serious of all challenges to English conquest which was the Nine Years War (1594-1603) led by the Ulster Chieftains under the leadership of Hugh O'Neill and Hugh O'Donnell. The English victory under Elizabeth left the process of mass land confiscation and colonization a relatively easy process for her successor, James I, although future conflict with the dispossessed and marginalized native Irish would become a feature in the following centuries. The mass influx of new Scottish and English settlers would leave a permanent mark on Irish history and a deeply complicating factor in the future for Irish nationalism.

In the decades after the Ulster plantations a deeply sullen "peace" descended upon Ireland with a dispossessed and oppressed native Irish population simmering with discontent and a deep feeling of injustice. This inevitably exploded in 1641 with a native Irish uprising against the mass land confiscations as well as discriminatory laws that deprived Catholics of even the most basic of rights. The rebellion would lead to an eleven years' conflict that would become known in Ireland as the Confederate Wars. The initial uprising brought outrage in England which was in the midst of a civil war and unable to respond militarily until 1649. In that year Oliver Cromwell and his victorious parliamentary forces invaded Ireland to begin a campaign of re-conquest that on a number of occasions bordered on genocide with numerous massacres of the civilian population as well as man-made famines that saw tens of thousands die of starvation.

It was a conflict where the taking of prisoners was more of an exception than the rule. The war was marked by a deep and vicious sectarian hatred which would leave an indelible mark on Irish history for centuries to come.

The Cromwellian victory which followed saw further mass land confiscations as well as a deepening impoverishment of the native population also sowed the beginnings of an Anglo- Irish landlord aristocracy that would last up until the early twentieth century. Despite the conclusive victory Irish resistance was able to slowly recover in the following decades to launch another war, this time not in support of independence but in support of an English Catholic king whom they hoped would reward their loyalty with a restoration of native rights and lands. The war would last from 1688 to 1691 and although the Irish armies fought with loyalty and distinction in the service of King James, the military superiority of the opposing English Protestant forces who claimed the throne proved too much. King James would abandon his Irish forces and flee to the European continent never to return leaving Ireland to face the full wrath of a new and vengeful Protestant monarch, William III.

The Treaty of Limerick which marked the final surrender of Jacobite forces in Ireland sent into exile almost 20,000 troops which would eventually fight in the service of France against English armies in the future. This was the first emergence of the concept of Ireland's "exiles" that would become as feature of later Irish American nationalism. Those who remained in Ireland became essentially second-class citizens unable to run for or hold public office or have any political say in their futures. The average Catholic would be more closely akin to Russian Serfs in the level of political and social control exercised by English and Anglo-Irish aristocracy.

The years after the Jacobite War up until the outbreak of the 1798 rebellion saw the growing entrenchment of the Anglo-Irish aristocracy and the growing impoverishment of the native Irish population. This time period was marked by the passing a number of politically and religiously restrictive laws. On top of these were laws which restricted the economic activity making it almost impossible for Catholics to economically improve their lot. An example of some of these laws were – Catholic exclusion from the legal profession and judiciary. Ban on Catholics running for parliament or other public office. Exclusion of Catholics from voting. No Catholic was

allowed to teach. No Catholic Church could be built of stone or be larger
than a Protestant Church. No Catholic was allowed to be educated abroad[1].

The years after the Jacobite defeat in Ireland and prior to the founding
of the United Irishmen was not a period that lacked physical violence
and resistance to the Anglo-Irish establishment. Secret agrarian societies
such as the Whiteboys who were active between 1761 and 1786 with acts
of violence against Anglo-Irish landlords who expelled Catholic tenants
from their holdings in preference to cattle grazing which was more prof-
itable. It is thought that many of the Whiteboys also took part in the later
rebellion of 1798[2].

The American Revolution saw some stirrings among the Anglo-Irish
establishment for greater economic freedom within the British imperial
structure but it was the French Revolution in 1789 that was to have a truly
profound impact on the future course of nationalism in Ireland. It would
be the ideas of Republican democracy and the exposure of these ideas to
radical Ulster Presbyterians and later to the Catholic peasantry that was
to provide the true ideological beginning of Irish Republicanism. The origins of militant Irish Republicanism stemmed from the French Revolution
and the violent revolutionary philosophy that it espoused. Theobald Wolfe
Tone, considered the father of Irish Republicanism, and his fellow United
Irishmen – Thomas Russell, Samuel Neilson, Robert Simms and Henry
Joy McCracken swore in the 1790s "never to desist in our efforts until we
have subverted the authority of England over our country and asserted our
independence". Wolfe Tone said it more succinctly when he stated that his
main objective was "To subvert the tyranny of our execrable government,
to break the connection with England, the never-failing source of all our
political evils and to assert the independence of my country – these were
my objectives."[3]

The United Irishmen movement was defeated with the bloody suppression of the 1798 rebellion. The greatest consequence of the rebellion was
that it set in motion the events which led up to the Act of Union in 1801

1   Kee, Robert. Ireland, a history. London. Weidenfeld and Nicolson. 1980.
2   Beames, Michael. Peasants and Power – The Whiteboy Movement and their con-
      trol in pre-famine Ireland.
3   Coogan, Pat, Tim. The IRA. London. Harper/Collins publisher. 1995. P. 5.

whereby the Irish parliament in Dublin was abolished and all Irish members
of parliament now had to sit at Westminster in London. However, there
was a second and more unforeseen consequence of the failed rising. The
remaining exiled leadership and members that fled to the United States set
in motion a tradition that would be the longest lasting transatlantic nationalist movement in U.S. history as well as being one of the most effective. At
the same time this tradition would often pose a constant thorn in the side
of many future White House administrations that would focus more and
more on building a strong Anglo-American world order. Intermittently
Irish-American nationalists would use tensions in this relationship to reap
the maximum benefits possible in the struggle for Irish independence.

The United Irishmen who arrived on American shores, while geographically far away from their native homeland, found a readymade ideological
home in the Jeffersonian political philosophy that formed the leading political opposition to the more conservative White House administration of
John Adams. While Thomas Jefferson and his supporters welcomed this
infusion of revolutionaries into their ranks with their pro-French revolutionary rhetoric there were others who were much more concerned. Adams
and his supporters feared being dragged into the bloody revolutionary
fervor sweeping Europe and saw these exiles as a dangerous and foreign
element that threatened the very Republic itself. One leading Federalist
described the newly arrived Irish political exiles as the "most god provoking
Democrats this side of hell". Another Federalist said that "Every United
Irishman ought to be hunted from the country as much as a wolf or tyger".
Just prior to the first mass arrival of United Irishmen exiles Harrison Otis
Grey during a debate in Congress in 1797 said "I do not wish to invite hordes
of wild Irishmen, nor the turbulent and disorderly of all parts of the world,
to come here with a view to disturb our tranquility". From the perspective
of the newly arrived Irish radicals the view of their newly adopted homeland is best summed up in a revolutionary rhyme from the time period –

> What have you got in your hand? A green bough. Where did it first grow? In America.
> Where did it bud? In France. Where are you going to plant it? In the crown of Great
> Britain[4].

4   Wilson, David A. United Irishmen, United States. Ithaca. Cornell University. 1998.

The stage was set early on for debate within U.S. society as to how recep-
tive it should be to an ideology whose loyalty was split between both sides
of the Atlantic and did not always correspond to U.S. national interests.

The first significant opportunity for Irish radicals to use their new
homeland as a base from which to attack the British Empire was in the
buildup to and during the War of 1812. Irish- American leaders built a political base within Jefferson's party in major urban centers of the northeast
which would continue to be the case in the centuries to come. One leading
United Irishmen figure at this time was William Duane who was editor
the Aurora newspaper in Philadelphia. Not only was the publication a
leading national Republican newspaper but it also promoted a far-reaching
vision of international revolutionary Republicanism in a struggle against
global empire and imperialism[5].

Two other leading United Irishmen figures in the U.S. at this time
period were William James MacNeven and Thomas Addis Emmet who
would become a close friend to Thomas Jefferson and was brother to Robert
Emmet who would be executed in 1803 while attempting a failed rebellion
and who would become eulogized in the annals of Irish martyrs for his
famous speech from the dock. Both men were viewed with such deep suspicion by Britain that Major- General John Skerrett, who fought the United
Irishmen successfully in Newfoundland, described both men as "two of
the most dangerous United Irishmen (who gave me much trouble during
Rebellion) have been very active and industrious in provoking the people
of the United States to wage war with England and said they would arm a
force of sixty thousand United Irishmen to aid them in this undertaking".

As far back as 1808, MacNeven had been requesting the formation
of an all-Irish militia to be known as the "Republican Greens". Although
the plan never came to fruition due mainly to financial reasons one can
speculate that this may have been the first attempt to sow the seeds of a
future Irish-American military force that could have been used in a potential war to liberate Ireland from British rule. When war finally did break
out in 1812 United Irishmen exiles placed an announcement in a New York
newspaper titled "Address to Irish-Americans" in the hope of encouraging

5   Taylor, Alan. The Civil War of 1812. New York. Alfred A. Knopf. 2010. P. 75-101.

Irish recruits into the struggle against Britain. Part of the address read "We have no interest but the safety of our country; nor ambition but to march with its defenders. Thrice happy in doing so, we avenge the wrongs of our dear native land". As Irish recruits answered the call official authorization was given for the formation of the Republican Greens which became part of the New York Regiment of Riflemen. A total of 1,600 Irishmen made up the newly formed Republican Greens. By the end of the war Irish-American participation and sacrifice helped in the early integration and acceptance of these "Wild Irish" exiles. It would not be the last time where Irish-American political grievance would correspond with American attitudes to Britain and its empire[6].

The years following the War of 1812 saw a somewhat lessening of revolutionary fervor and more of a focus on assimilation and the cause of Catholic Emancipation back in Ireland. Before 1829 Catholics were denied the right not only to be elected to British parliament but to even vote for a candidate. Daniel O'Connell took up and led the cause for Catholic Emancipation which was to dominate the Irish political arena throughout the 1820s. For the Anglo-Saxon Protestant ruling establishment in the U.S. the Irish issue and the presence of Catholic Irish emigrants in American society were perceived as no immediate threat to American identity because of the small number of Irish emigrants then living in the U.S. This was to all change in the 1830s and particularly during the 1840s.

A number of factors led to a significant increase in Irish emigration to the U.S. throughout the 1830s. Firstly, the relative cheapness of travel was a major factor. For as little as one shilling an Irish man or woman could cross the Irish Sea, work for a few months as a migrant worker in Britain and save enough money to buy transatlantic passage to the U.S. As the U.S. was growing and expanding so too was the availability of cheap land. Since most of the land in Ireland was owned by absentee British and Anglo-Irish landlords this was a very attractive feature indeed[7]. Finally, growing agrarian violence by secret societies such as Captain Rock and Ribbonmen caused

6   Ingham, R., George. Irish Rebel, American Patriot. CreateSpace Independent Publishing Platform. 2014. P. 221-237.
7   Mitchell, Brian. 1996. The Ordinance Survey Memoirs; a Source for Emigration in the 1830s. History Ireland. Vol. 4 (Issue 4).

widespread violence and reprisals where British troops on a number of occasions were brought in to quell the growing violence. These organizations were some of the first violent secret oath bound organizations to appear in Ireland since the United Irishmen. One big difference was that their central cause surrounded the issue of land ownership as opposed to the cause of Irish independence. However, these secret agrarian organizations did provide a blueprint for future revolutionary movements such as Clan-na-Gael[8].

Unlike other immigrant groups that would arrive in later generations the Irish immigrants of the 1830s did not attempt to immediately assimilate to the point of becoming mere pawns of the established Anglo-Protestant political establishment. Irish immigrants played a major role in the most tumultuous year of the decade in 1834. Reasons for Irish violence varied from labor and economic discontent to outright hostility to African-Americans and the growing Abolitionist movement. On top of this these discontented Irish communities faced growing hostility and eventually physical attacks from nativist mobs who feared the arrival of large number of Catholics and a group that refused to accept and play a subservient role to the established order[9].

During the 1840s as a result of the catastrophic famine in Ireland immigration of Irish Catholics to the U.S. would reach unprecedented proportions. Nativist antagonism and violent response became inevitable. Attacks on Catholic convents, anti-Catholic conspiratorial literature and conflict between Catholic and Protestants over public school policy accompanied this initial wave of nativism. The worst example of the violent confrontation came in 1844 in Philadelphia where Irish immigrants faced off against nativist rioters in three days of brutal rioting. After the state militia was called in to quell the violence approximately twelve people were dead not including four militia men themselves[10]. As nativists organized politically so too did Irish Catholics who began the early stages of building up major urban political machines in the cities of

---

8   Donnelly, James. Captain Rock. The University of Wisconsin Press. Madison. 2009.
9   Prince, E., Carl. Society for Historians of the Early American Republic. The Great "Riot Year": Jacksonian Democracy and Patterns of Violence in 1834. Vol. 5, No. 1, 1985. P. 1-19.
10   Milano, Kenneth. The Philadelphia Nativist Riots. History Press. Charleston. 2013.

the northeast. Irish emigrants had the major benefit of political experience from O'Connell's campaign in Ireland for Catholic Emancipation and later Repeal attempts which put them at a major advantage compared to other ethnic groups at the time. While many of the newly arrived Irish were of poor peasant stock and poorly educated they were far from politically naïve. These political enclaves would provide a major base of operations and support for Clan-na-Gael in the years to come[11].

The year 1848 was one of liberal revolutions which swept Europe as a largely middle-class idealistic new generation attempted to overthrow monarchies and establish democratic republics in their steads. In Ireland a new organization of mostly young middle-class Catholics who called themselves Young Irelanders split with the moderate leadership of Daniel O'Connell believing that Ireland had no longer a future within the British Empire and instead espoused the ideal of a violent revolution to establish a Republic. As the famine and the terrible consequences it brought with it started to eat away at the fabric Irish society the Young Irelanders attempted a desperate rebellion which ended in inevitable disaster. Too many sympathetic to the cause were starving and struggling to merely survive to even worry about the political ideal of a Republic. Just like the United Irishmen a half century before the new generation of political refugees landed on the shores of the United States among the multitudes of starving and emaciated Irish. Just like the United Irishmen the new exiles we're not afraid to carry their ethnicity into the political arena.

From the late 1830s to the early 1840s Anglo-American relations were tense with the rise of American expansionism throughout the continent with the annexation of large parts of Mexico in 1848. Many Americans who believed in Manifest Destiny also looked north to the wide open and sparsely populated region of British-Canada. While for most of the 1840s Irish- American nationalism focused on non-violent efforts toward Catholic Emancipation and Repeal of the Union conditions during the decade did offer hope to those of a more violent revolutionary disposition.

11   Murphy, F., Angela. Immigration and Ethnic History Society. Daniel O'Connell and the "American Eagle" in 1845: Diplomacy, Nativism, and the Collapse of America's first Irish Nationalist Movement. Vol. 26 (No. 2). 2007. P. 3-26.

Anglo-American tensions arose out of major crises involving the still undefined U.S.-Canadian border. In 1837 U.S. citizens supported a failed bid
by Canadian rebels to achieve independence from Britain causing a major
international incident known as the Caroline Affair. Violent Incidents continued into 1838 and were not finally settled until the Webster-Ashburton
Treaty of 1842. Irish-American nationalists would be at the forefront of
proponents for Continental Union during the nineteenth century[12].

Prior to the outbreak of the 1848 rebellion in Ireland a new revolutionary consciousness was emerging among the Irish-American community.
This new generation was very aware of the United Irishmen legacy that
preceded them in the U.S. which they viewed as a legacy of pride and as a
cause of inspiration for the Irish Republican cause. Many of these exiles saw
a deep affinity to American Republican rhetoric and viewed the U.S. as a
site for aid and possible future intervention in the cause of Irish independence. The term "Irish-American" was one which was deeply embraced as the
new generation of Irish revolutionaries saw no contradiction in this dual
identity. With this newfound sense of confidence and reinforced identity
Irish- American nationalists lobbied hard on behalf of the Irish nationalist
cause. This new focus resulted in the formation of the Irish Republican
Union. The avowed purpose of the new organization was "to promote revolutions for the establishment of Republican Governments throughout
Europe, especially in Ireland". The new organization went straight into
making plans for the formation of an Irish Brigade which would be filled
with men "ready and willing to embark in her battle".

This new revolutionary fervor did not go unnoticed by the American
political establishment as the fear of been drawn into direct confrontation
with the British Empire became a very real prospect. Son of former U.S.
president, Robert Tyler, warned against the prospect of an Irish army of
invasion as a breach of the American constitution. The Irish Republican
Union attempted to adapt to the situation by emphasizing no threat to
the U.S. constitution or their newly adopted homeland while at the same

---

12   Stevens, Kenneth. Border Diplomacy – The Caroline and McLeod Affairs in
      Anglo-American-Canadian Relations, 1837-1842. University of Alabama Press.
      Tuscaloosa. 1989.

time never abandoning plans to dispatch military assistance to Ireland. In prospect for future revolutionary action a new fundraising body called the American Provisional Committee for Ireland was established. This creation of a new and virulent form of Irish-American Republicanism is best summed up in the words of Young Irelander Thomas Mooney when he said the purpose of Irish-Americans should be to "plant the Republican Tree of America on the Hill of Tara". This new mobilization of Irish revolutionary activists saw a growing alliance with former O'Connellites and even the Catholic Church. The increased activities of Irish revolutionaries put British Canada on alert against possible invasion. The collapse of the movement in Ireland amid horrific famine and a disastrously timed and planned rebellion marked an ignominious collapse of the revolutionary movement in the U.S.

Before continuing further with Irish revolutionary machinations in the US during this time period we much first analyze the social and political impact of the Irish famine on those immigrant communities both already established in America and those arriving. The horrific Irish famine which lasted from 1845-49 was a watershed moment that gave birth to a uniquely Irish-American nationalism that differed in many respects to Irish nationalism in the U.S. prior to the famine and also the type of nationalism back in Ireland. Well known Irish-American historian Thomas Browne researched the formation of this nationalism and concluded that it was formed through "Loneliness, poverty and prejudice". These three factors were prominent in the U.S. amidst hostile nativism and the horrific conditions of urban ghettos and low paying and often dangerous employment. On top of this many came over with no family whom they either had to leave behind in Ireland creating a great sense of guilt or who may have died in the famine creating a deep sense of loss and a rage for vengeance. In Ireland, while oppressed, they at least were an overwhelming majority on the island which provided some sense of belonging and psychological security. In the U.S. they continued to face discrimination and poverty but were now also a minority in a vast country and an unfamiliar urban setting.

Regional differences were quickly forgotten among Irish immigrants as the community welded itself into very tight knit ethnic enclaves. The deep sense of grievance was even greater than that back in Ireland at having been driven into "exile". This image of the exiled Irish natives been driven from their home by the ruthless Anglo-Saxon landlords and British political establishment was a uniquely Irish-American creation. The conditions from which many had fled and now lived in major urban ghettos created a deep sense of shame and disgrace and an urge to improve their lot in their newly adopted country as well as impacting and changing conditions back in their native land. This sense of inferiority and desire to prove themselves would spill over to the arena of Irish nationalism where these new immigrants would seek to be just as dedicated to Irish independence despite living thousands of miles away.

As opposed to other immigrant groups in the U.S. at this time Irish Americans clung fiercely to a Gaelic identity which stood in direct opposition to the established Anglo-Saxon institutions and ruling class. This combination of deep antagonism to Britain and anything Anglo-Saxon, the experience of the benefits of American democracy which the Irish were particularly quick to adapt to and the urban experience over time created a unique outlook on Irish nationalism. This outlook was uncompromising and ideologically "pure" and "untainted" by the restraints of British political, social and economic oppression in Ireland, the reality of a large loyalist population in the north of Ireland and a population in Ireland that on many occasions veered between focus on land reform and moderate limited Home Rule within the British Empire as opposed to an independent Republic. Beneath all of this was a deep psychological and historical trauma which was passed down from generation to generation through a vibrant oral tradition as well as literature, theatre and ethnic societies and institutions of which Clan na Gael would become the most notable[13].

With the collapse of the revolutionary attempts in Ireland Irish-American revolutionaries turned to other strategies which included increased involvement in urban machine politics and overt displays of Catholic and cultural nationalism and identity. Along with these displays of nationalism came overt internal dissension within the ranks of the Young Ireland exiles over those seeking a long-term strategy toward achieving Irish independence and hawks seeking immediate revolutionary action. This dissension was on many occasions to cripple the Irish- American

---

13   Browne, N, Thomas. The Review of Politics. The Origins and Character of Irish-American Nationalism. Vol. 18 (No. 3) July, 1956. P. 327–358.

nationalist movement right up until the formation of the Fenian movement in 1858[14].

While the years 1848-58 are sometimes known as the era of Irish-
American "armchair Republicans" there were those who moved with
purpose and direction toward establishing a new revolutionary movement along the lines of the United Irishmen and Young Irelanders. At the
forefront of this resurgence was individuals such as James Stephens, John
O'Mahony and Michael Doheny. The center of this new resurgence was
the exile community in New York. New York of the 1850s was a hive of
Irish revolutionary activity. As astute British observers correctly saw that
one of the main results of the failed revolution of 1848 "was to change the
base of Irish revolution from Ireland to America". There were central factors why New York was the chosen location for these new revolutionary
efforts. Firstly, and most obviously, New York contained the largest concentration of Irish people in the world outside of Ireland. Secondly, Irish
revolutionary fervor in New York was by no means the only game in town.
Other European leaders such as Giuseppe Garibaldi and Lajos Kossuth
were making highly publicized tours of the U.S. espousing revolutionary
republican ideals identical to those of Irish revolutionaries. Rubbing elbows
with such revolutionary figures could only have inspired and encouraged
new efforts to establish a republic in Ireland.

The first step toward this new wave of Irish Republicanism was the
establishment of the Emmet Monument Association in Boston in 1855. The
main purpose of the new association was to act as a focal point for uniting
elements of the now defunct Young Ireland movement in an effort toward
reestablishing and organizing a viable revolutionary movement that could
actually impact events in Ireland. The new association had affiliates as far
away as Cincinnati. The motivations of the new organization were evident
early on when twenty members were arrested in early 1856 for attempting
to encourage migration to Ireland with the intent of fermenting revolution
in violation of the 1818 Neutrality Act.

---

14   Belchem, John. The Past and Present Society. Nationalism, Republicanism and
     Exile: Irish Emigrants and the Revolutions of 1848. (No. 146). 1995. P. 103-135.

An individual who was an early driving force behind the Emmet
Monument Association was one Joseph Denieffe. Although initially modest
in scale Denieffe's efforts marked the first time that impetus for Irish revolutionary organizing emanated from the U.S. rather than from Ireland. A
rebellion that had been planned by the Association for 1855 had proved far
too premature and unrealistic and inevitably never materialized. However,
in 1857 two events occurred that would provide temporary encouragement to Irish radicals in the U.S. The first of these events were the Indian
Mutiny which shook the very foundations of British rule in India. Events
in India caused a major stir among Irish Republicans in New York who
hoped the conflict would open up opportunities for a planned rebellion
in Ireland while the British were heavily engaged in India. In the end the
rebellion did not last long enough and was finally suppressed after approximately fourteen months.

The second international event that provided temporary encouragement to Irish Republicans during this time period was the Crimean War.
For the first time Irish-American radicals would reach out to a non-US
government for military assistance in aiding rebellion in Ireland. In this in-
stance help was sought from Russia. Contact was made with the Russian
embassy in the U.S. and promises of military aid was given although never
received. The end of the Crimean War brought to an end any hopes of assistance from the newly found ally.

Although the Emmet Monument Association was soon dissolved
after successive failures and disappointments it did provide an important
bridge between the Young Ireland exiles and the eventual emergence of the
Fenian movement. It set in place the basic structure of a nationwide organization with the outline of important fundraising networks. It was this
financial support that provided the impetus for the foundation of the Irish
Republican Brotherhood in Ireland and her sister organization in the U.S.,
the Fenian Movement[15].

As one would expect the driving force behind the formation of the
Fenian movement were the older members of Young Ireland exiles from the

15   Brundage, David. Irish Nationalists in America – The Politics of Exile, 1798-1998.
     Oxford University Press. New York. 2016. P. 88-99.

previous generation. The central figures behind the new movement were John O'Mahony and Michael Doheny who founded the Fenian movement on Saint Patrick's Day in 1858. Just like previous Irish revolutionary movements in the U.S. the central purpose of the new movement was to achieve and independent Irish Republic through armed revolution. The immediate task for the Fenian movement was to resurrect and unite defunct and fractured Irish revolutionary societies throughout the U.S. as well as carry out fundraising on a large scale. The potential of the movement was seen in the first six months when almost $1,000 was raised[16].

The early development of Fenianism was interrupted with the onset of the American Civil War. While it would have been easy for many in the Fenian leadership to have viewed the war as a major inconvenience and disruption many actually viewed it as an opportunity and actively encouraged mass Irish participation in the Union cause. The benefit of having thousands of Irishmen trained the art of war and battle hardened by the heat of conflict would be of major benefit to the cause of Irish independence at the end of the war. The Irish- American press in general also promoted mass Irish participation. The Irish military commitment was severely tested with the slaughter of the Irish Brigade at Fredericksburg, Antietam and later at Gettysburg. The belief began to become commonplace that Irish immigrant soldiers were being used as little more than cannon fodder in the Union war effort. This growing resentment reached boiling point in July of 1863 with the Draft riots and an outburst of the worst rioting in U.S. history. As well as anti-draft sentiment the growing realization that the end of slavery which was marked in January of the same year with the Emancipation Proclamation would see the arrival of millions of former slaves onto the labor market. Such a realization contributed to the growing fear of cheap labor flooding the U.S. economy and competing with already poorly paid unskilled Irish workers.

Throughout the war Fenianism did not just immerse itself in the conflict against the Confederacy. Instead, it continued its agitation for the Union to declare war on Britain as a result of the British support for the

16   Kee, Robert. The Green Flag – A History of Irish Nationalism. Penguin Books. London. 2000. P. 299-311.

Confederacy through the sale of naval vessels used to sink Union shipping. The high point of this agitation came early in the war during the Trent Affair. Leading Fenian John O'Leary felt war with Britain was inevitable as he declared "a feeling, almost universal in the ordinary mind, that another war than that of words was fast becoming inevitable". Despite the best Fenian efforts there would be no direct conflict between the U.S. and Britain for the duration of the war as the Confederacy began it's painful and bloody collapse after the Battle of Gettysburg in 1863[17].

Fenian hopes of a U.S. war with Britain did not end with Union victory in the civil war. The focus for most American historians during the Reconstruction era is the struggle for African- American rights and the reintegration of the South into the Union. However, another major event occurred during this time period. The Fenian movement emerged from the Civil War as a more invigorated, confident and militarily potent force. At this point Andrew Johnson was president and he carried a well-known hostility to Britain as a result of her actions during the recent war. This, added to the fact that Anglo-American relations remained at a dangerously low point as a result of the Alabama Claims where the U.S. claimed reparations from Britain from sinking caused by the CSS Alabama which was manufactured in England. The combination of these three factors created the perfect circumstances for a major Fenian effort toward armed rebellion. Thomas Sweeney, Secretary of War for the Fenians, reported that the U.S. government was "perfectly well aware" of Fenian military preparations in the form of arms purchases and recruitment.

The decision to invade Canada caused a major split with the Fenian movement. A faction led by John O'Mahony favored supporting a rebellion in Ireland while a second faction led by William Roberts favored attacking Canada and using it as leverage to gain Irish independence. While on first reading the Canadian invasion plan may seem a bizarre strategy there were a number of advantages to such an approach. Firstly, Canada was part of the British Empire and shared a very long and open border with the U.S. British military presence in Canada was minimal and relied mainly on

---

17   Hernon, Joseph. Celts, Catholics and Copperheads. Ohio State University Press. 1968. P. 11-59.

poorly trained local militias for security. Secondly, there was a large Irish immigrant population in Canada which the Fenians hoped would be sympathetic and supportive of such a plan.

In 1866 the Fenians began a number of raids that would continue into 1871 when it would eventually end. The high point of the raids came early on in 1866 when General John O'Neill led the Fenians to victory at the Battle of Ridgeway. From the victory at Ridgeway until 1871 the raids were largely ineffective. little if any support was received from Irish-Canadians and they all ended up with eventual retreats back across the U.S. border. When the U.S. eventually gained the necessary concessions it was looking for through negotiation and the Treaty of Washington in 1871 it clamped down hard on Fenian activities. While the O'Mahony faction of the movement would eventually have its planned rising in Ireland in 1867 it ended up being a disaster with no lasting consequence. At this point the Fenian movement lay in disarray as a result of military defeats, internal division and growing public disenchantment among Irish- Americans. It was in the midst of this failure and collapse that Clan-na-Gael would emerge to take up the mantle for the next generation of Irish-American revolutionaries[18].

The United States was a very natural home and base for Irish revolutionary republicanism to take root. The main reason was the Irish attraction to U.S. republican democratic institutions. As well as this there was also a deep attraction to American Republican rhetoric. This deeply held embrace not just helped in overall assimilation but highlighted the passionately held grievances toward conditions in Ireland which offered a stark contrast to their new homes in the U.S. Revolutionary Irish republicans distinguished between diasporic nationalism and full integration and assimilation. This allowed revolutionaries to be both American and Irish at the same time and members to continue to be different without feeling that they were outsiders. This embrace of American republican values and rhetoric made Irish-American revolutionaries "A kindred and congenial

---

18 Sim, David. American Nineteenth Century History. Filibusters, Fenians, and Contested Neutrality: The Irish Question in U.S. Diplomacy, 1848-1871. Vol. 12, No. 3, September, 2011. P. 265-287.

element"[19]. Periods in U.S. history when Irish revolutionary republicanism did not correspond with foreign policy, in particular Anglo-American relations, made them a very difficult group to deal with as their beliefs and rhetoric constantly harkened back to the beliefs and foundation of the American republic itself, providing the growing pro- British American establishment with uncomfortable reminders of the basis on which their own Republic was founded.

19   Lynch, Timothy. "A Kindred and Congenial Element": Irish-American Nationalism's Embrace of Republican Rhetoric. Vol. 13, No. 2, 2009. University of St. Thomas (Center of Irish Studies).

CHAPTER 2

The Birth of Clan na Gael

It was early in the decline of the Fenian movement that a number of leading figures realized that a new beginning was necessary and that this would involve establishing a new organization. The main figure in the early efforts was one Jerome Collins. Collins was a native of Dunmanway, County Cork and became a member of the Fenian movement early on. After his involvement in a failed attempt to free Fenian prisoners jailed in Britain he was forced to flee to the United States[20]. Among the deeply divided and antagonistic factions of Fenianism Collins seems to have been one of those rare figures that were held in high esteem by almost everyone. A number of years after Collins's early and tragic death on the doomed Jeannette Polar Expedition John Devoy described him as the "greatest of the Fenians" and "One of the best and purest men I ever knew, and no Irishman of his time had a finer intellect. The Clan-na-Gael had every right to be proud of its founder and the nationalists of Cork are right in decorating his grave once a year when they pay tribute to the dead who were true to Ireland"[21].

Although the late 1860s saw increasing factionalism within Irish-American nationalism conditions overall were not altogether negative toward the establishment of a new organization. As stated earlier Anglo-American relations in the aftermath of the Civil War were at its lowest point since the War of 1812. In the White House sat a president who was not only hostile to Britain for her assistance to the Confederacy during the recent war but was also willing to turn a blind eye to Irish nationalist activities involving arms purchases, recruitment, fundraising and eventual

---

20   Isacsson, Alfred. Always Faithful – The New York Carmelites, the Irish People and Their Freedom Movement. Vestigium Press. New York. 2004. P. 8.
21   Herlihy, Ronnie. 2009. Jerome Collins. History Ireland. Vol. 17 (Issue 4).

invasion of Canada. So it was that Jerome Collins along with other former leading figures of the collapsing Fenian movement came together on 20 June 1867, on Hester Street in New York to form Clan-na-Gael, the name literally meaning "family of the Gael". The purpose of the new name was to address the issue of factionalism and division and to push home the point that all members were Irishmen regardless of their differences and that these differences were secondary when compared to the overall cause of Irish independence. The location of New York for the founding of the new movement was also no accident. The city contained the largest concentration of Irish people in the world outside of Ireland and would remain a hotbed of Clan activity for generations to come. Although Jerome Collins was the founder of the new movement it would be John Devoy and later Joseph McGarrity who would become the dominant figures in the history of the movement.

Just like the defunct Fenian movement the Clan's aims were the "attainment of the complete and absolute independence of Ireland by the overthrow of English domination by means of physical force". There would be one major difference between the Clan and its Fenian predecessor, however. Unlike the Fenian movement the Clan would be a secretive revolutionary movement. During their heyday the Fenians were known for their public meetings, open fundraising and declarations of plans in the Irish-American press for armed rebellion. Such openness bordered on naivety if not outright incompetence. Inevitably the Fenians were open to easy infiltration by both British and American intelligence services. One of the most glaring examples was the case of the notorious British spy Henri Le Caron. Le Caron, who's real name was Thomas Miller Beach, not only infiltrated the Fenian movement but reached the highest levels of the organization where he for years passed on planning for the raids to Canada and Britain. This gave the British the advance warning needed to neutralize the Fenian threat. Le Caron would go on to infiltrate the Clan and provide a harsh lesson on internal security.

New members of the organization went through masonic style initiation rituals and ciphers were used in official communications. After the initial ceremony member's candidates were placed before the local President and a charge concluding with the following words were read – "With this assurance and understanding, as you do that the object of this organization is the freedom of Ireland, will you submit yourself to our rules and regulations and take our obligations without mental reservation?"

The candidates then took the oaths repeating the following phrases after the president – "I _____, do solemnly and sincerely swear, in the presence of Almighty God, that I will labor while life is left in me to establish and defend a republican form of government in Ireland. That I will never reveal the secrets of this organization to any person or persons not entitled to know them. That I will obey and comply with the constitution and laws of Clan-na-Gael and promptly and faithfully execute all constitutional orders coming to me from the proper orders to the best of my ability. That I will foster a spirit of unity, nationality and brotherly love among the friends of Ireland. I furthermore swear that I do not belong to any other Irish revolutionary society antagonistic to this organization and that I will not become a member of such a society while connected with Clan-na-Gael; and finally, I swear that I take this obligation without mental reservation and that any violation hereof is infamous and merits the severest punishment So help me God". (Candidate kisses the book)[22].

The Clan was made up of camps and clubs spread throughout the major urban centers of the northeastern United States where major Irish population centers were concentrated. Each club was given a number and a public name like the Napper Tandy Club or the Emmet Literary Society. Such names allowed meetings and gatherings to occur without bringing unwelcome attention as to the true revolutionary nature of the organization. Each individual camp had assigned to it both a senior and junior guardian responsible for its day-to-day administration. The clubs in individual states were divided into districts. These regions then elected delegates who, along with a chairman and a secretary, made up the National Executive Committee. There also existed a Revolutionary Directory consisting of three members of the Clan and three members of the Irish Republican Brotherhood, the Clan's sister organization back in Ireland. The Directory

22   Pollard, H.B.C. The Secret Societies of Ireland. The Irish Historical Press. Kilkenny, 1998.

was not established until 1877 and had as its central purpose the coordination of revolutionary activity on both sides of the Atlantic[23].

As Clan-na-Gael emerged from the ashes of the dying Fenian movement it took on a much different character from its predecessor. While
aims and objectives were identical to the Fenian movement, Clan-na-Gael
was from the beginning a much more professional revolutionary organization with a tighter control over membership, more secretive in its inner
workings and a dedication to keep out of the public eye as much as possible. Although the Clan was not immune to mistakes such as occasional
infiltration and factionalism it for the most part learned the costly lessons
from the Fenian movement.

In the United States Clan membership transcended socio-economic
boundaries with members who we're not just working class but also phys-
icians, professors, businessmen and even politicians. Most of the Clan activity throughout the country took place in and around saloons which were
the center of social gatherings and activities in many Irish communities
in America. These saloons were not just locations for the consumption of
alcohol as thought of today. In the Irish context they were places of social
gatherings such as wedding receptions, family gatherings for baptisms, holy
communions and confirmations. They were also places for political gatherings and organizing to get a local Irish candidate elected to city council
or higher national office. It was a natural location for Clan activities.

An excellent case study of a typical Clan branch was researched by
author Dennis Clarke in his book "Erin's Heirs – Irish Bonds of Community".
In his case study he looked at one Mike McGinn of the Philadelphia branch
of the Clan. McGinn emigrated from County Cavan in Ireland in 1897 and
joined the local Clan branch on his arrival in Philadelphia in the same year.
From this we can assume that McGinn's revolutionary credentials back in
Ireland were confirmed and significant enough to gain access to the movement. Philadelphia at that time and right up until the 1940s would be a
hotbed of Clan activity and home of the most radical wing of the movement.

23   Funchion, Michael. Chicago's Irish Nationalists 1881-1890. Loyola University. 1973.
      Chicago. P. 51.

Like most new arrivals that became Clan members they would have been set up with employment and even given assistance to open new businesses such as saloons. One such individual within the Clan who would have provided such assistance was Patrick O'Neill. O'Neill himself was also a leading fundraiser for the Land League in Philadelphia. When McGinn approached O'Neill for loan to establish a new saloon in an Irish neighborhood in South Street. The venture really turned out to be a joint venture among Clan members who pooled their money together to buy the premises. The new saloon was but one of a number of Clan ventures throughout the city. The bars were usually located near railway stations, ball parks and major transit exchanges, locations which increased both their regular patronage and their usefulness and Clan centers of influence and communication.

Over the years McGinn's hard work and loyalty to the Clan paid off as he earned greater respect within the movement. He soon gained more responsibility over such activities as recruiting, organizing new branches and fundraising. One of the most important of these responsibilities were to transmit money collected in the United States to Ireland. McGinn was responsible for one of the largest Clan fundraising events in America. Each year on the anniversary of the death of Irish patriot Robert Emmet the Clan would hire one of the largest theaters in the city and present an evening of music and oratory. This event along with regular dance events, raffles, picnics, sports competitions kept money rolling in and made Philadelphia one of the most successful branches of the Clan.

Each branch of Clan na Gael would in many ways mirror the old Chieftain and Clan systems of earlier centuries of Irish history in structure. The basic structure of the old Irish Clan system was the Chieftain, the fine who were the extended Clan who vowed to protect the Chieftain and wage war when necessary and the duiche which was the territory ruled over by the Chieftain[24]. In the case of Clan na Gael the local leader or "Chieftain" was usually determined by their revolutionary credentials and past involvement in revolutionary activities. This was much in the same way as an ancient Chieftain would often

24   Dorney, John. Irish Clans in the Sixteenth century. The Irish Story. 2017. Available online <https://www.theirishstory.com/2017/08/15/irish-clans-in-the-sixteenth-century/#.Xy1azIhKjIV>

be chosen based on past martial achievements. The fine in the case of the Clan were usually those directly underneath the local Clan na Gael Chief and directly responsible for organizing fundraising events as well as political lobbying and distribution of propaganda material. All were active members of the organization. Finally, you had the duiche which was the territory "ruled" over by the local Clan branch and the Irish community contained within it. The sense of loyalty and ethnic identity would certainly have been heightened in a multi-racial and multi-cultural environment that was the makeup of nearly all major American urban centers during this time period and certainly today.

Lessons were also learned from the earlier generation of the Catholic Association and the later Repeal Movement in Ireland which can be argued to have been Europe's first truly mass democratic movement. Just like these earlier movements, under the leadership of Daniel O'Connell, membership and appeal crossed class boundaries. Any financial contribution was encouraged. In Ireland peasants would give as little as a penny to the cause which would give them a steak in the political prospects of the movement. Financial contributions in the case of Clan na Gael was a way for contributors and members to have a stake and a say in events in Ireland, a country that many felt resentful at having to leave due to economic and political circumstances. The image of "Erin's exiled sons and daughters" was strongly encouraged by Clan na Gael propaganda.

The financial success of the Clan, particularly in Philadelphia, gave the organization the ability, when the situation arose, to take part in secret electoral financing in Ireland, organize anti-British demonstrations and to raise money for arms and bombing campaigns against British forces in Ireland as well as targets in Britain itself. McGinn in many ways epitomized Clan-na-Gael as an organization. McGinn evolved his role within an American urban environment and strong Irish communal ties. He became the kind of leader that was part of the very fiber of the local community. He relied on persuasion and personal appeal to exert an image of folk hero, freedom fighter and community leader. The Clan was not just a stand-alone revolutionary movement, it became part of the very fabric of Irish America for decades[25].

25   Clark, Dennis. Erin's Heirs – Irish Bonds of Community. University Press of
      Kentucky. 1991. Lexington. P. 144-156.

CHAPTER 3

1870s – Phoenix Rising

Political conditions in Ireland during the 1870s, while not conducive to armed insurrection aimed at establishing a full republic, did see major movements towards at least increased independence. The Home Rule movement started to gain increased momentum thanks primarily to an emerging new generation under the leadership of Charles Parnell. Parnell and his companions started to use the very un-British and ungentlemanly tactic of obstructionism in the British parliament in order to bring attention to political and social issues in Ireland. Although Parnell would go on to become the most important nationalist figure in Ireland between the death of Daniel O'Connell and the war of independence he could not have been more different in social background and political tradition to future Clan na Gael leaders such as John Devoy and Joseph McGarrity. Parnell was raised within the Anglo-Irish Protestant tradition of landed aristocracy. While many in his class would be advocates of achieving increased control of domestic affairs in Ireland through an Irish parliament none of this meant breaking the bonds with the British Empire. Parnell would remain a life-long opponent of violence despite developing political connections with Clan na Gael during what would become known as the Great Departure[26].

The Irish Land League would also emerge during the 1870s agitating for land reform and using for the first time a tactic called boycotting which was used against non-compliant Anglo- Irish and English Landlords. From the perspective of Anglo-American relations things looked no brighter in terms of launching a rebellion. With the Treaty of Washington in 1871 all outstanding disputes between the Unites States and Britain were settled amicably with the prospect of any future war ever less likely. Although the

26   Lyons, F.S.L. Charles Stewart Parnell. Oxford University Press. New York. 1977.

1870s did not see armed revolution in Ireland it was nonetheless one of gaining strength for Clan-na-Gael. As rival Fenian factions and political refugees started coalescing around the Clan membership would grow to around 11,000 members by 1877[27]. The first major building block of the decade came in 1871 with the arrival of what became known as the "Cuba Five". Among the arrival of these five new political refugees would be the greatest leader in the Clan's history, John Devoy.

On 19 January 1871 a group of Irish rebels were released from British prisons on the condition that they would not enter any part of the British Empire until their sentence expiration date had been completed. The five members consisted of John Devoy, Jeremiah O'Donovan Rossa, Charles O'Connell, Henry Mulleda and John McClure. These five men, particularly Devoy and Rossa were the most unrepentant and dangerous opponents of the British Empire with already a long history of armed opposition and conspiracy behind them. For these five men the United States was an obvious destination from which to continue the struggle for Irish independence.

The importance of the arrival of these men did not go unnoticed to Irish-Americans and those wishing to curry favor with the Irish electorate in the United States. Democratic representatives from Tammany Hall as well as Republicans gathered to meet the new arrivals as they sailed into New York Harbor. Irish fraternal organizations including the Knights of Saint Patrick competed with each other to be the first to greet the arriving heroes. Devoy stood out among the arriving exiles. Devoy conducted an interview with a Spanish journalist both in Spanish, which he had some knowledge, but switched to speaking French which the journalist also had knowledge of. Devoy's early years serving in the French Foreign Legion came to serve him well in his future endeavors. The arrival as a whole proved a spectacular propaganda success that rallied many divergent factions into the fold of Clan-na-Gael who took the lead in organizing the overall event.

At this point it is best to delve more into the monumental figure of John Devoy who would come to dominate Irish-American nationalism until his death in 1928. Devoy was born in County Kilkenny in 1842. His

---

27   Funchion, Michael. Chicago's Irish Nationalists, 1881-1890. Loyola University. Chicago. 1973. P. 51-52.

father was a farmer and laborer which was the common occupation for many Irish Catholics of the time period. In later years Devoy's family moved to Dublin where his father would take up employment working in a brewery. It was this move to Dublin that would open up many new opportunities for what was becoming a more intellectually and politically aware young mind.

During his time in Dublin Devoy worked full time to support his family during the day and at night attended the Catholic University. During these early years in Dublin the increasingly politically aware Devoy came more and more into contact with the Fenian movement whose aims and objectives he came to sympathize more and more with. In 1861 Devoy took the momentous decision to join the Fenian movement. Prospects of rebellion were dim during this time period so Devoy took the unprecedented decision of joining the French Foreign Legion in order to gain the necessary experience he felt was required for the eventual and inevitable rebellion. The decision to join one of the most psychologically and physically demanding military forces in the world and to serve in the most inhospitable parts of northern Africa says a lot about the mentality of Devoy. From almost the beginning of his revolutionary career he threw himself wholeheartedly into the cause of Irish independence and from day one never wavered in that commitment.

When Devoy arrived back in Ireland after a year in the French Foreign Legion he was designated a Fenian organizer in Naas, County Kildare. After the arrest of many in the Fenian leadership in 1865 Devoy was appointed Chief Organizer of Fenians in the British Army in Ireland. His central focus was to recruit Irish members of the British Army to the Fenian cause. This was the first major indicator as to the high esteem that Devoy was held within revolutionary circles in Ireland. His stock was further increased when Devoy organized the prison escape of leading Fenian, James Stephens, from Richmond Prison in Dublin.

The Fenian movement attempted to launch an armed rebellion in 1866 which turned out to be an unmitigated disaster and resulted in Devoy's arrest and imprisoned in Mountjoy prison. After being convicted of treason and sentenced to fifteen years' penal servitude in Portland prison Devoy continued his rebellious activities through organized prison strikes. He became such an irritant and threat to prison authorities that Devoy was eventually moved to Millbank Prison in London, far removed from his Fenian colleagues. The conditions for prisoners, in particular Irish political prisoners, in Victorian Era British prisons can be described as little more than barbaric during this time with conditions being closer to the medieval era than the nineteenth century. Devoy would stay in Millbank until his eventual release in 1871[28]. While others would be driven mentally insane and leave prison broken men Devoy's experience, If anything, strengthened his revolutionary commitment.

In 1869 a wide section of the Irish population organized a campaign for the amnesty of Fenian prisoners serving extremely harsh sentences in Irish and British prisons. Under the leadership of John Nolan the remaining Fenian leadership organized an extremely effective public relations campaign that exposed the often brutal treatment of Fenian prisoners' in English prisons. Mass meetings were organized and one held in Cabra in Dublin was estimated to have attracted as many as 200,000 people eventually forced the British government into releasing thirty leading Fenian prisoners in 1871, one of which was John Devoy. While prison authorities would certainly have been glad to see the back of Devoy, in hindsight the British released what would turn out to be its most enduring, bitter and effective opponent of British rule in Ireland to have been seen in generations and would remain so until his death in 1928[29].

With the domestic situation lacking the conditions needed for an uprising Clan-na-Gael looked in other directions to attempt to force the situation and take the lead in creating such circumstances. As with earlier Irish radicals leading up to and during the Crimean War the Clan looked to Russia for assistance and aid. The 1870s saw rising tensions between the British and Russian empires. As Russian influence in central Asia grew, as well as its desire for warm water ports on the Indian Ocean, the British feared possible aggression toward India. Tensions were further exasperated with rebellions in the Balkans in 1876 which threatened the already slowly collapsing Ottoman Empire. Britain's great fear again was the spread of

28   Golway, Terry. Irish Rebel – John Devoy and America's Fight for Ireland's Freedom. St. Martin's Griffin. 1999. New York. P. 1-41.

29   Kee, Robert. The Green Flag – A History of Irish Nationalism. Penguin Books. London. 2000. P. 358.

Russian influence into southeast Europe which would unsettle the balance of power on the European continent threatening a possible conflict in which Britain would inevitably be dragged into[30].

Being very aware of international conditions the Clan sent a delegation to the Russian minister in Washington to discuss possible plans for support of a military nature in a possible rebellion in Ireland. Just as during the Crimean War the Russians showed little interest. This lack of interest was based on a solid knowledge of the political situation in Ireland which the Russians knew was more focused on issues of land reform and Home Rule. With the international situation in a precarious position the Russians did not want to be seen as the one who would provoke the British into taking retaliatory action that could lead to full scale war. In the end the Berlin Conference of 1878 eased Anglo-Russian tensions therefore ending the Clan's hope of a major British military entanglement with the Russian Empire[31].

With the domestic situation in Ireland and internationally looking less and less conducive to armed insurrection the Clan took it upon themselves to take the initiative to launch a major show of organizational ability and a propaganda coup. In 1876 the Clan planned and executed what would turn out to be not only one of its best planned operations but also one of the greatest and most audacious prison escapes in modern history. Australia had long been a location of exile and imprisonment for generations of Irish rebels. As far back as 1798 United Irishmen prisoners were sent to the colony and in 1804 many of those same men rose in rebellion against British colonial authorities to stage the first armed insurrection in Australia. Although it ended in failure with brutal retributions Irish political exiles remained a constant thorn in the side of British authorities in Australia.

After later waves of Young Irelander exiles it would be the turn of Fenian prisoners who planned from their earliest days' escape from the harsh Australian environment. It would be the relentless John Devoy who would take the lead in organizing the first successful mass escape of

30   Hopkirk, Peter. *The Great Game: The Struggle for Empire in Central Asia.* Kodansha International. Tokyo. 1992.

31   Funchion, Michael. *Chicago's Irish Nationalists, 1881-1890.* Loyola University. Chicago. 1973. P. 52.

numerous Fenian prisoners. The catalyst for the escape seems to have been a letter received by Devoy from James Wilson who was a prisoner that time in Australia asking for an attempt to be made to organize a prison break. After debate within the ranks of the Clan it was Thomas Fennell who suggested the purchase of a ship. A whaling ship called the Catalpa was purchased for $5,500 and manned with twenty-two sailors it set sail in April 1876 from New Bedford, Massachusetts. Since this was well before the creation of the Panama Canal and the base of Clan strength lay in the northeast of the United States the journey to Australia would be almost 10,000 miles. One must also keep in mind that the British navy was the most dominant in the world at this time and truly "ruled the waves". The plan was audacious in the extreme.

When the Catalpa finally docked in Freemantle in Australia. Both John Breslin and Thomas Desmond went ashore under false names to make prearranged contacts with the Fenian prisoners. After arranging, a time, date and location for the escape the wheels were set in motion. On 17 April at 8.30 a.m. a total of six Fenian prisoners escaped from their work party and made it by a small boat to the Catalpa that was docked in the local bay. The prisoners included Thomas Darragh, Martin Hogan, Michael Harrington, Thomas Hassett, Robert Cranston and James Wilson. While the relief must have been palpable it was just the beginning of what would be an epic escape.

Soon into the escape the Catalpa was tracked down by the British warship the Georgette. The Clan men raised the America flag and declared that any act of aggression against the Catalpa would be a declaration of war against the United States. The captain of the Georgette, uncertain of how exactly to proceed and not wanting to cause an international incident veered on the side of caution and returned to Freemantle. For the remainder of the journey the Catalpa avoided British naval ships and eventually reached New York in August.

The arrival and reception for the escaped prisoners was something not seen in New York for many years. The Clan arranged for the escaped men to be brought in carriages to Rossa's hotel this was turned into a site for widespread celebration. The Irish World newspaper, the main voice of Clan-na-Gael, reported "Rossa's hotel, on which the green flag was hoisted immediately on the arrival of the news, became the center of attraction for nationalists. A constant stream of visitors kept pouring in throughout the day, and the 'Catalpa six' would have been quickly tired out but that the satisfaction of being free and compatriots did not allow any other feeling to affect them. All were in the garb of sailors, provided them onboard the Catalpa".

The spectacular escape and the newspaper reporting that accompanied it sent a surge of pride and renewed purpose through the ranks of Clan-na-Gael. The Clan had proven it had the ability not just to strike at the British empire but to do so thousands of miles away. The success showed a logistical ability as well as the possibility to influence directly events in Ireland at some stage in the future. Membership and donations to the Clan swelled in the weeks and months after the event. The organization spread rapidly as far as San Francisco and New Orleans. Perhaps just as importantly John Devoy emerged as the main driving force behind the Clan[32].

John Devoy and the Clan's newfound resurgence in confidence soon manifested itself in perhaps one of the most ambitious and in the end unrealistic plans. Very soon after the Catalpa success Devoy became informed through reliable sources of the invention and tests being carried out by another Irishman, John Holland, of what would be the forerunner of todays submarine. In the aftermath of the famous rescue mission on the Catalpa money poured into the Clan in the form of donations. These donations were used to set up what became known as the Skirmishing Fund. This would be a financial pool from which Clan branches could draw upon. Devoy later wrote that "Holland was well informed on Irish affairs and was anti-English and with clear and definite ideas of the proper method of fighting England. He was cool, good- tempered, and talked to us as a schoolmaster would to his children". After meeting with Holland Devoy envisioned a weapon that if properly mastered could cripple the British navy.

Early disagreements within the Clan about the ideas of financing the submarine project saw O'Donovan Rossa, who opposed the plan, pitted against the rising star of John Devoy. Devoy's position within the Clan saw

---

32   Stevens, Peter. The Voyage of the Catalpa. Carroll and Graf Publishers. New York. 2002.

his vision win out in the end against Rossa who at this stage of his life was beginning to be seen as unstable, borderline alcoholic and out of touch with the new rising generation of nationalists. In other words, Rossa was seen by many as a leftover of a bygone age. In May of 1879 Holland was given the go ahead with the project of creating a weapon that was hoped would neutralize the strongest branch of the British military and the key to its empire, it's navy.

Early on the project faced major problems. The first failure was the inability of the Clan to keep the project a secret. Numerous foreign governments caught wind of the project which included Britain who kept a particularly close eye on the project. To make matters worse regular reports and updates appeared in New York newspapers along with the inconvenient exposure of Clan involvement. It was the New York Sun newspaper who gave the submarine it's enduring nickname, the Fenian Ram.

Despite the unwanted exposure Holland's work progressed and by 1881 he was ready to test out his new submarine. Rossa and his supporters within the Clan raged against the massive cost of the project which was estimated to be approximately $60,000. He argued that it would have been better spent financing bombing campaigns in Britain. The launch and early testing of the Fenian Ram proved a huge success and by mid-1883 Holland was cruising in New York harbor at depths of up to 50 feet.

Despite these successes the Fenian Ram was still a long way off from taking to the open oceans to sink British shipping. With no foreseeable benefit on the horizon some within the Clan began to argue that the submarine should be sold and the money recouped used for more direct revolutionary purposes. At this point the Skirmishing Fund had little more than $15,000 in its account, hardly enough to carry out major operations.

One late night in November 1883 members of the Clan used a tugboat to pull away the Fenian Ram from its mooring and put it into hiding in New Haven. It turned out that it was a faction of the Clan under the instruction of Breslin that decided to use the submarine themselves. However, it soon became apparent that none within the Clan had the technical experience to operate the submarine and the whole event became a fiasco. To make matters worse the Clan even had the audacity to contact Holland to ask for help in operating the submarine that they had stolen from him. Needless to say, Holland was infuriated. He vowed to "Let her rot on their hands" before he would help them. From that point the Clan cut off all financing for the project. Both Holland and the Clan now went their separate ways. The Clan abandoned the Fenian Ram in New Haven. It would not be until 1916 that the submarine reemerged at Madison Square Garden as part of an exhibition to raise money for the victims of the Easter Rising. Today it sits in Paterson Museum. It was somehow fitting that the submarine the Clan wasted so much money in financing would end up returning so much of that money to pay for the aftermath of a rebellion that they played such a central role in organizing[33].

As the 1870s came to an end Clan-na-Gael consolidated its position as by far the largest and most well-organized Irish-American revolutionary movement. Other groups, including remaining Fenian factions, either amalgamated with the Clan or disappeared entirely from the political scene. Despite these domestic successes in the United States, it was a barren decade when it came to organizing what was the central purpose of the Clan's entire existence, a successful rebellion in Ireland against British rule. As the decade came to an end debate began to emerge with the Clan as to a possible change in strategy that in the short term fell short of armed insurrection. It became impossible to ignore the political conditions then existing in Ireland. The mass popular movements in Ireland during this time period did not involve advocating armed rebellion, instead mass debate and protest surrounded the issues of Home Rule and land reform. These were political aims that fell far short of the Clan's desired aim of a republic but did offer opportunity in other ways. Voices began to emerge within the leadership ranks of the Clan that the best way forward was to align itself with the popular mass movements in Ireland in the short run while continuing to plan and lay the groundwork for a future republic. It would be these voices that would gain the upper hand and lead the Clan into the 1880s. However, this decision would not come without opposition from the die-hard militants of the Clan and it would be a cause of dissension and factionalism in the coming years.

---

33   Goldstone, Lawrence. Going Deep – John Philip Holland and the Invention of the Attack Submarine. Pegasus Books. New York. 2017.

CHAPTER 4

The New Departure

By the end of the 1870s political opinion among the three main strands of Irish politics began to coalesce along the lines of forming a broad front to achieve the central aims of Home Rule and land reform that would see major land transfers from Anglo-Irish and English landlords back to the Irish peasantry. The year 1879 would be a momentous milestone in Irish and Irish- American history and one that would have lasting consequences for Clan-na-Gael. Charles Parnell as leader of the moderate Home Rule movement never flinched in attempting to reach out to revolutionary republicans. He was a young leader who broke with the older generation of leaders in being more forceful and confrontational in making demands for major political and social reform in Ireland. This first outreach came in 1877 when Irish-American journalist and close friend to John Devoy, James O'Kelly, met with Parnell during two long conversations during which was discussed the topic of political collaboration with Clan-na-Gael in the U.S. and her sister organization the Irish Republican Brotherhood in Ireland.

This first contact was to prove that Parnell held no stigma in working with militant Irish Republicans. O'Kelly reported back to Devoy approvingly of the meetings with Parnell – "With the right kind of support behind him and a band of real nationalists in the House of Commons he would so remold Irish public opinion as to clear away many of the stumbling blocks in the way of progressive action". For Devoy Parnell held the possibility of opening up mainstream Irish politics to the influence of Clan na Gael. At the same time Parnell was very well aware of the huge financial resources offered by the Clan and how that could further the cause of both Home Rule and the Land League[34].

---

34   Kee, Robert. The Green Flag – A History of Irish Nationalism. Penguin Books. London. 2000. P. 367-368.

At this point it must be worth noting the pivotal role played by Kelly during the New Departure on behalf of Irish-American revolutionaries. O'Kelly was a boyhood friend of Devoy dating back to the pre-Fenian days for both. Both O'Kelly and Devoy were sworn into the Fenian movement together. Like Devoy O'Kelly would also join the French Foreign Legion in order to gain military experience for a future rebellion in Ireland. With the failed Fenian rising of 1867, internal factionalism and the inability of the IRB to launch an armed uprising in the years following O'Kelly became disillusioned and eventually immigrated to the U.S. where he took up a career in journalism in New York. He never forgot the cause of Irish independence and soon made contact with Clan-na-Gael and his lifelong friend John Devoy. From an Irish revolutionary standpoint O'Kelly's credentials were impeccable. His standing among the IRB in Ireland and the Clan in the U.S. contributed toward O'Kelly becoming a leading figure in Irish revolutionary circles for decades to come. His opinion and viewpoint was always to be taken seriously.

O'Kelly was then a logical choice to become the Clan envoy to the IRB. Although O'Kelly was advocating what was essentially a major ideological compromise he never swayed from his revolutionary roots. In 1879 O'Kelly proposed providing military aid to the Zulus in their war against Britain. In 1880 he would further try to persuade the Clan and IRB to arm Irish tenants in their land agitation against British landlords. Both proposals were ultimately rejected. Despite this Devoy would hold O'Kelly's suggestions and viewpoints in the highest regard. In the years to come O'Kelly would become a member of the Land League's Central Committee and later on become essentially the Home Rule Party's foreign policy spokesperson. During this entire time period O'Kelly remained an unrepentant revolutionary and member of Clan-na-Gael. The Clan had invaluable access at the highest levels of Irish political life that was critical to developing policy and reading the Irish political situation in attempts to launch future armed rebellions[35].

35   McGee, Owen. 2008. Originator of the New Departure. History Ireland. Vol. 16 (Issue 6).

On the face of it the Clan was compromising most ideologically by joining what would become the "New Departure". Its avowed purpose was to achieve an independent Irish Republic through armed rebellion. As a result of this new political strategy the Clan was essentially, at least in the short term, giving up prospects of launching a rebellion. This did not go down easily with many hardliners within the Clan. In reality, however, the Clan and IRB continued to secretly prepare for an uprising. When the details of the New Departure were published in the New York Herald in October 1878, it triggered off intense debate within the Clan membership. Although Devoy at this stage was leaning toward the new political alignment he needed to bring along the grass root membership with him. To clarify the situation and ease concerns of the Clan membership Devoy visited Europe and had two meetings with Parnell in order to clarify the conditions of the new alliance. According to Devoy he clarified to Parnell that while the focus should be on land reform that this should not interfere in attempts for an uprising. According to Clan sources they also managed to get a pledge from Parnell that he was in favor of eventual Irish independence[36].

This meeting must be looked at in detail in order to fully access. Firstly, it is possible that the nature of the discussion and Parnell's response was made up or manipulated in order to placate more radical members of the Clan na Gael membership back in the U.S. by reassuring them that revolutionary Republicanism was not being merely used or manipulated by moderate nationalists in Ireland for their own political purposes. Devoy was a master after all at balancing the different political currents and factions within the Clan. However, it is also conceivable that the conversation took place as described by Devoy in which case we must ask the question was Parnell being genuine in his belief of eventual Irish independence or was he merely placating Devoy in order to continue his access to Clan na Gael's financial resources? It is likely in hindsight that Parnell aided Devoy in telling him exactly what he wanted to hear and gave him the means to bring the Clan along with him in the political alliance known as the New

36 Kee, Robert. The Green Flag – A History of Irish Nationalism. Penguin Books. London. 2000. P. 168-169.

Departure. Also, it is likely that the politically astute Devoy may not have fully believed and trusted Parnell and fully intended to further the Clan's ultimate revolutionary goal when the moment presented itself. Essentially, both men used each other in the short term while having differing long term political goals.

In relation to remaining loyal to the principles of armed revolution Devoy also had a number of secret meetings with the IRB during his time in Ireland. Devoy proposed and was supported by the IRB in organizing joint arms smuggling operation to arm the 25,000 members of the Brotherhood. The Clan would provide $25,000 needed for the operation. The guarantee from Parnell coupled with the promise of funds for arming the IRB placated many of the more militant and suspicious within the ranks of the Clan who feared a political and ideological sellout. From Devoy's perspective it was a masterful display in turning a hardened revolutionary movement into a more ideologically flexible and adaptable movement responsive to the needs of both the Irish-American membership as well as the domestic wing of the movement, the IRB. He played his hand deftly in remaining true to revolutionary principles while taking part in the mainstream political process with more moderate political and social elements of Irish society[37].

After having met with and come to agreement with the leader of the Home Rule movement Devoy took the next logical step of meeting with Michael Davitt, leader of the Land League. It was Parnell who arranged the meeting between the three heads of the largest political movements in the country at that time. Devoy spent a large part of the meeting listening to Davitt and his descriptions of the deteriorating conditions among the peasantry, especially in the west of the country which was traditionally the poorest. Devoy already had an established relationship with Davitt. The year before in 1878 Devoy helped organize a lecture tour for Davitt in the U.S. in which he publicized the struggle for land reform and raised funds for the Land League. As well as this Davitt had a strong revolutionary background. In 1867 Davitt was involved in a failed Fenian raid on Chester Castle in order to obtain arms. In 1870 he was eventually captured and

---

37   Golway, Terry. Irish Rebel – John Devoy and America's Fight for Ireland's Freedom. St. Martin's Griffin, New York. 1998. P. 112-113.

imprisoned on treason charges and served fifteen years penal servitude in Dartmoor prison. Most of Davitt's imprisonment was in solitary confinement where he was treated with brutality on many occasions. On his release Davitt continued his revolutionary activities when he joined the new Irish Republican Brotherhood and went on to become a member of its Supreme Council in 1877. As a member of the IRB he was a continual advocate of the Land issue arguing the need for IRB involvement and support. In 1879 Davitt would go on to be the leading founder of what would become known as the Land League. These credentials in many ways left Devoy with much more of a common bond with Davitt that he would ever have had with the more aristocratic Anglo-Irish Parnell[38].

During the meeting Devoy informed both Davitt and Parnell than the IRB was in opposition to such an alliance but that the Clan was in full support. This was of enormous significance to both Parnell and Davitt as it was more important that Clan-na-Gael were on board that the IRB. The central reason was the enormous financial resources that the Clan could bring to the upcoming political struggle. The IRB at this point were politically insignificant and totally reliant upon its sister organization in the U.S. The refusal of the IRB to support the New Departure may well be seen not only as an ideological disagreement but also an attempt to assert some sort of independence and give itself a voice that was increasingly drowned out by Devoy and the more politically powerful and influential Clan na Gael organization. It would ultimately prove a futile gesture.

Devoy did not give up on the IRB and continued to try to bring them on board in the new political alliance. Although Devoy toured IRB strongholds throughout the country he was unable to bring the membership along with his aims and objectives. During a meeting on 1 June between the three main figures Devoy would later insist that Parnell agreed to the conditions put forward by the Clan in return for Irish-American support[39]. These conditions were likely the same ones sent by the Clan leadership directly to Parnell in late 1878 which were as follows – 1. Abandonment

---

38   Sheehy-Skeffington, Francis. Michael Davitt. MacGibbon & Kee. London. 1967. P. 26-81.

39   Golway, Terry. Irish Rebel – John Devoy and America's Fight for Ireland's Freedom. St. Martin's Griffin. New York. 1998. P. 120.

of a Federal demand, and substitution of a general declaration in favor of self-government. 2. Vigorous agitation of the land question on the basis of a peasant proprietary, while accepting concessions tending to abolish arbitrary evictions. 3. Exclusion of sectarian issues from the platform. 4. Irish members to vote together on all imperial and home questions, adopt an aggressive policy, and energetically resist coercive legislation. 5. Advocacy for all struggling nationalities in the British Empire and elsewhere[40]. These Clan demands give an excellent insight as to where exactly the organization stood in both a practical and ideological sense during this critical moment in Irish and Irish-American history. The Clan saw a huge revolutionary potential in the Irish peasantry and saw the land issue as the main vehicle in which to move forward the cause of a republic. They did not turn their back on parliamentary politics but instead argued for a more aggressive and confrontational stance within the British parliament. The mention of the issue of sectarianism was tacit acknowledgement for one of the first times in Clan history of continuing religious strife in the province of Ulster for which it had few practical solutions. Perhaps the hope was that the land issue would help unite in some way poor Catholic and Protestant tenant farmers under the banner of land reform. The final point of advocating for other nationalities under British rule is perhaps one of the most interesting. On first reading this may seem somewhat of a less important almost innocuous final demand. However, unlike the IRB, the Clan was taking on a more global anti-imperial role that would become more and more evident in the decades to come and which would set it somewhat apart from its counterparts in Ireland who paid but limited lip service to such global struggles. One can take this global anti-imperial stance as very much a consequence of the Clan's American experience and connections with political exiles from around the world who would take up residence in the U.S. over the centuries.

Although Devoy indicates that Parnell acquiesced to Clan demands many historians today seem to agree that this was little more than lip service. Parnell never formalized the relationship between Clan-na-Gael and

---

40   Pollard, H.B.C. The Secret Societies of Ireland. The Irish Historical Press. Kilkenny. 1998. P. 57.

the Home Rule Party. From Parnell's perspective doing so would only have given ammunition to his conservative opponents in Britain and loyalists in the north of Ireland to portray him as either the dupe of nefarious revolutionaries or even worse, that Parnell himself was a secret republican using the cloak of Home Rule. While Devoy would continually defend the New Departure to the Clan and Irish-Americans more broadly, for Parnell it was a simple case of gaining access to the large financial resources that the revolutionary movement in the U.S. could offer. It could also be argued that both Devoy and Parnell very much tried to use each other to achieve their own limited objectives by riding the wave of a popular national issue in land reform. In the end both Home Rule and a republic were too incompatible to last in alliance for long[41].

Parnell's hopes would come to fruition in 1880 as the Clan played a major role in organizing a U.S. tour for him in order to highlight the Land League and the campaign for major land reform. During his tour of the U.S. Parnell tended to use forceful and even violent language in order to appeal to Irish-American nationalists. In Cincinnati Parnell allegedly stated during a speech "When we have undermined English rule, we will have paved the way for Ireland to take her place among the nations of the earth. None of us will be satisfied until we have destroyed the last link which keeps Ireland bound to England". The pinnacle of Parnell's visit came when he addressed the U.S. House of Representatives on 2 February. The growing power and influence of the Clan in the U.S. was highlighted when they arranged a secret meeting with select Democratic Congressmen in order to put forward a resolution asking for Parnell to address the House which was eventually passed.

During Parnell's highly publicized tour of the U.S. another less well covered tour was taking place. With the help of the Clan-na-Gael Michael Davitt carried out a tour that would end up taking him from New York to San Francisco. As stated earlier Davitt's credentials among revolutionary Irish-Americans were impeccable with his reputation preceding him. While Parnell was never fully embraced by many within the Clan membership

---

41 Golway, Terry. Irish Rebel – John Devoy and America's Fight for Ireland's Freedom. St. Martin's Griffin. New York. 1998. P. 120.

Davitt was seen very much as one of their own. With Clan help Davitt hoped his tour would revive flagging Land League organizations in the U.S. and reinvigorate vital fundraising efforts upon which the land struggle heavily relied. At one of his many meetings and speeches Davitt declared "teaching peasants and all people that the land was made for them and not for 10,000 lazy Englishmen....and that they are to rely upon themselves alone and not upon foreign or hostile legislators". Davitt not only helped revive failing branches of the movement but along with the Clan helped found new branches throughout the country. In the end Davitt's tour helped sustain the Land League during a time of slow growth and internal disagreement over direction. The British government were obviously following Davitt's activities in the U.S. and viewed him as enough of a threat that when he returned to Ireland in 1881 his ticket-of-leave was revoked, and Davitt was arrested[42].

It seems very likely that Parnell had an ulterior motive to his U.S. visit. It could not have been palpable to the leading figure of Irish nationalism at this time not to have control over the vital purse strings that was the life blood not only of the land struggle but also Parnell's beloved aim of achieving Home Rule. Parnell proposed early on his U.S. tour that each branch of the Land League in the U.S. sent its money directly to Ireland and not through Clan-na-Gael. The Clan were in a dominant enough position to kill any plan of bypassing Irish American revolutionaries and thus taking away their main point of political leverage over Parnell and the Land League. Parnell would change tactic and demand that the Land League fund raise directly in the U.S. thus, bypassing the Clan altogether again. Parnell achieved a limited success when the Land League established a formal organization in the U.S. known as the National League of America. This success was shallow indeed as the leadership of the new organization was dominated by Clan na Gael members.

Between 1879 and 1882 Clan membership reached an estimated 40,000 members. Each member paid 25 cents a week to his local branch or camp. Along with fundraising events and donations from major donors the Clan's

---

42   Janis, Ely. A Greater Ireland – The Land League and Transatlantic Nationalism in Gilded Age America, University of Wisconsin Press. 2015. P. 17-50.

financial clout was substantial. This would mean that the Clan would remain a force within Irish nationalism for decades to come despite setbacks and divisions[43]. It was impossible to ignore tensions within the New Departure between Clan na Gael and the Home Rule movement. Parnell's maneuvers in the U.S. in attempting to gain control over fundraising and financial resources was a direct challenge to the Clan which they managed successfully to stave off. The tactic by Parnell was a precursor to a similar attempt some forty years later when Eamon De Valera would successfully wrest financial control from Clan na Gael causing a damaging split within the organization. In many ways the Land League was caught in the middle between these two contesting forces. While Home Rulers saw the Irish peasantry as vital in creating a mass popular base in achieving Home Rule the Clan saw them as a potential revolutionary force that would provide the basis for a future rebellion. Clan na Gael and the Home Rule movement, while technically political allies, were nevertheless in a contest to win over the political allegiance of the Irish people.

43 Keyes, Michael. 2009. Money and Nationalist Politics in Nineteenth Century Ireland; From O'Connell to Parnell. History PHD. National University of Ireland. Maynooth.

CHAPTER 5

From Politics to the Bomb

As stated earlier divisions began to arise within Clan na Gael corresponding with the movement's increased involvement in the political arena. From the late 1870s well into the 1890s two distinct factions began to form. One faction viewed the New Departure and the objective of Home Rule as a step in the direction of eventual independence and possibly laying the groundwork for a future rebellion at an undefined future date. Leader of this wing of the movement was the indomitable John Devoy.

On the opposite end of the spectrum were the hardline militants who disavowed the political path as little more than an ideological sellout to the long-held belief of planning for an armed rebellion as soon as possible. If conditions were not ripe for such an uprising, it was the responsibility of the Clan to initiate and instigate the necessary conditions through violent action. The main voice for this wing of the movement was the undying and ever present Jeremiah O'Donovan Rossa[44]. This deep-seated distrust of parliamentarianism would be a feature of the Clan and broader militant Irish Republicanism for generations to come. With Rossa in advanced age and representing a very much older generation a younger element of uncompromising radicals were emerging in opposition to the political path being taken by Devoy and others. One such leading figure was Alexander Sullivan. He was an individual who would turn out to be arguably the most controversial figure in Clan history. He was a lawyer based out of Chicago and was a figure that could command both great loyalty and hatred. He had shot and killed a Superintendent of Schools over objections to bibles

---

44 Osborne, David. 2013. The Terrorist Cell: An Historical and Evolutionary Study of Irish Terrorist Cells, 1881-1896. PHD Thesis. Massey University. <https://mro.mas sey.ac.nz/bitstream/handle/10179/5761/02_whole.pdf>

in the classrooms during his early days. He somehow ended up being acquitted on a technicality. This was an early indicator to a level of violent ruthlessness that would be part of Sullivan's tenure within the Clan. By 1881 Sullivan had become the undisputed leader of the Clan in Chicago. Sullivan would become the leading voice of the militant wing of the Clan during the 1880s. As a result of Sullivan the center of radical Clan activities moved from Philadelphia to Chicago for the duration of the decade where he could maintain maximum control[45].

The early sign of tension between both wings of the movement came in letter sent by Sullivan to Devoy in September 1880 – "I fear our work and money are wasted while the IRB is under control of men who lack activity and brains. I must confess for myself that I am sorely disappointed at affairs in Ireland, especially when I am forced to believe that there never was better material there to form a revolutionary organization. Unless a change was made, my judgement is that the home connection ought to be dropped. We could do something if alone. We can do something unless home management is changed".

The letter from Sullivan to Devoy in striking in a number of ways. O'Sullivan was intelligent enough not to come out directly and attack Devoy who was a very popular figure within the Clan and in Irish-America more broadly. His criticism of the IRB was not without grounds. The two leading figures within the Irish Republican Brotherhood at this time were Charles Kickham and John O'Leary. By the early 1880s Kickham was largely deaf almost blind. He spent a large part of his time in literary pursuits and would become a well-known novelist, poet and journalist. He would end up dying at the young age of 54 in 1882. O'Leary was viewed with suspicion by many Clan members because of his strongly held atheist views. Radical Clan members were particularly frustrated by him as a result of his conservative views when it came to armed rebellion. The conditions O'Leary set forth as necessary before any uprising should be attempted was seen by many as nearly impossible to achieve or least many years into the future.

---

45   O'Brien, Gillian. 2015. "A diabolical murder": Clan-na-Gael, Chicago and the murder of Dr. Cronin. History Ireland. Vol. 23 (Issue 3).

Other significant events occurred during this time period which played directly into the hands of the radical wing of Clan-na-Gael. The years 1880-81 saw a heightening of the Land War in Ireland with evictions increasing rapidly alongside a No Rent Campaign instituted by the Land League. Violence was the almost natural result of the worsening condition and the British government responded, as it traditionally did in Ireland, with the introduction of a coercion bill which suspended habeas corpus. The imprisonment of Michael Davitt infuriated many Irish members of parliament who proceeded to cause mass disruption to proceedings through obstructionist tactics. The resulting turmoil resulted in a number of Home Rule members actually being ejected from parliament. More radical elements of the Land league wanted Home Rule members to withdraw completely from parliament in protest. Parnell's response was typically restrained and more conservative and he refused to back the No Rent Campaign. From the point of view of many within Clan-na-Gael Parnell's decision and actions during this tumultuous time period was an indication of his total lack of commitment to the more revolutionary aims of the New Departure. It now became very apparent that Parnell fell far short of the hopes that the Clan leadership had held for him.

With the IRB in apparent stagnation and the Home Rule Party falling far short of the hoped for revolutionary direction radical elements led by Rossa, and in particular Sullivan, began to view the situation as needing more direct and violent revolutionary action. One of the most important meetings in Clan history took place from 3–10 August 1881, at Palmer House, Chicago. The choice of Chicago was no mere coincidence. As already stated it was the base of power of Sullivan and the most radical wing of the Clan movement. Two hundred members representing the fifteen Clan districts came together to elect Alexander Sullivan as Chairman of the newly reformed Executive Committee. Other members elected to the committee were Michael Boland, Denis Feeley, James Treacy and James Reynolds. All were considered as belonging to the more radical wing of the Clan. The gathering was a major coup and represented a more militant takeover of the Clan. One can only assume that the elections were the result of months of prior groundwork and canvassing on behalf of what was essentially Sullivan's chosen candidates.

The takeover was further enhanced with the selection of the three American members of the Revolutionary Directory. The sitting members of the Directory were Dr Carroll, William Hynes and of course John Devoy. Devoy stepped down for personal and financial reasons while both Carroll and Hynes tendered their resignations but stated they would continue in their positions if requested by the newly elected Executive Committee. The gesture was ignored and instead Sullivan, Boland and Feeley were installed on the Revolutionary Directory. The takeover was now complete.

At this juncture it is perhaps pertinent to ask where exactly Devoy was politically and even mentally during this political takeover of the Clan? As already stated Devoy was going through personal financial problems which required his attention during this critical time period. However, is this enough to fully explain his absence and failure to build a block strong enough to stave off O'Sullivan's takeover of the Clan? The O'Sullivan faction take over had been many months in the making and it is hard to believe that the well-connected and politically astute Devoy was not aware of what was happening. Assuming this to be correct we can look as Devoy's absence from a number of different perspectives.

Firstly, Devoy may have allowed the takeover to occur and at the same time distance himself from events giving political cover in order to put pressure on the Home Rule movement by highlighting his personal importance and gaining more concessions in terms of support for future independence. Parnell saw the takeover of the Clan by its radical wing and the ensuing violence that would follow as seriously jeopardizing his own credibility and political future as well as the overall potential of achieving Home Rule. On top of these potential dangers a more militant leadership of Clan na Gael would be far less likely to give financial support to a political movement aiming for anything less than full Irish independence.

A second possibility, although less likely, is that Devoy had lost popular support within Clan na Gael and stepped back to let events play out. When the situation deteriorated with a failed military campaign, as he felt it inevitably would, he would step back into the fold to regain control and take the movement forward.

With the new leadership now in place it was time to discuss strategy. The obvious calls were to wage war in the near future. However, the stagnant position of the IRB in Ireland and the peasant focus and the Land War seriously limited the options available. During the course of discussions the idea of launching a bombing campaign in Britain were first discussed. While the Clan did not specifically endorse a bombing campaign it did press for support for an "active policy". While relations and attitudes to the Home Rule movement cooled significantly the Clan did continue to promote the idea of friendly cooperation with the Land League. The belief that the greatest revolutionary potential lay with the Irish peasantry was greatly enhanced during the ongoing Land War where violence was spreading rapidly and the idea of harnessing this energy for revolutionary purposes was very much to the fore of Clan thinking[46].

The idea of a bombing campaign using dynamite was not a new one within Clan ranks or broader terrorist style revolutionary movements operating in Europe at this time. During the Civil war many Irish soldiers who later would become members of the Fenians and Clan-na-Gael became exposed to such technological developments as landmines and clockwork explosives. During the conflict Bernard Janin Sage wrote "The Organization of Private Warfare: Bureau of Destructive Means and Measures" which advocated the effectiveness of "bands of destructionists and captors" in winning a war. The idea was quick to take hold in the Fenian movement in the immediate post-Civil War years. O'Donovan Rossa was quick to take up the concept of this new type of warfare when he established a Brooklyn Dynamite School to teach members in the art of explosive manufacturing[47].

By the time of the Clan conference in Chicago and the takeover of the movement by the radical wing O'Donovan Rossa and Patrick Crowe had essentially broken with the Clan and formed an organization called the United Irishmen. Rossa stated in the weekly newspaper of his new organization –

> "I believe in all things for the liberation of Ireland. If dynamite is necessary for the redemption of Ireland, then dynamite is a blessed agent that should be availed of by

---

46 Funchion, Michael. Chicago's Irish Nationalists, 1881-1890. Loyola University. Chicago. 1973. P. 116-171.

47 Kenna, Shane. War in the Shadows – The Irish-American Fenians who bombed Victorian Britain. Merrion Press. Sallins. 2013.

the Irish people in their holy war, and speaking in all soberness, I do not know how dynamite could be better use than blowing up the British Empire".

By 1881 former students of the Dynamite school were setting off bombs in Liverpool, London and Salford in England. These bombers were given the technical skills necessary to make these bombs on site in Britain itself. The bombs used were described as "a simple outside sheet of sheet iron, about ten inches square, the inner compartment contains the clockwork movement that at the time fixed, liberates a knife which cuts a string and let's fall a spring onto the percussion cap causing the machine to explode". The clockwork mechanism was quite an innovation for the time period. The innovation did not belong to Rossa however. A chemical expert was hired early on by the name of Professor Mezzeroff, whose real name was Richard Rogers, who professed himself as a Russian nihilist. The bombing campaign led by Rossa and the United Irishmen organization would last until February 1885. By this time Rossa and his organization had all but reintegrated back into the Clan who were now following the path of launching its own dynamite campaign[48].

Clan-na-Gael was vexed to say the least with Rossa's decision to carry out independent action outside the direction and leadership of the movement. During the early stages of Rossa's bombing campaign, the Clan leadership decided on their own bombing campaign in Britain. There may have been a number of reasons for this. Firstly, the need to be seen as the leading Irish-American revolutionary movement was essential for fundraising purposes and necessary to beat off any competition for these financial resources where the real strength of the Clan lay. Secondly, the need to keep in line young militant members from either joining Rossa's splinter organization or establishing their own independent groups. By this stage British authorities were well aware of Clan-na-Gael and their abilities. – "It's systematic proceedings in America and the secrecy which attends its projects, and correspondence with its agents in the United Kingdom and Australia it has proved itself a more formidable than any of its predecessors". In many ways it was Rossa's actions that forced the hand

48   Gantt, Jonathan. 2006. Irish-American Terrorism and Anglo-American Relations, 1881-1885. The Journal of the Gilded Age and Progressive Era. Vol. 3, No. 4.

of the Clan leadership to commence their campaign perhaps somewhat earlier than they had planned.

Between 1881 and 1883 Clan-na-Gael returned to its roots of a movement totally dedicated to violent insurrection in Ireland. The 1883 convention in Philadelphia ended Clan support for the Land League in Ireland and its branches in the U.S. A new organization to be known as the Irish National League of America was formed in order to coordinate the activities of all Irish- American revolutionary organizations. There is little doubt at this point that the declaration and new organization was an outreach to Rossa and his supporters in an attempt to coordinate activities and heal the breach within the movement. As expected, the Clan dominated the new organization with Alexander Sullivan becoming the president of the new body.

The Philadelphia conference also served another purpose. Behind the scenes in a more secretive environment it was finally decided to funnel funds behind a dynamite campaign in Britain. Voices advocating a more moderate approach with continued support for Parnell's Home Rule approach was drowned out as radical militants were now in the majority. The Clan also decided to use its financial power in a more aggressive way than it had ever done before. The IRB had always struggled financially and if it wanted to remain a viable organization then it needed Clan-na-Gael financial support and weapons imports. This would give the Clan the upper hand in the relationship and made the IRB more subservient to the military and political wishes of her American sister organization.

With the balance of power between Clan-na-Gael and the IRB firmly based in the U.S. the Clan began to exert more and more pressure on the Brotherhood to become more relevant and active in Ireland. In order to assist and encourage increased IRB activity the Clan sent $40,000 to Ireland. This financial assistance as well as pressure from the Clan changed the IRB's attitude toward the dynamite campaign to one of full support. Tensions still remained between both the Clan and IRB as the IRB deeply resented being subordinate to what was the foreign based wing of the republican movement. It must be remembered that the IRB Supreme Council viewed itself as the provisional government of Ireland. As a result, only they had the sole right to determine when a revolution would occur as they were closest to not only the political situation in Ireland but to the Irish people themselves. Relations would remain cool until after 1887 then the IRB again would establish a supportive relationship with the moderate wing of Clan na Gael.

Just like the United Irishmen organization under Rossa dynamite was to be the preferred weapon of the Clan's British bombing campaign. The organization was to become very innovative in the development of military technology. Men such as Thomas Bullen designed a torpedo boat back in the 1870s with the hope of sinking British shipping. It did manage to stay under water for up to three hours despite its ultimate failure. The bombs themselves saw the innovative use of nitroglycerin compounds in various configurations. The earlier mentioned Mezzerhoff provided his expertise to the Clan and went on to teach many of their operatives, such as Thomas Mooney and Edward O'Donnell in the manufacture and use of dynamite out of the dynamite school in Brooklyn. Mezzerhoff was fond of lecturing his students on how at a cost of $150 twenty men could successfully undertake a devastating bombing campaign of London.

Those who actively carried out the bombing campaign were either first or second generation Irish emigrants to the U.S. Those who were from Ireland were radicalized through their direct exposure to British rule and the poverty and unjust land system that the majority of the Irish peasantry lived under. Those born in the U.S. became radicalized as a result of their membership of the Clan. This would have involved attendance to secretive Clan meetings and public propaganda events and classes. Those born in America would also have had parents and/or grandparents who some forty years earlier had fled horrific famine conditions in Ireland resulting in vengeance being a major motivating factor[49].

The organizational structure of the bombing campaign was to be based upon a system of cells. Although this system was used before under the Fenians it would be Clan na Gael that perfected its effectiveness. These cells operated as semi-autonomous irregular fighting units that operated in

---

49   Osborne, David. 2013. The Terrorist Cell: An Historical and Evolutionary Study of Irish Terrorist Cells, 1881-1896. PHD Thesis. Massey University. <https://mro.massey.ac.nz/bitstream/handle/10179/5761/02_whole.pdf>

major British urban centers. They would range in size from two to twelve men with a cell leader coordinating day to day operations. They operated with discretion and blended into their urban environment to the point of becoming part of the landscape around them. The ultimate aim of the bombing campaign was to cause maximum disruption to British civilian life and keeping the issue of Irish independence at the forefront of British politics. The hope was also to cause civilian pressure on the government to ultimately disengage from Ireland[50].

The British government was aware of the Clan bombing campaign that was about to commence. Arguably the greatest breach of Clan security came with the infiltration into its ranks of one of the most damaging spies in its history. Henri Le Caron, whose real name was Thomas Miller Beach, was a British agent who had infiltrated the ranks of the Fenian movement as far back as 1865. Due to extremely relaxed nature of internal security Le Caron was able to gain access to highly classified information relating to the Fenian raids on Canada. He remained an ever-present feature of the Irish-American nationalist movement. It would be Alexander Sullivan who opened up a second door of opportunity by offering Le Caron membership of Clan na Gael. Le Caron would go on to become a close confidant of Sullivan in the years ahead. Le Caron would remain a secret agent until he finally revealed his true identity in 1889 after returning to Britain in the aftermath of passing on hundreds of reports to British intelligence on the inner workings of the Clan. Le Caron's first warnings of the Clan bombing campaign came too late to affect the immediate upcoming attacks[51].

The early bombings carried out by O'Donovan Rossa's wing of Clan na Gael commenced in 1881 with attacks on Salford Barrack in Manchester, a failed bombing attempt of London Mansion House and bomb attacks on Liverpool barrack and Town Hall. As can be seen Rossa choose military and political targets over that of civilian targets. These choices of targets showed how Rossa was very much from a generation that did not view

---

50   Osborne, David. 2013. The Terrorist Cell: An Historical and Evolutionary Study of Irish Terrorist Cells, 1881-1896. PHD Thesis. Massey University. <https://mro.mas sey.ac.nz/bitstream/handle/10179/5761/02_whole.pdf>

51   Cole, J.A. Prince of Spies – Henri Le Caron. Faber and Faber publishers. London. 1984.

civilian targets as legitimate or morally justifiable[52]. This would change when the Clan entered the campaign.

The early actions of Rossa and later Clan bombers did not go unnoticed by the more militant elements within the Irish Republican Brotherhood. A younger generation of more radical members of the IRB became frustrated at the lack of opportunity being given with the older and more conservative leadership of the organization and decided to take independent action based on the examples of their Irish-American counterparts. On 13 March 1881, Russian Czar Alexander II was assassinated which made news all over Europe. More militant elements of the IRB saw the huge international impact of a targeted assassination on a high-ranking public official. The arrest of Parnell and the faltering of Land League ambitions just added to the frustration and feelings of the need for radical action to bolster the cause of independence.

Out of this frustration was born what would become known as the Irish National Invincibles. The new organization was funded by John Walsh and P.J Sheridan. Walsh himself sat on the Supreme Council of the IRB and was suspected as having close links with Rossa. A major source of recruits for the Invincibles were the IRB itself. As opposed to using the bombing strategy of Rossa and the Clan it was decided to carry out targeted assassinations, with the priority being the highest-ranking British official in Ireland which was at this time Lord Frederick Cavendish who was Chief Secretary of Ireland.

On 6 May 1882, the Invincibles struck with the assassination not just Lord Cavendish but also the Permanent Undersecretary, Thomas Burke. Both were stabbed to death while walking in Phoenix Park in Dublin. In the aftermath of the assassinations the British backlash was rapid and severe with the arrests and executions of the assassins in the aftermath of the killings. With this the Irish National Invincibles quickly collapsed. However, in its short existence it carried out what would be the highest profile assassination of a British official in Irish history. It can be strongly argued

52   Kenna, Shane. War in the Shadows – The Irish-American Fenians who bombed Victorian Britain. Merrion Press. Sallins. 2013.

that Clan na Gael while not directly involved were certainly an inspiration for the use of more violent direct action against British rule in Ireland[53].

In 1883 following the Phoenix Park assassinations the Clan would launch its most daring and in the end disastrous campaign to date. At the commencement of the campaign the Clan issued the following communique to its active members – 1. Hereafter no member shall by interview or in any manner appear in the public press, or speak or write to anyone not a member, of any matter, person or event, engaged in or arrested member for revolutionary operations. 2. Senior Guardians shall in their sound discretion have power to publish information calculated to deceive the enemy. 3. Camps may, when it is deemed prudent, change their present names and locations for others less suspicious, without attracting public attention to the change. 4. No person who is not a member for at least three years and who antecedents, prudence and courage is not fully known, shall be accepted and sent forward for any work of a revolutionary character. 5. In localities favorable to the work, camps shall institute schools for the manufacture of explosives and other warfare. 6. Camps shall procure, as far as possible, the names, photographs and residences of detectives, and keep a list of the same. 7. All books and papers, when the same cannot be satisfactorily secured, must be destroyed or cancelled. 8. It is made the duty of every camp to utilize every method of raising funds for the Special Fund by picnics, balls, parties and fairs, and contributions from outside confidential sources[54].

From the beginning of the Clan's formal bombing campaign, they succeeded is establishing an atmosphere of fear with bomb attacks that went beyond political and military targets. Locations that were targeted were such things as gasworks, bridges, train stations, newspaper offices, the Tower of London as well as politically symbolic targets like Scotland Yard. However, setbacks would dog the Clan's campaign with arrests and resulting disruptions made early on.

---

53 Osborne, David. 2013. *The Terrorist Cell: An Historical and Evolutionary Study of Irish Terrorist Cells, 1881-1896*. PHD Thesis. Massey University. <https://mro.mas sey.ac.nz/bitstream/handle/10179/5761/02_whole.pdf>

54 Pollard, H.B.C. *The Secret Societies of Ireland*. The Irish Historical Press. Kilkenny. 1998.

In January of 1883 the Clan launched attacks in Glasgow and London.
Dozens of injuries resulted in these attacks. The London underground was
attacked in October which resulted in seventy casualties. British authorities
reacted quickly to spreading public fear of further attacks by expanding the
Irish Special Branch with more experts in dealing with political violence
and revolutionary organizations. Special Branch in both Ireland and Britain
activated their network of spies and informants which resulted in a number
of tipoffs in their favor. A number of bombs attacks were prevented and
arrests resulted. March 1883 saw the arrest of Clan members Denis Deasy
and Patsy Flanagan were arrested in Britain and Timothy Featherstone
in Cork. From that point things only got worse for the Clan. Although
intermittent attacks continued it seems that the arrests bore fruit and the
arrested members seem to have given up information under interrogation
that more than likely would include what we would classify today as torture. Businesses in Cork were raided which were probably used as fronts
to transfer money and resources from the U.S. to distribute among Clan
operatives. British authorities were rapidly gaining an insight into the Clan
operation in Ireland and Britain. The year 1883 would see the further dismantling of Clan networks with the arrests and convictions of Thomas
Gallagher and three other Clan members who went on trial and were
sentenced to life imprisonment. Further arrests in Liverpool and Glasgow
would see the year end disastrously for the Clan campaign.

The year 1884 saw a significant falloff in attacks as a result of the arrests.
High profile attacks on Scotland Yard and London train stations did not
cover the fact that continued arrests of important operatives such as John
Daly, James Egan and William McDonnell saw the Clan campaign stutter
to its inevitable conclusion. Attacks in 1885 on the Tower of London and
outside the House of Commons saw the final actions of a failed campaign.
British intelligence had the final say with the discovery of a dynamite stash
on Harrow Road in London[55].

In total twenty Clan members would be arrested for their involvement
in the bombing campaign. These men would suffer terrible conditions in

---

55   Kenna, Shane. War in the Shadows – The Irish-American Fenians who bombed
      Victorian Britain. Merrion Press. Sallins. 2014.

Victorian prisons. A number of prisoners suffered mental breakdowns. Denis Deasy would die in custody. One of those arrested was Thomas Clarke who would be a future leader of the 1916 Rising and signatory of the declaration of independence the same year. Clarke recalled years later his horrific prison experience –

> "Had anyone told me before the prison doors closed upon me that it was possible for any human being to endure what Irish prisoners have endured in Chatham Prison, and come out of it alive and sane, I would not have believed him....we treason/felony prisoners were known as..." the special men" ...kept, not in ordinary prison halls but in penal cells – kept there so that we could be more conveniently persecuted, for the authorities aimed at making life unbearable for us. The ordinary rules regulating the treatment of prisoners, which, to some extent, shield those from foul play and the caprice of petty officers, these rules as far as they did that, were in our case set aside. This was a scientific system of perpetual and persistent harassing.... harassing morning, noon and night, and on through the night, harassing always and at all times, harassing with bread and water punishments, and other punishments with "no sleep" torture and other tortures. The system was applied to the Irish prisoners and to them only., and was especially designed to destroy us mentally or physically – to kill or drive insane[56]".

As the beginning of the bombing campaign the Clan had a number of advantages – 1. technical training and advancements in the field of bomb making as provided by the Brooklyn Dynamite School. 2. Significant financial resources to support such a campaign. 3. An organizational structure based on a system of cells that on the face of it seemed secure and efficient. The question then must be asked, why did it all go so wrong? Firstly, on arrival in Ireland and Britain Clan operatives made contact with the domestic Irish revolutionary circles. The organization in Ireland had been infiltrated by a number of informants who passed on vital information to British authorities. As well as this the British were continuing to receive updates from Le Caron in the U.S. as to Clan decision making and planning. Once captured many of these young operatives were not equipped to stand up to the intense interrogation and torture inflicted by their captors and ended up giving important information leading to

56   Clarke, Thomas. Glimpses of an Irish Felon's Prison Life. Maunsel and Roberts. Dublin. 1922.

further arrests. In essence, the Clan organization in the U.S. failed by al-
lowing Le Caron access to the highest ranks of the Clan and the IRB in
Ireland failed by having informants within its ranks that led to the collapse of the dynamite campaign. The fact that many of the Clan operatives in Britain had American accents at a time when very few Americans
lived there also made them stand out and easier to identify.

The fact that American citizens were using the U.S. as a base to carry
out bombing attacks in Britain was obviously going to raise tensions between both nations and an expectation on the behalf of London that the
U.S. should respond with a major clamp down on Clan na Gael. Discussions
were carried out early on between Secretary of State James Blaine and
British minister Edward Thornton. Based on these discussions the British
concluded that both governments were in "complete harmony" as to the
criminal nature of Clan na Gael activities within the U.S. When the British
intercepted a ship containing explosives bound from Boston to Liverpool
British complaints elicited further guarantees from Blaine – "National,
State and Municipal are all engaged in the work of discovering the wicked
authors of the dynamite plot. It was a stealthy, secret crime and it is not
believed that any considerable numbers of accomplices were engaged in
it. No pains or expenses will be spared in the detention and prosecution
of the guilty parties".

The British for the most part took seriously these American guarantees but tensions between both nations were increased with the arrests
and imprisonments of U.S. citizens. From February 1881 to February 1882
American officials in Britain intervened in dozens of cases involving Irish-
American citizens being arrested by British authorities. The issue of these
prisoners also became a hot button domestic political issue within the
U.S. Politicians wishing to court the Irish vote highlighted and, in many
cases, applauded the heroic efforts in struggling against what many saw as
British tyranny. The issue now became much more complicated for the
Federal government in Washington as the issue was not just one between
two nations but instead between two governments and a large voting block
within the U.S.

As bombings continued throughout 1882-85 relations between Britain
and the U.S. became more strained. Continued British complaints brought

only a limited American reaction. The British efforts to portray Clan activities as a common threat to both nations fell on deaf ears. The primary reason being that historically Irish-American nationalism had never posed a threat to the U.S. as it often lived side by side with a deeply held American patriotism by most Irish- Americans as seen in participation in the Civil War and later conflicts.

Two major factors must be considered to fully understand the U.S. response to the Clan at this time. Firstly, the Republican Party and its president during the early 1880s was still very much the party of Lincoln. President Chester A. Arthur was a Brigadier General during the Civil War at a time when the British were considering giving official recognition to the Confederacy and supplying battle ships used to sink Union shipping during the conflict. Many within the Republican party still held an enmity toward the British empire and had little sympathy for the security problems being caused by Clan activities and little incentive to intervene on her behalf.

On a second front by the 1880s the Republican party was beginning to undertake major efforts to woo Irish voters into its ranks. In 1884 several prominent Irish-American leaders supported James Blaine's candidacy for the Republican nomination. During the 1884 presidential contest the Arthur administration feared that public comments criticizing Clan na Gael attacks in Britain would put in jeopardy Irish votes and refused to press for stricter laws against explosives trafficking. In response to this gesture Alexander Sullivan temporarily suspended bomb attacks in Britain for the duration of the campaign. When Arthur lost the Republican nomination to Blaine who himself went on to lose the presidential election to the Democrats he turned on Irish-Americans and the Clan in particular. Arthur was deeply resentful and advocated strong anti-terrorist legislation. His urgings of "prompt and thorough" action against transatlantic terrorism fell on deaf ears. The British by this point had lost patience and faith in Arthur.

The incoming Democratic administration under President Grover Cleveland could hardly have proved any more effective than the Republicans considering that Irish-Americans were one of the most important voting blocs within the party with control over a number of urban political machines that was vital in Democratic electoral victory and fundraising. The new Secretary of State Theodore Frelinghuysen paid lip service to dealing with "overt acts of hostility against a friendly nation" but at the same time considered British evidence as at best circumstantial as to American connections and involvements in the bombing campaign.

As the Clan na Gael bombing campaign entered its final year in 1885 headlines in the New York Times such as "London's Great Terror" forced many in Congress to the conclusion that some sort of substantive response was required in order to allay growing American public concern over the issue. On the same day as the final bomb attack in London Democratic Senator Thomas Bayard of Delaware introduced a resolution stating "indignation and profound sorrow" at the recent attacks. Bayard announced that the U.S. had to be clear and strong when it came to upholding the rule of law and declaring America's "horror and detestation of such monstrous crimes against civilization". The Bayard resolution passed 63 to 1 but failed to pass the Committee on Foreign Relations. The greatest consequence of these debates during the Clan bombing campaign of the 1880s was that it laid the foundation of a future extradition treaty known as the Blaine-Pauncefote Extradition Treaty which was ratified in March 1890.

The fear of Irish-American bombers lingered long after the end of the Clan campaign in 1885. Fears surrounding the U.S. visit of Joseph Chamberlain in 1887 caused a huge security headache for both U.S. and British authorities. The visit, as stated by the British ambassador to the U.S. was considered "very obnoxious to the Irish here". Queen Victoria's Jubilee in 1887 saw rumors swirl of a 150 Clan dynamite army ready to attack at a moment's notice. As late as November 1888 the British government was still pressurizing the U.S. to punish and shutdown Irish- American publications for "murderous threats against English officials".

By the end of the 1880s the official American position on transatlantic terrorism was best stated by historian Murney Gerlach when he claimed that both the British and U.S. governments "Fervently desired an end to Irish-American terrorism". In December 1889 President Harrison labeled terrorists as the "avowed enemies of social order". Despite these public announcements many in the American political establishment never spoke with a unified voice when it came to violent Irish-American nationalism. This was greatly hampered by political considerations when it came to the

Irish vote, the popularity of the idea of Irish independence not just within Irish-American but also broader American society. As well as this there was also the long-held tradition in American society dating back to Thomas Jefferson that held anti-imperial and anti-colonial views that very much aligned with Irish-American aspirations for an independent democratic Republic along American lines[57].

57   Gantt, Jonathan. 2006. Irish-American Terrorism and Anglo-American Relations, 1881-1885. The Journal of the Gilded Age and Progressive Era. Vol. 3, No. 4.

CHAPTER 6

The Case of Dr Cronin

The disastrous end of the Dynamite Campaign saw a major questioning and eventual challenge to the leadership of Alexander Sullivan and his supporters. It was an opportunity that the more moderate wing of the movement had been waiting for. At the head of this opposition was John Devoy who remained infuriated at Sullivan's treatment of the IRB whom he saw as vital in a future rebellion. Devoy's dislike for Sullivan also had a deeper element to it. The failure of the Clan leadership made up of Sullivan and his supporters to provide funding for his Irish Nation newspaper which Devoy saw as an essential component of the Clan's propaganda campaign was also a factor. It would also seem that Sullivan felt threatened by Devoy's popularity amongst the rank-and-file membership and his constant attacks on individuals such as Rossa and other more militant members of the movement. Devoy always felt himself to be a purer revolutionary than the more politically ambitious Irish-American leadership as exemplified by Sullivan. The personal affront at being excluded from both the Executive Committee and Revolutionary Directory would also have played a major factor in Devoy's growing animosity toward Sullivan. With these conditions in place Devoy, along with John Breslin and James Pallas, formed the center around which opposition to Sullivan began to form.

Opposition to Sullivan pointed toward heavy handed tactics that bordered on intimidation at what was perceived as Sullivan's takeover of the Clan. The image of Sullivan as a corrupt machine politician was carefully fostered in a well laid campaign that was used to undermine Sullivan's leadership. The attacks against Sullivan took a particularly vicious and dangerous turn when allegations of theft of Clan funds for personal use began to emerge. The leading voice of these allegations was one Patrick Cronin, often simply referred to as Dr Cronin[58].

Cronin was an immigrant to the U.S. from Canada where his parents had originally emigrated from Ireland. After settling in the Midwest after the Civil War Cronin went on to become a medical physician who would become a frequent feature in high social circles in his hometown of St. Louis. It was during his time in St. Louis that he became a member of Clan na Gael. In 1882 he moved to Chicago where he took up a new position in Cook County Hospital. Cronin quickly became an active member in a number of charitable societies and was prominent in the Catholic Church as a singer in the choir. During his time in Chicago, he changed his membership from the St. Louis to the Chicago branch of the Clan. After a while Cronin set up his own private practice with the vast majority of his patients being of the Irish-American extraction. Cronin went on to quickly become a popular and active member of the Chicago Irish community.

On the face of it Cronin and Sullivan could not have been more different in character and personality. While Cronin was a socially conscious and popular figure Sullivan was a much more Machiavellian individual who operated in a politically underhanded and corrupt manner and was prone to violence as seen earlier in his life. It would become almost inevitable that both individuals would come into conflict[59].

Early on during his time in Chicago Cronin took up the cause of the Devoy faction of the Clan. The issue of Sullivan's embezzlement of Clan funds arose as early as 1882 when a member by the name of P.W Dunne first brought up the issue publicly. To settle the matter Sullivan chose his close friend Father Maurice Dorney to look over Clan accounts for any misappropriation of funds. Unsurprisingly the accounts were all found to be in order. Soon after Dunne was expelled from the organization. In many ways the event acted as a warning against anyone who was thinking of challenging Sullivan or questioning Clan finances. It would take more than this show of strength to discourage Cronin.

58   Funchion, Michael. Chicago's Irish Nationalists, 1881-1890. Loyola University. Chicago.

59   O'Brien, Gillian. 2015. "A diabolical murder": Clan na Gael, Chicago and the murder of Dr. Cronin. History Ireland. Vol. 23 (Issue 3).

Cronin spend the following weeks and months going from one Clan camp to another gathering information and listening to members. At the end he claimed to have gathered enough evidence to prove large scale corruption headed by Sullivan himself. Sullivan was quick to react and with the leadership packed with supporters he commenced proceedings to expel Cronin from the organization. However, Cronin would not quietly accept his fate. Cronin's inevitable expulsion had the opposite effect that Sullivan had hoped for. Cronin went on to establish his own rival Clan camp and he allied himself even closer to the Devoy faction. The campaign against Sullivan continued unabated with Cronin quickly becoming his most outspoken critic. Thanks to Cronin Chicago quickly became the center of the dispute and growing opposition to Sullivan's leadership. Since Chicago was not only Sullivan's powerbase but his hometown his anger and rage only grew as the years passed and it became apparent that Cronin was not going anywhere. By 1886-87 Sullivan began to seriously consider the assassination of Cronin. Although Cronin picked up on the rumors it says a lot as to his character that he refused to relent in his attacks and criticisms of Sullivan.

The growing antagonism between the Devoy and Sullivan factions of the Clan came to a head during the Clan convention in June 1888. Devoy immediately went on the attack and listed four specific charges – 1. Violation of their oaths of Membership and Office 2. Misappropriation of funds of the United Brotherhood. 3. Betrayal of Trust and of the interests of the United Brotherhood. 4. Malfeasance in Office. It became apparent very early on that the convention would not bring about the hoped for healing of divisions. The central issue was the charge of the theft of between $100,000 and $128,000 from Clan accounts and the falsifying of financial records between 1881 and 1884. A six-man jury was established with Cronin on the prosecution side.

The trial itself took place in Buffalo, New York. This was probably based on the idea that removing the proceedings outside of Sullivan's powerbase of Chicago would mean less chance of intimidation or undue influence on Clan members involved in the proceedings. As expected the atmosphere throughout the trial was intense and heated. Some members, including Devoy, attended the proceedings armed fearing a violent response from Sullivan should the proceedings go against him. During the case a number of witnesses came forward that included the families whose members were in British prisons as a result of the failed dynamiting campaign. Under Clan rules these families were to receive financial assistance for the duration of the imprisonment of the family member. When these families approached Sullivan for financial assistance they were either refused or received paltry financial sums. Many on the Clan jury were appalled, and it turned out to be a major turning point in the proceedings. However, most within the Clan did not want to see a major split within the movement. Sullivan was acquitted of all charges while other members such as Michael Boland were censured for financial irregularities. The result was a mere political gesture that attempted and ultimately failed to heal the deep divisions within the Clan. In the end no one was left satisfied.

Cronin was furious in the aftermath of the decision and was determined to show that the trial was little more than a sham. Cronin declared to a close friend "I will do my duty...I am alone, a single man, I have no wife or children to feed and consequently do not fear to die. No one will be injured by my death. I will do my duty fearlessly, come what may." This momentous decision was to have sad consequences for Cronin and monumental consequences for Clan na Gael[60].

At the same time as tensions continued on the domestic front for the Clan matters only continued to become more critical as the 1880s came to a close. In Ireland Charles Parnell was coming under severe public pressure in Britain as a result of a number of articles in The Times newspaper titled "Parnellism and Crime". The articles accused Parnell of having close link with secret revolutionary Irish organizations which included Clan-na-Gael. As expected, Parnell denied all allegations and a special parliamentary commission was established to investigate the matter. As already discussed, Parnell did indeed have connections with the Clan and behind closed doors paid lip service to future rebellion. Proceedings would take a total of fourteen months to complete and in February of 1889 one of the most dramatic moments in Clan history was to occur. The British

60   Chicago. 2015 O'Brien, Gillian. Blood Runs Green – The Murder That Transfixed
       Gilded Age Chicago. University of Chicago Press.

spy Le Caron travelled to England and publicly revealed himself as a long standing informant.

Le Caron revealed that he met Parnell on a number of occasions and that Parnell was perfectly aware of the Clan's aims of using violence to achieve Irish independence. It then became quickly apparent that it was Le Caron himself who was providing the information that made up the basis for The Times articles that attacked Parnell and that this information was also used in the arrests of Clan bombers and interception of explosives in transport and safe locations. Without doubt Le Caron's access to such high-level information was as a direct result of his close relationship with Alexander Sullivan. The news of Le Caron being a spy sent shockwaves not just through Clan na Gael but through the broader Irish American community in general. On the face of it the revelation of Le Caron should have put Sullivan in severe jeopardy since it was, he who admitted the spy into the highest ranks of the Clan and provided him with highly secretive and sensitive information. Sullivan was anxious to divert from his obvious culpability in the matter and quickly looked for a scapegoat. Dr Cronin became the obvious target and outlet for Sullivan's violent rage and frustration. Sullivan soon set in motion a plan to murder Cronin.

On 4 May Cronin was called out to an accident at an icehouse where it was claimed a young man was seriously injured. Being the medical professional that he was Cronin responded without hesitation and quickly left in a waiting buggy. As the hours passed without Cronin returning it soon became apparent that he was missing. The initial response of police was somewhat slow as detective Daniel Coughlin was assigned to the case. The urgency of the case was soon amped up when several patrolmen reported the unstable passage of a horse and cart carrying a large trunk through the streets of Chicago late on the same evening as Cronin's disappearance. The day after the report the same trunk was discovered with blood stains and tufts of human hair.

Despite the evidence of a violent ending to Cronin's life rumors began to circulate in the press that Cronin may have been a British spy and that he actually fled to Canada. Other newspapers reported that he left as a result of an ill-fated affair. It would be unsurprising if Sullivan did not deliberately plant these stories to throw investigators off the trail. Despite the lurid newspaper stories, it started to become apparent to most observers that Cronin likely met a violent end.

The disappearance of Cronin took its inevitable course when on 22 May when his body was discovered in a sewer in Lake View. In an eerie turn of events his face was discovered peering through the bars of the sewer. His corpse was swollen, and he had been stripped of all his belongings. After the body was identified, it was taken to the morgue at Lake View police stations. News quickly spread with the first reaction being one of shock which later turned to outrage as the details of Cronin's murder began to slowly emerge.

The case was further blown open when just two days later the scene of the murder was discovered by the Carlson family who rented out a vacation cottage at Lake View to a person by the name of "Frank Williams". After the cottage was vacated the Carlson family discovered blood stains and broken furniture. They reported it to the police almost immediately. From this point onward the Cronin case started to develop rapidly. Soon after it was discovered that the horse and buggy used in the transport of Cronin's body from the murder scene actually came from a stable regularly used by the police themselves. The horse and buggy matched the description in the newspaper of the one used by Cronin to travel to his last known location. This indicated straight away that someone from within the police force may have been involved. Further investigation revealed that Detective Coughlin, the chief investigator on the case, was involved. Coughlin was arrested on 27 May and soon after Patrick O'Sullivan was taken into custody. As a result of information retrieved by both men as well as intense further investigation all signs led back to Camp 20 of Clan na Gael, whose head was Alexander Sullivan himself. After further arrests of those involved Sullivan himself was arrested on 11 June.

The scene was now set for one of the biggest trials in Chicago's history. Four Clan members in total were brought to trial – Coughlin, Beggs, Burke and O'Sullivan. There was not enough evidence to directly connect Alexander Sullivan to the murder. The case had gained such wide media attention that by December of 1889 thousands of newspapers were reporting on the trial. Public opinion turned quickly against the accused and many believed the accused to be guilty. The trial lasted a total of seven weeks and became a media circus with every twist and turn being reported in detail by the media.

As the case proceeded it became more and more of a disaster for the Clan as the inner workings of the movement became public. As deep corruption became revealed it deeply damaged the image of an idealistic nationalist movement so carefully nurtured by the Clan for decades. Many Chicagoans both inside and outside the organization became more and more reluctant to defend the cause of Irish republicanism. Although sections of the Irish community in Chicago defended the accused broader society in Chicago demanded justice.

The court room drama ended on 12 December and the jury started their deliberations. While Coughlin, Sullivan and Burke were found guilty and sentenced to life imprisonment Beggs was acquitted of all charges. The three convicted individuals were sent to Joliet prison to serve their prison terms. Daniel Coughlin waged an ardent campaign for a retrial of the convicted and although O'Sullivan died in prison of tuberculosis Burke was allowed to enter the dock in 1893. He was cleared of all charges and released. There may be some cause to assume that bribery of the jury may have been involved in the final decision. So ended one of the most damaging episodes in Clan history[61].

Sullivan was forced to reduce his role and public profile for a number of years after the Cronin case. Tensions and public distain toward Sullivan grew to such an extent that he felt obliged to leave the U.S. altogether for a two-month trip to Europe in 1896. On his return Sullivan made one last effort to regain some of his former influence within the Clan and broader politics in general. Sullivan gave his support to Carter Harrison for Mayor of Chicago in return for him being able to choose the police chief. The plan was that by such a maneuver Sullivan would be able to remove the police officers involved in securing the convictions of Coughlin and others. Harrison refused the offer outright. Harrison later recalled Sullivan as being "obliterated" and "flabbergasted" as the response. At this point Sullivan must have seen the writing on the wall. His former political clout

---

61   O'Brien, Gillian. 2015. "A diabolical murder": Clan na Gael, Chicago and the murder of Dr. Cronin. History Ireland. Vol. 23 (Issue 3).

and influence was all but gone and more than that, he was now seen as a political liability and pariah. On a professional level Sullivan's legal career never recovered from allegations of corruption and a bribery case involving jurors in the Coughlin case. Although he was cleared of the charges his reputation was tarnished. With the death of his wife in 1903 all the fight seems to have gone out of Sullivan. He lingered on as a forlorn and lonely figure until he finally died in 1913. There would be no traditional Irish outpouring for a fallen chieftain as so often seen for such events in the past. The Clan would attempt to move on from and forget the legacy of Sullivan's tenure as leader[62].

As would be expected the case surrounding the murder of Dr Cronin and the following fallout marked the decline and eventual end of the Sullivan leadership of the Clan. The high profile case occurred at the height of what today we know as the Gilded Age. One of the features of the period was a strong and growing aversion to corruption. While this aversion was primarily focused on politics, particularly urban political machines, the stories of financial misdeeds within Clan na Gael under the leadership of Sullivan was quickly identified in the public mind as a mere extension of this. Many non-Irish Americans believed that the veneer of a romantic nationalist organization striving for the freedom of a small country from British rule was but a guise for financial misdeeds and misappropriation of funds.

Within the Irish-American community itself and particularly within the Clan the issue was more complicated. The period of Sullivan's leadership showed a growing tension between American and Irish born nationalists. Many Irish born nationalists perceived Sullivan and many of his U.S. born supporters as being deeply attached to the local and national politics of the U.S. to the detriment of the ultimate and central cause of Irish independence. Urban machine politics which many Irish Americans played a central role in creating and maintaining was seen as having a deeply corrupting influence which attracted the politically ambitious sorts of Alexander

62   O'Brien, Gillian. Blood Runs Green – The Murder That Transfixed Gilded Age Chicago. University of Chicago Press. Chicago. 2015. P. 204-207.

Sullivan and others. John Devoy and his "purist" supporters saw this as not merely a distraction but detrimental to the cause of Irish independence.

As the 1880s came to a close the Clan could look back on a decade of disappointment and setbacks. The failed dynamite campaign and the controversy of the Cronin murder on the face of it would seem irreparable to the Clan's image and possible future role in the broader Irish independence movement. However, there were some causes for optimism. The 1880s saw in Ireland the emergence of what became known as the Gaelic Revival. This involved the reemergence of the Irish language, culture and literature. This not only reinvigorated the sense of Irish identity but also interest in pre-colonial Ireland and the long historical struggle against British rule. With the continued arrival of hundreds of thousands of Irish emigrants throughout the 1880s it did not take long for the Gaelic Revival to reach American shores.

This cultural revival saw the emergence of plays, Irish language classes and literature that portrayed a longing for a bygone era of an Ireland free from British rule and cultural influence. These combined together to form an increased consciousness and identity generated by bitter memories of famine and British misrule in Ireland that was further increased by bouts of anti- Irish and anti-Catholic sentiment in American society. By financially supporting and/or being actively involved in nationalist organizations in the U.S. many Irish-Americans felt part of the broader Irish movement for independence. This coming together would not only help in the cause of Irish independence but also help improve opportunities in American society in general through political organization and common cause. Despite the setbacks of the 1880s Clan na Gael benefited enormously from the cultural revival as many Irish-Americans looked past the failures with a continued dedication to the cause of "home[63]".

63   Ni Bhroimeil, Una. Building Irish Identity in America. Four Court Press. Dublin. 2003.

CHAPTER 7

Domestic Rebuilding and Global Anti-Imperialism

The beginning of the 1890s started as inauspiciously as the 1880s had ended. After the failure to pass the first Home Rule bill through the British parliament in 1886 the Home Rule suffered a further devastating blow with the death of Charles Parnell in 1891 which was preceded by a major split in the party after a divorce scandal which implicated the leader. By this point the New Departure was fundamentally dead with Clan na Gael now rededicating itself to a purer revolutionary format after seeing the failure of constitutional nationalism and the restrictions placed on its advancement by a British parliament.

After the decline of the Sullivan faction of the Clan John Devoy was now able to reassert control of the movement providing the organization with a badly needed popular and unifying figure. After the disappointments and failures of the 1880s the movement received a boost with the arrival in the U.S. of perhaps it's second greatest figure, after Devoy, in the Clan's history. Joseph McGarrity was just 19 years old when he arrived as an immigrant in the U.S. in January 1892. Unlike many previous Clan arrivals on U.S. shores McGarrity came from the town of Carrickmore in County Tyrone, one of the nine counties of Ireland's ancient province of Ulster. Ulster had been the last of the ancient Irish kingdoms to fall under British rule. It had also been the birthplace of the 1641 rebellion as well as seeing significant violence in the 1798 rebellion. Following British control of the province and the formation of the sectarian Protestant Orange Order the province had become over time one of the most violent and volatile regions in Ireland with regular riots between Catholics and Protestants and anti-Catholic pogroms in Belfast and other major urban centers. McGarrity grew up with a distinctly different experience from Devoy and others. McGarrity harbored less of a romantic nationalism and more of a hardened reality when it came to revolutionary violence. McGarrity's experience of the failures and shortcomings of the Home Rule Party while growing up left him with a deep and enduring hostility to constitutional nationalism which he saw as a betrayal of Ireland's right to full independence. By the time of his youthful arrival McGarrity was already a hardened revolutionary with a tunnel vision of violent revolutionary Republicanism. Nothing would ever shake him in that aim up until his death in 1940.

McGarrity lost little time in becoming involved in Irish revolutionary activities and within his first year became a member of Clan na Gael. From that point onward his hard work and dedication would see him rise rapidly through the ranks of the Clan. On a personal level his strong work ethic would see him become a very successful businessman and a leading figure in Irish circles in his newly adopted home in Philadelphia which in the years to come would become the home of the more revolutionary and violent wing of the Clan[64].

One of the most urgent issues facing the Clan was to find a relevancy in conditions that were far from conducive to revolution in Ireland. The failure of the first Home Rule bill in 1886 and the untimely death of Charles Parnell in 1891 following a major political split resulting from a divorce scandal involving the leader left few political avenues to pursue. On the face of it this should have driven many in Ireland into looking for a political alternative that Clan na Gael would have hoped would have been revolutionary Republicanism. However, major land reform legislation was passed by the British parliament in 1885 and 1887 that saw major transfers of land to the Irish peasantry. Along with land reform the Congested District's Board was established to alleviate major economic distress in places like the west of Ireland. The British intention was to "Kill Home Rule with Kindness" and along with that Irish Republicanism. As a result the 1890s saw a major slackening off of revolutionary activity in Ireland with support falling off significantly. Clan na Gael needed to find new direction and outlet for its revolutionary anti-imperial messaging and this new direction was to be found on the global stage with the growth of American imperialism and the British embroilment in the Boer War.

64   Tarpey, Marie. 1971. Joseph McGarrity, Fighter for Irish Freedom. Studia Hibernica. No. 11, P. 164-180.

The decline of the nationalist movement in Ireland was marked by a further split within Clan na Gael on 7 May of 1891 with the formation in New York of a moderate breakaway organization known as the Irish National Federation of America. The new president of the organization was none other than Dr Thomas Addis Emmet who was the grandnephew of the Irish revolutionary martyr Robert Emmet. The main purpose of the new organization was "For the purpose of aiding in the advance of Home Rule for Ireland and for representing in this country the Irish people under the leadership of the majority of the Irish members of Parliament". Under the competent leadership of Emmet, the organization quickly grew thanks primarily to the support of the Catholic Church which had little sympathy with secret oath bound organizations like Clan na Gael whom they saw as a threat to their own role and influence within Irish-America. The success of the new fledgling INFA would be short lived however. The defeat of a second Home Rule Bill in the British House of Lords all but finished off the prospects of Home Rule for almost a decade and led to the demise of the INFA by the early 1900s.

The split between the moderate and militant wings of the Clan and the INFA had a number of long-term consequences. Firstly, although one could easily view the split as being negative and detrimental to the Clan's overall prospects for launching a revolution in Ireland it in many ways had the opposite effect. With the moderates leaving the movement it meant that those that remained were those totally dedicated to armed insurrection and as a result greater consensus existed as to aims and objectives freeing up the leadership from crippling paralysis and infighting over strategy and political direction. The objectives were now clear, armed insurrection as soon as the conditions presented itself. Secondly, the failure of the Home Rule Bill in 1893 and the demise of the INFA was interpreted by many Irish-Americans as a final indictment of constitutional politics and attempting to win greater independence within the confines of the British imperial structure[65].

---

65   Brundage, David. Irish Nationalists in America – The Politics of Exile, 1798-1998. Oxford University Press. New York. 2016. P. 129-132.

The 1890s saw the continued revival of Irish literary and cultural nationalism following on from the 1880s. The establishment of the Gaelic
League in Ireland in 1893 which promoted the revival of the Gaelic language
as well as in Irish history. The arrival of the Gaelic League in the U.S. was
a trigger for Irish-American fraternal organizations such as the Ancient
Order of Hibernians to start lobbying for the teaching of Irish history in
parochial schools. Irish history was inevitably taught through the lens of
an almost continuous struggle against British rule and a harkening back
to an idyllic pre-colonial era of an island of "Saints and Scholars". Needless
to say the crossover of membership between Clan na Gael and organizations such as the Gaelic League was overwhelming. The Gaelic Athletic
Association founded in the late 1880s and its arrival on U.S. shores just
further reinforced a newly empowered Irish-American identity which
would later manifest itself during the Clan's most important and influential period from 1916- 21[66].

With the nationalist cause in Ireland at a low ebb and prospects for
armed revolution almost non-existent the Clan had to find ways to keep
itself and the cause of Irish independence at the forefront of Irish-American
politics and culture. The prime way during the 1890s that this was achieved
was to take up the growing anti-imperial movement and sentiment sweeping
the U.S. as the result of political and military expansion beyond the North
American continent. The Clan was quick to connect the cause of Irish
independence to a global struggle not just against the British empire but
the growing and expansionist U.S. republic. A fine line would have to be
walked as the Clan was always anxious to prove its undying loyalty to the
U.S. and was ardent in it aims of projecting the image that its opposition to
American global expansion was a show of loyalty to the true ideals of the
Republic and not a betrayal to the objectives of setting up an Irish Republic
which the Clan saw as hand in hand with true American Republicanism.

During this time period the Clan wedded itself ever closer to the
Democratic Party who took up the anti-imperial cause of American
Republicanism while the Republican Party who in years gone by courted

66   Ni Bhroimeil, Una. Building Irish Identity in America. Four Court Press.
     Dublin. 2003.

the Irish vote very much followed the path of "dollar diplomacy" and the capitalist path of foreign expansionism[67]. Of the number of foreign expansionist issues during this time period the one that most took hold of the Irish-American imagination was the issue of Cuba. Cuba shared an historical similarity with Ireland of being a Catholic Island nation with a long history of anti-colonial struggles against Spanish rule. By highlighting the similarity in the Cuban struggle and the rights of the Cubans to a free and independent Republic the cause of Irish independence was kept to the forefront of Irish-American opinion[68].

In the same year as the start of the Spanish-American War and a year before the outbreak of the Boer War there occurred in Ireland and among Irish-Americans widespread commemoration ceremonies marking the centenary of the United Irishmen rebellion of 1798. With Clan na Gael by far the largest and best known of the Irish revolutionary movements in the U.S. the organization took the opportunity not only to lead and organize nationwide ceremonies but also to put themselves forward as the natural inheritors to the United Irishmen tradition. The moment was also used to heal old divisions and reunite with old factions that remained outside of the Clan na Gael fold. Events were held all over the U.S. where major Irish communities existed and celebrations included nationalist parades and public picnics all of which were used as recruiting and fundraising events for the Clan. With growing momentum all it would take was a major event to catapult the Irish Republican cause back to the forefront of the Irish and Irish-American imagination[69].

A less well-known part of the world during this time period where the 1798 centenary celebrations were taking place was in South Africa. By 1896 there were approximately 1,000 Irish immigrants living in the Transvaal region. The celebrations not only celebrated Irish separatism but showed

---

67   Baron, Harold. 1957. Anti-Imperialism and the Democrats. Science & Society. No. 3, P. 222-239.

68   Doyle, David. 1968. American Catholics, Racism and Imperialism: A Select Study of Responses to the Issues as Involved in American Expansion, 1890-1905. Marquette University. Master's Thesis.

69   McMahon, Richard. 2016. Irish Chicagoans, Nationalism, and the Commemoration of Rebellion in 1898. Eire-Ireland, Vol. 51. P. 218-242.

a deep solidarity with the Boer cause and independence. By the time of
the outbreak of the Boer war in 1899 there existed a small but dedicated
network of Irish separatism in South Africa[70].

No event more clearly manifested the Clan's new global approach to
the struggle against the British Empire than the Boer War. If Ireland was
not ready for revolution, then the Clan would seek out existing global
struggles against Britain and carry the Irish colors into battle. While technically speaking the Boers were descendants of the first Dutch colonial
settlers who first settled in South Africa back in 1652 and that the native
Africans of the region were brutally exploited and endured mass land confiscations Irish-American nationalists were to view the Boers as the victims
of British imperial expansion while the suffering of native Africans was
almost completely ignored. British interests in South Africa commenced
with their annexation of Natal in 1843. Continued British expansion into
the African interior led to inevitable conflict with the Boers and the start
of what became known as the First Boer War from 1880-81. Although the
Boers gave a good military account of themselves and inflicted a number
of defeats on the British they were able to maintain their independence
only under certain conditions set by the imperial government in London.
The most important of these conditions was that the Boers had to allow
British immigration into their Republics.

Conflict between the Boers and newly arriving British settlers was
made inevitable with the discovery of diamonds and gold which triggered
a tidal wave of newcomers who saw themselves as British subjects and not
Boer citizens subject to Boer law. The Boer governments failed to give full
voting rights to the new settlers. Imperial capitalist interests in Britain,
most notably the very wealthy Cecil Rhodes, started propagating the idea
of annexing the now very affluent Boer Republics. The idea of using the
failure to give voting rights to the new settlers was used as a pretext for pressurizing the Boer government into an impossible position making war ever
more inevitable. A faction of the newly arrived British settlers attempted an
uprising that became known as the Jameson Raid in 1895, named after its
ill-fated leader Dr Leander Jameson. Although a total failure the event led

70   Fallon, Donal. 16 Lives – John MacBride. Dublin. The O'Brien Press. 2015. P. 61-64.

to a deterioration in diplomatic relations between Britain and the Boers. Although formal negotiations were undertaken between both governments in relation to giving full voting rights to British immigrants the imperial government in London ordered troops to amass at the border of both the Transvaal and Orange Free State. Paul Kruger, the indomitable President of the South African Republic, issued an ultimatum on 9 October 1899, ordering the British government to remove all troops from her borders within forty-eight hours. If the British did not do so the South African government would declare war. When Britain failed to remove her troops war was declared and Britain invaded[71].

Ireland saw the revitalization of the Clan's dormant sister organization the Irish Republican Brotherhood in response to a wave of anti-imperial sentiment resulting from the British invasion of the Boer Republics. Sentiment was best summed up during this time period when a popular ballad became common on the streets of Dublin –

> God save the Boer Against the British hordes God bless the brave Boers' swords, God save the Boers! May their high battle-tide, Still swelling far and wide Crush British greed and pride, God save the Boers!

> Oh! Freedom, Justice, Right, Rise, Mammon's minions smite, God save the Boers! Nerve every heart and hand Till, from their fatherland Boers drive the base brigand. God save the Boers!

In 1899 the Irish Transvaal Committee was formed. The main purpose of the Committee was to raise funds for propaganda purposes opposing the war as well as raising money for an Irish ambulance corp. The Committee also orchestrated anti-recruitment campaigns discouraging young Irish men from joining the British army as well as large protests in support of the Boer war effort[72].

The Irish Republican Brotherhood became very aware of the possibilities that the Boer War held in the advancement of their own separatist

---

71   Pakenham, Thomas. The Boer War. Avon Books. New York. P. 3-116.
72   McCracken, Donal. Forgotten Protest. Ulster Historical Foundation. Belfast. 2003. P. 49-52.

agenda and yet again the idea of "England's difficulty was Ireland's opportunity". The widespread network of spies which had penetrated the ranks of the IRB soon meant that the British government was quickly informed on plans to export arms to the Boers which resulted in an increased naval presence around major Irish ports. The IRB increased its "treasonable" literary output with pamphlets dissuading Irish men from joining the British war effort. British intelligence proved up to the task and managed to intercept a large amount of the material before it reached the streets. Although the IRB did find a new purpose and direction that helped reinvigorate it as an organization it proved fairly ineffective within the tightly held environment of British occupied Ireland. Clan-na-Gael would have no such difficulties[73].

Before focusing on Irish-American reaction and involvement in the Boer war we must first look at the official U.S. governmental policy toward the conflict. The State department was mostly favorable to the British position and was hopeful of a short conflict. It was hoped that a British victory would turn out more favorable to U.S. business interests and foreign policy objectives. As the war dragged on Boer victories increased and the portrayal of the Boers in the domestic media as a brave underdog fighting against overwhelming British imperial might akin to the American Revolution made the government's pro-British stance more difficult to defend. Irish-Americans and the broader U.S. anti-imperial movement began to heavily criticize the U.S. government for supporting the crushing of a Republic by an imperial monarchy. Although the U.S. was technically neutral it was a major source of military supplies and aid for the British Army. American capitalist interests who were already active in South Africa prior to the outbreak of the war hoped that a British victory would open up the South African market and act as a launch pad for further expansion into the African interior where it was hoped raw materials and further mineral wealth lay ready to be exploited[74].

With the outbreak of the Boer War in 1899 the Clan found fertile grounds to exploit and further the Irish republican cause. As already

---

73   McGee, Owen. The IRB – The Irish Republican Brotherhood from the Land
     League to Sinn Fein. Four Court Press. Bodmin. 2007. P. 279-83.
74   Noer, Thomas. Britain, Boer and Yankee. The Kent State University Press. Kent.
     1978. P. 69-71.

mentioned, Irish-America was in the midst of a major cultural and literary revival first started in Ireland and brought over by a constant and steady flow of immigrants. The defeat of the Sullivan faction which mired the Clan in corrupt domestic urban politics in the U.S. at the expense of furthering the republican cause in Ireland and the split with moderates more focused on moderate Home Rule demands strengthened the hand of hardened revolutionaries such as Devoy and McGarrity.

Conditions in the U.S. for the Clan to fully exploit the Boer war was a sharp contrast to the stifling conditions under which the IRB operated in Ireland. The Catholic Church in the U.S., which had a strong Irish influence during this period, showed sympathy to the Boer cause which increased further the Clan's moral stance against imperialism. One high profile Catholic figure was Bishop James Ryan of Illinois who held the opinion of condemnation on the British invasion of the Boer Republics. Ryan went as far as supporting a petition for the U.S. government to mediate in a peace settlement to end the war. Ryan went on to express his feelings and emotions that "The soul of America is with the Boer", that "The Republic is in danger" and that U.S. citizens "Throughout its length and breath, to your feet with a hail. To the Boer, God bless him, and God speed him". It is hard to imagine a high-profile religious figure in Ireland during this time period speaking out so publicly on such a matter[75].

One of the leading Irish American publications at this time which strongly supported the Boer War effort and the wider anti-imperial cause was the Irish World newspaper edited by Patrick Ford. The publication was to prove a further legitimizing factor in the Clan's international anti-imperial stance as well as its more specific opposition to British rule in Ireland even though the Irish World itself never came out directly in support of revolutionary violence. The Irish World from early on in the war carried numerous reports of the "heroic" deeds of the Boers along with reports of pro-Boer protests in the U.S. and Ireland that passed resolutions of sympathy and an "undying hatred for England". During the time

---

75   Strauss, Charles. 2008. God Save the Boer: Irish American Catholics and the South African War, 1899-1902. U.S. Catholic Historian, Vol. 26. P. 1-9.

period of the Boer War the total readership for the Irish World was approximately 125,000[76].

The leadership of the Clan felt that conditions were conducive to take direct action on behalf of the Boers in the war against Britain. As usual the attempt was to be used not just to help the Boer cause but also for propaganda purposes to keep alive the flagging separatist cause in Ireland as well as reinvigorating the Irish-American public. The efforts for Irish Republican direct involvement in the Boer originated in Ireland and in particular from the driving force and ambitions of John MacBride.

Born in Westport in County Mayo in 1868 John MacBride was born into a lower middle class background. From his early years MacBride was involved in a number of cultural and Gaelic sporting organizations that included Celtic Literary Society and the Gaelic Athletic Association. Since cultural organizations such as these would have inevitable attracted militant Republicans such as those of the Irish Republican Brotherhood it is very probable that MacBride was first introduced to revolutionary politics during this time period of the 1880s. Although he still occasionally flirted with moderate Home Rule politics and even attended the funeral of Charles Parnell in 1891 MacBride seems to have committed himself to revolutionary politics in 1895 when he joined the Irish National Alliance which was made up of former Clan na Gael members and former Fenians who were frustrated with the inactivity and strategy of the Irish Republican Brotherhood. Although the INA would be a short-lived organization MacBride became a leading member and even travelled as a delegate to the Irish National Alliance Convention held in Chicago in 1895. Although not recorded it is possible that MacBride came into contact with members of Clan na Gael during this time period as it was a common strategy for the Clan to promote membership of other organizations to observe proceedings and report back on any possible opportunities of alliance or threats

76   Ni Bhroimeil, Una. 2004. The South African War, empire and the Irish World, 1899-1902. Retrieved from <https://dspace.mic.ul.ie/bitstream/handle/10395/1528/N%C3%AD%20Bhroim%C3%A9il%2c%C3%9A.%282004%29%20%27The%20South%20African%20War%2c%20empire%20and%20the%20Irish%20World%2c%201899-1902%27%20%28Book%20Chapter%29.pdf?sequence=2&isAllowed=y>

of competition for membership and fundraising. MacBride was now an emerging figure within republican circles and came to the notice of British intelligence after the Chicago convention. He would remain under periodic monitoring right up until his execution in 1916[77].

Although MacBride would become the driving force and public face of the Irish Transvaal Brigade it was actually Belfast man Dan O'Hare and Dick McDonagh from County Kerry who first proposed the idea. Both men lived in the Transvaal and had deep roots and connection in the Irish community. The initial formation of what would become known in the media as "MacBride's Brigade" was made up of a mixture of Irish from Ireland as well as Irish living in South Africa. Even at this early stage there were a few Irish-Americans involved. These small number of American volunteers were attracted as much by adventure as by any Irish nationalist or anti-imperialist ideology. The newly formed Brigade was an extraordinary event in many ways. Although Ireland had a long history of exiles fighting in the service of other countries Ireland was by the 1890s and integral part of the British Empire and Britain's oldest colony. Being technically British citizens, the cost of capture would almost certainly be court martial and sentencing to death by firing squad[78].

Prior to the Clan's direct involvement in the Boer War in 1900 the leading American figure was the colorful John Fillmore Blake. Blake has been described more akin to Buffalo Bill than to your traditional Irish revolutionary figure and seems to have been attracted more by adventure and romanticism than to any deeply held ideology. Although he served thirteen years in the U.S. sixth cavalry he spent most of it on garrison duty at Leavenworth with brief interludes of war against the defiant but ultimately hapless Native Americans. Blake would eventually leave the military and end up in South Africa fleeing a failed business venture. He quickly became caught up in Irish nationalist rhetoric and the Boer cause[79]. The following poems popular in the Irish community at the time would have caught the imagination of individuals like Blake and others –

77 Fallon, Donal. 16 Lives – John MacBride. The O'Brien Press. Dublin. 2015. P. 18-41.
78 McCracken, P., Donal. MacBride's Brigade. Four Court's Press. Dublin. 1999. P. 22-25.
79 Fallon, Donal. 16 Lives – John MacBride. The O'Brien Press. Dublin. 2015. P. 29-30.

From land to land throughout the world The news is going round That Ireland's flag triumphant waves On high o'er English ground. In far off Africa today The English fly dismayed Before the flag of green and gold Borne by MacBride's Brigade[80].

Another major consequence of the Boer war and one which was specific to Irish Americans was how the conflict marked the beginning of a close relationship with German America that would endure right up until the end of World War One. On an official level the German government actively supplied weapons to the Boers throughout the war. Ever since German unification in 1871 British attempts to prevent the newly emerging continental power from becoming a global empire was done so to prevent any threat to her own imperial dominance. The new and vibrant German nation wanted to take her "place in the sun" as a global power along with the likes of Britain and France and deeply resented the insult of being denied what many Germans saw as their rightful and natural position as a world power. The Boer War gave the opportunity to give the British a bloody nose without risking outright war. German Americans, like their Irish counterparts, took the same position.

As well as sharing a deep Anglophobia both the Irish and German Americans shared other common bonds. Both sets of immigrants were some of the earliest non-Anglo Saxon European immigrants to settle in the U.S. prior to the large influx of southern and eastern Europeans from the 1890s onwards. Both groups settled in the same cities of the northeast and lived in relative harmony for generations. As well as this most of the German immigrants, like their Irish counterparts, were from rural and Catholic backgrounds which made social interaction and intermarriage easier. Both groups would also have worked together when circumstances arose in the newly emerging urban machine politics of major northern cities which the Irish were to perfect in the years ahead. Familiarity and interaction between Irish and German America was well established prior to the Boer War and would be further enhanced during the conflict.

The Boer War gave for the first time a genuine cause to come together for purposes that both German and Irish nationalism had a stake in. During the course of the Boer War both groups came together to hold pro-Boer

80   Fallon, Donal. 16 Lives – John MacBride. The O'Brien Press. Dublin. 2015. P. 22.

and anti-British rallies and protests, gather petitions, fundraise and procure weapons and volunteers for the Boer war effort. Although their efforts did not prevent an eventual British victory it was the first concerted effort to influence American foreign policy which was viewed by both Irish and German Americans as dangerous and would reach fever pitch during the time period 1916-17. Clan na Gael, in particular John Devoy, developed close political links with German nationalist elements in the U.S. in the hope that at a future date German assistance could be used to further the cause of Irish independence by influencing domestic politics in the U.S.

CHAPTER 8

The Road to Insurrection

From the decline and eventual defeat of the Sullivan faction of the Clan back in the 1880s John Devoy had remained the undisputed leader of the organization. The split and formation of the INFA only occurred when the more moderate Home-Rule faction of the Clan was unable to wrest control of the Clan from Devoy. The years following the Boer War saw the emergence of younger more militant members of the Clan. Foremost among this new generation was Joseph McGarrity. McGarrity's newly emerging wing of the movement found its powerbase located in Philadelphia where it would remain until McGarrity's death in 1940. In the years after the Boer War up until the end of the Irish War of Independence Devoy and McGarrity would remain united in the common cause of creating and supporting the conditions for revolution in Ireland. In the end the patriarch of the Clan was always more willing to accept short term compromise to achieve long term objectives. This would in the end set Devoy on a collision course with the younger more uncompromising McGarrity who saw any political compromise short of the establishment of an Irish Republic as a total betrayal.

One of the first major initiatives undertaken primarily by McGarrity after the Boer War was to re-establish links with the almost dormant Irish Republican Brotherhood back in Ireland. The IRB faced many problems in Ireland at this time with the chief among them being severe lack of funding. As always British intelligence kept the organization under close observation through informants. Mark Ryan was the main contact point for the distribution of Clan funds to the IRB and it is highly probable that intermediaries used to contact IRB chief organizer P.T Daly were working for British intelligence. From the beginning the Clan plan to revitalize the IRB was going to be challenging to say the least[81].

---

81   McGee, Owen. The IRB – The Irish Republican Brotherhood from the Land League to Sinn Fein. Four Court Press. Bodmin. 2007. P. 307.

Realizing how vulnerable the links between the Clan and the IRB were
to British infiltration and remaining tensions between the two organizations
dating back to the failed bombing campaigns of the 1880s it was decided
that Thomas Clarke would become the trusted link between both branches
of the Republican movement. The choice was a well thought out and astute
decision. Clarke's revolutionary credentials were impeccable. Clarke, although born in England in 1858 of Irish parents, spent his childhood in
Dungannon in County Tyrone. In 1878 Clarke joined the IRB. After being
involved in an attack on members of the Royal Irish Constabulary in 1880
Clarke fled to the U.S. in order to avoid arrest. It was during this period in
hiding in the U.S. that Clarke was introduced to Clan na Gael and became
a known figure within revolutionary circles in the U.S.

During this time Clarke settled in New York, joined Clan na Gael and
associated himself to the more radical wing of the Clan under Alexander
Sullivan. He received instruction in the use of dynamite before being sent
to take part in the bombing campaign in Britain in 1883. While in transit
with a supply of nitroglycerin Clarke was arrested and sentenced to penal
servitude for life. After years of solitary confinement, torture that included
physical beating and food and water deprivation Clarke was eventually released under a general amnesty for Irish political prisoners in 1898. Clarke,
who was always a small frail man, survived these years which had killed
or broken younger and physically stronger men. Unable to find employment after his release from prison Clarke returned to New York where
he reconnected with Clan na Gael, became secretary to John Devoy and
became editor to the Gaelic American, a Clan publication. With strong
revolutionary credentials, links and connections to both the IRB and the
Clan there could have been no better choice for the main intermediary
between both wings of the revolutionary movement[82].

During his time in Ireland Clarke was much more than just a simple
carrier of information between the Clan and the IRB. Clarke was looked
upon as a folk hero by many younger members of the IRB and he soon
developed a close working relationship with a rising light within the

---

82   Connell, Joseph. 2012. Thomas Clarke returns to Dublin. History Ireland. Vol. 20
     (Issue 1).

revolutionary movement in Ireland, Sean MacDiarmada. This sentiment was conveyed in a communication in 1908 Clarke sent to Clan member James Reidy in New York –

> "There is a splendid set of young fellows – earnest, able and energetic, around Dublin, with whom it is a pleasure to work, fellows who believe in doing things, not in gabbing about then only. I'm in great heart with this young, thinking generation. They are men; they will give a good account of themselves"[83].

This communication sent by Clarke is interesting for a number of reasons. First of all, Clarke is clearly indicating a rising and more energetic younger membership of the IRB. This new generation was very much the product of the literary and cultural revival begun back in the 1880s and still thriving in the early twentieth century, with Dublin at its center. On a wider international scale the Romantic Nationalist movement was sweeping the European continent creating rising nationalistic fervor of which Irish nationalism was no exception. The cultural and literary revival in Ireland was certainly a product of this. This new generation with Thomas Clarke as its leader would reinvigorate the lackluster and almost dormant IRB leadership. The days of the "Armchair Republicans" was at an end. A newer and more militant generation demanded nothing less than armed rebellion. For the first time since the Clan was created in 1867 there was a generation in Ireland emerging that were both intellectually and psychologically ready for rebellion and only awaited the material assistance and circumstances to launch an uprising. It would be Clan na Gael that would provide the vital last piece of the revolutionary jigsaw.

In Clarke's communication with Reidy he also indicates a generation not just anxious for revolutionary action but one which was a "thinking generation", meaning they were politically indoctrinated with Republican ideology and an actual vision of revolution and a post independent Irish republic. Clarke's decades of revolutionary experience gave him the ability to identify revolutionaries of ability and action. He opened up the doors of the IRB to younger individuals of outstanding ability which included

---

83   MacAtasney, Gerard. Sean MacDiarmada. Drumlin Publications. Manorhamilton. 2004. P. 43.

his protégé Sean MacDiarmada but also others like P.S O'Hegarty and
Bulmer Hobson. MacDiarmada would actually spend the years prior to
the 1916 Easter Rebellion riding around the country on his bicycle from
rural parish to parish, village to village and town to town reorganizing and
recruiting members to dormant branches of the IRB.

On top of Thomas Clarke's many attributes he also brought with him
the financial clout of Clan na Gael. Through choosing Clarke as the inter-
mediary to the IRB the Clan had achieved a monumental coup. They had
for the first time managed to put in place a member that was in all but name
head of the IRB. Clarke's organizational ability, skill in choosing younger
talent and appeal as an impeccable father-like figure to a rising more militant younger generation brought the prospects of rebellion as close as it
ever had been since the Clan's creation[84]. Yet again it was Ireland's exiled
sons that were taking the lead in advancing the cause of an Irish Republic.

Coinciding with the emergence of the IRB was the reemergence of
the Home Rule movement. In 1900 both wings of the divided Home Rule
party reunited under the leadership of John Redmond. Just like previously
the Party quickly reinvigorated the political base of the movement with
the objective and promise of attaining Home Rule. Previously dormant
and inactive branches nationwide became active again.

At this point the ruling Conservative Party in Britain had been in
power for almost a decade and had little sympathy for Home Rule demands in Ireland. Most in the Conservative party, including an increasingly
vocal and well-organized Ulster Protestants in the north of Ireland saw
any devolution of the Irish Act of Union as a threat to the empire. Instead
of taking reactionary measures that may well have only added to calls for
Home Rule in Ireland the Conservative Chief Secretary of Ireland, Arthur
Balfour, introduced a policy which became known as "Killing Home Rule
with Kindness". This policy involved the introduction of the Land Purchase
Act which provided loans for the Irish peasantry to buy their own land.
Congested District Boards were also created whose central aim was to help
the desperately poor areas which included most of the west of Ireland. In

---

84   Moran, Farrell, Sean. Patrick Pearse and the Politics of Redemption. The Catholic
     University of America Press. Washington D.C. 1997. P. 71-75.

1898 the Local Government Act was passed which gave a lot more local political decision-making power to rural districts and towns.

While in the late 1890s and early years of the 1900s the IRB did become more organized and invigorated with a newer more motivated and talented groups of revolutionaries there were still many limitations. The rise of the Home Rule Party deflected much potential support from the IRB and the British policy of "Killing Home Rule with Kindness" effected Irish revolutionaries much more than it did the Home Rule Party. The IRB and Clan na Gael always relied heavily on the revolutionary potential of the Irish peasantry and the British reforms more positively affected this group than any other section of Irish society.

Despite these obstacles the Clan's drive to reinvigorate and push the Irish republican movement down the path to armed insurrection had many factors in the U.S. that facilitated Irish-American nationalism. Irish-American nationalist sentiment had firmly fallen behind the support of full independence. Through the efforts of Clan na Gael, particularly the Clan's main mouthpiece The Gaelic American, which was founded in 1903 and edited by John Devoy, the idea for Home Rule had been denigrated. During the early 1900s Devoy and the Clan started reaching out much more to the upper strata of Irish-American political elites to get them to use their power and influence much more in the cause of Irish independence. Although the central focus of the Gaelic American was on Irish national issues it also brought attention to "various other lands struggling under Britain's yoke".

The first decade of the twentieth century saw Clan membership grow steadily. The growing influence of the Irish vote in major urban areas and growing support of the Clan among Irish- American political elites like Congressman William Bourke Cockran put the Clan in a strong position coming into a critical period of the independence movement[85]. Being out of reach of British intelligence and what was seen as the corrupting influence

---

85   Bornemann, Sara Bethany, "Political activism and resistance in Irish America: The Clan na Gael 1912-1916. 2018. Electronic Thesis and Dissertation. Paper 2940. Retrieved from <https//ir.library.louisville.edu/etd/2940>

of Home Rule propaganda the Clan was able to operate without virtually any competing ideology and alternative political options.

The one major fundraising effort made by John Redmond and the Home Rule movement in the U.S. occurred in 1910 through its American outreach organization, the United Irish League of America. Although there were Irish-Americans in the upper echelons who stayed loyal to the ideal of Home Rule the Clan bitterly attacked Redmond's message of a Federalist relationship within the British Empire. After a particular interview with The Daily Express where Redmond attempted to explain his federalist position the headlines next day were "THE NEW HOME RULE – MR. REDMOND COMES OUT AS A BRITISH PATRIOT-IMPERIALISM –LOCAL GOVERNMENT, THAT'S ALL". From the moment the story broke Redmond spent the remainder of his visit essentially on the defensive. The Clan fully exploited the situation to benefit its own position of full independence being the only true option and the failure of Home Rule to give any meaningful political freedom[86]. While most of Irish America were for full independence many in broader U.S. society held a more pro-British viewpoint and were more favorably inclined toward a peaceful Home Rule settlement. The election of 1912 would bring to power a President that was not only more pro-British in sentiment but one that was also hostile to the whole concept of ethnic nationalism within the United States. Woodrow Wilson would preside over the most critical period in the history of Irish American nationalism and his election in 1912 would prove the most important in Clan na Gael history[87].

---

86   Meleady, Dermot. John Redmond. Irish Academic Press. Sallins. 2014. P. 179-182.
87   Bornemann, Sara Bethany, "Political activism and resistance in Irish America: The Clan na Gael 1912-1916. 2018. Electronic Thesis and Dissertation. Paper 2940. Retrieved from <https//ir.library.louisville.edu/etd/2940>

CHAPTER 9

Woodrow Wilson, Clan na Gael and the Election of 1912

Woodrow Wilson was born into an Ulster Scots family in Staunton, Virginia in 1856. For most of his life Wilson would be more at home in academic surroundings as he entered the University of Virginia Law School in 1879 and four years later as a graduate enter John Hopkins University. During his time at John Hopkins Wilson would study Political Science, History, and German language as well as economics. In 1886 Wilson would receive his PHD with his dissertation titled "Congressional Government: A study in American Politics". The work was an indicator on where Wilson's real passions lay, politics and history.

After lecturing for short spells as Cornell University, Bryn Mawr College and Wesleyan University Wilson would end up in 1890 at Princeton University where he would establish himself as one of the foremost Political Scientists of his day. As Wilson's reputation grew over the years as an expert in the field of Political Science and his reputation as a popular lecturer and public speaker spread beyond the boundaries of Princeton he soon came to the attention of local Democratic political bosses as a possible candidate for the Governorship of New Jersey. After the approach was made Wilson accepted the Democratic nomination and in 1910 went on to defeat his Republican opponent. After just two years Wilson had come to such prominence within Democratic circles that he was nominated as their presidential candidate in 1912. After winning an extremely tense and close Primary process Wilson would go on to win a famous victory in what would turn out to be one of the country's most important Presidential elections that would shape U.S. politics and foreign policy for generations to come[88]. Few

---

88   Heckscher, August. Woodrow Wilson. Maxwell MacMillan International. New York. 1991. P. 136-253.

presidents had entered the office of the Presidency more intellectually or academically prepared than Wilson which in many ways were the keys to so much of his political success.

Wilson's first up close connection to the Irish-American community during his rise to political power was his choice of Joseph Tumulty as a political adviser during his election campaigns to the New Jersey governorship and later presidential campaigns. Prior to and during the Wilson administration Tumulty would be one of the leading Irish-American figures in the U.S. Tumulty would serve Wilson as his Private Secretary from 1911 to 1921 as one of his most loyal and faithful members of his administration. What Tumulty was able to give Wilson was a connection to and an insight into the Irish-American voting block which was so important to the electoral success of any Democratic candidate, particularly one coming from the northeast of the country. Being personally raised from childhood within the tightly knit Irish community in Jersey City and learning his political trade in the well-oiled Democratic machine of the state it would be safe to assume that Tumulty was introduced to Irish nationalism from a young age and rubbed shoulders with Clan na Gael figures from the time period. In his own autobiography in 1921 Tumulty would even make reference to "a devoted friend of mine, a fine, clean cut Irishman, who stood high in the ranks of Clan na Gael"[89]. While there is no proof or reason to believe that Tumulty was ever a member of Clan na Gael or a believer in Irish revolutionary politics he would show in later years a certain level of sympathy towards the cause of Irish-American nationalism. The best example of this was when Tumulty tried to pressure Wilson to ask for leniency for Roger Casement who was convicted for treason on attempting to import arms into Ireland.

While on the election trail Wilson was never averse to trying to court the Irish vote by highlighting his own Irish roots. The contradiction of his Ulster-Scots roots being historically deeply antagonistic and hostile to the native Irish Catholic tradition seems never to have been pointed out or picked up on by Democratic Irish American voters. Despite this cultural

---

89   Tumulty, Joseph. Woodrow Wilson as I knew him. Doubleday, Page and Company. 1921. P. 75.

background Wilson was certainly not anti-Catholic in any meaningful sense of the word. In a campaign speech in 1912 to the Friendly Sons of Saint Patrick Wilson clearly stated in relation to the issue of immigrants that "the country should be divested of all prejudices". However, later in this same speech Wilson went on to strongly attack the whole concept of what he referred to as "hyphenated Americans". By default, he was also attacking ethnic nationalism within the U.S. in the strongest terms. In another speech just a week later to Polish-Americans Wilson would further state "Is it not time to stop the practice of prefixing some race before the names of these Americans? I somehow feel that America is bigger than the continent on which it has been placed. The first Americanism is that we must love one another – forget race and creed". For possibly the first time a modern Democratic presidential candidate refused to appeal to Irish-American nationalist sentiment and out-rightly attacked the whole concept of an Irish-American identity[90].

On top of this open hostility to ethnic nationalism in the U.S. Wilson also had strong Anglophile leanings that would certainly not endear him to Clan na Gael. From a Political Science perspective Wilson held a deep admiration for the British political system. One of his favorite books were Bagehot's "English Constitution" which he read many times over the years[91]. Wilson's Anglophile tendencies were cultural as well as political as he once expressed to his wife that before going into politics that they both should live in Britain for a period[92].

Clan na Gael efforts during the 1912 election was its first major attempt to exert political influence on a national level. The trigger for the start of

90   Wolfensberger, Don. 2007, March 12. Woodrow Wilson, Congress and Anti-Immigrant Sentiment in America. An Introductory Essay by Don Wolfensberger for the Congress Project Seminar "Congress and the Immigration Dilemma: Is a Solution in Sight?" Woodrow Wilson International Centre for Scholars. Retrieved from   <https://www.wilsoncenter.org/sites/default/files/immigration-essay-intro.pdf>

91   Heckscher, August. Woodrow Wilson. Maxwell MacMillan International. New York. 1991. P. 76.

92   2. Potter, Gary. 2014. Woodrow Wilson, The Great War and Our World Today. Available online <http://catholicism.org/woodrow-wilson-the-great-war-and-our-world-today.html>

this contentious relationship seems to have been the 1912 Democratic Convention when the Irish dominated Tammany Hall clashed with Wilson on a number of issues with foremost being the issue of supporting Irish independence or at least accommodating the issue. Wilson showed particular dislike toward leading Clan na Gael member Daniel Cohalan. Coholan was a strident opponent of Wilson's nomination which was a slight Wilson never forgot and one which would manifest itself in the years to come when it came to dealing with Irish-American nationalists[93]. With the exception of the Mexican intervention in 1912 Wilson paid little attention to foreign policy issues until the outbreak of World War One in 1914. The Irish Question would force him to pay attention when the issue exploded with the Easter Rising of 1916.

Since 1912 is the first time period that Daniel Cohalan has been mentioned it is worthwhile taking a more detailed look at a Clan na Gael figure that would become one of the most important individuals in the movement during the critical time period of 1912-20. Cohalan was born in 1865 in Orange County, New York. After graduating from Manhattan College in 1885 Coholan would go on to a successful legal career before entering politics. As a Democrat Cohalan would become Grand Sachem of the Tammany Society from 1908-11. The society was the main instrument of political patronage for the Democratic Party in New York and already had a long history of corruption and cronyism. For Cohalan to have achieved such a position showed an adeptness at navigating such an environment.

Cohalan's success in operating within the corrupt world of Tammany Hall saw him rewarded by being appointed to the New York Supreme Court by Democratic Governor John Alden Dix. Coholan had always been involved in a number of Irish American organizations with Clan na Gael being the most prominent. A strong relationship soon developed between Devoy and Cohalan which would see both men become leading figures in the movement, particularly in the more American wing of the Clan. Despite Cohalan's obvious skills as an astute political operator, organizer and fundraiser he also had the unfortunate ability of developing deep

93   Duff, John. 1968. The Versailles Treaty and the Irish-Americans. The Journey of American History. Vol. 55, No. 3. P. 583.

antagonisms of those who disagreed or opposed him. On the American front this was particularly apparent with the ire he drew from Woodrow Wilson and the future Irish leader Eamon De Valera who saw him as little more than a political opportunist and product of corrupt urban machine politics. This last criticism is somewhat unfair to Cohalan as his tenure as New York Supreme Court Justice was more to do with local party politics, and he had nothing personally to gain from involving himself in conspiratorial revolutionary activities. In fact, he had much more to lose if his activities were ever fully revealed to public scrutiny[94].

With this seeming assault on ethnic identity in the U.S. with the election of Wilson the alliance between German and Irish Americans began to coalesce as they combined their powers as voting blocs into an alliance that dated back to the era of the Boer War and was reinvigorated not only with Wilson's election but also growing Anglo-German tensions and Irish nationalism. Both groups were very aware of prioritizing the need to show and espouse loyalty not just to their native lands but also to the newly adopted home. At a joint Irish and German rally, Devoy claimed "We love America more than we hate England, and it is our love for America which governs our actions".

What both Irish and German Americans were attempting to do was reverse what was a growing Anglo-American alliance that had steadily been taking place over the previous decades. The Clan had to deal with regular attacks from nativists with accusations of being "Un- American" and of having "divided loyalties". There were even accusations that Irish and German-American connections to nationalist causes in Europe would eventually draw the U.S. into "foreign entanglements". John Devoy was acutely aware of the fine line Clan na Gael would have to walk in terms of maintaining visible loyalty to the U.S. while at the same time driving forward the Irish nationalist agenda. Fortunately for the Clan they had at this moment an astute and some would even say cunning leader in the personality of John Devoy.

---

94 Doorley, Michael. Justice Daniel Cohalan 1865-1946: American Patriot and Irish-American Nationalist. Cork University Press. Cork. 2019. P. 5-335.

Through a well thought out and planned propaganda campaign Clan na Gael kept in high public visibility the cause of Irish nationalism. This was achieved through the very regular use of media and public relations campaigns which included large scale rallies and direct political lobbying which were covered in many media outlets beyond just Irish and German American media. The fact that most Clan members were also members of other Irish fraternal organizations such as the Ancient Order of Hibernians and the Friendly Sons of Saint Patrick meant that the Clan was able to use and manipulate these organizations towards its own end.

From the pages of the Clan's newspaper, the Gaelic American, Devoy carried out constant attacks on the British claiming a vast Anglo conspiracy that was attempting to demean the cause of Irish nationalism. He would also argue that the British and their supporters in the U.S. were very capable at advancing an anti-Irish American agenda as well as subverting the American Republic in general. The Gaelic American deeply embraced the Gaelic cultural and literary revival then taking place in Ireland and Irish-America as a process that would "de- Anglicize Ireland"[95].

On a broader national level Clan na Gael sought to exert direct influence on Anglo-American relations. The opportunity to do so was in relation to Irish-American opposition to the proposed Root-Bryce Treaty. John Devoy and Clan na Gael had always been aware of its duty to prevent any joint Anglo-American alliance, particularly one of a military nature. As far back as 1907 Devoy was warning the American public against British diplomatic efforts in the form of Ambassador James Bryce to encourage the U.S. into a formal military alliance with Britain. When a formal pact known as the Root-Bryce Treaty was negotiated and making its way through the Senate Devoy and Clan na Gael spared no efforts to scuttle its progress.

What would turn out to be one of the Clan's greatest foreign policy achievements Devoy spearheaded a very well organized and coordinated nationwide lobbying and propaganda campaign highlighting the risk the proposed treaty had in dragging the U.S. into a foreign war. Devoy's tenacity is

95   Bornemann, Sara Bethany. "Political activism and resistance in Irish America: The Clan na Gael 1912-1916. 2018. Electronic Thesis and Dissertation. Paper 2940. Retrieved from <https//ir.library.louisville.edu/etd/2940>

no better highlighted than at one point he spent six straight weeks lobbying Senators in Washington. During one such lobbying effort Devoy had a poignant and somewhat entertaining exchange with Senator John Sharp Williams of Mississippi. When Williams accused Devoy of being a "hyphenated American" the following exchange took place – Devoy – "Aren't the Anglo-Saxons hyphenated?" Williams – "Yes, but I am not Anglo-Saxon. I'm a Welshman. But my people have been in America for a hundred and fifty years". Devoy – "Judging by that standard Sitting Bull has a better record".

Devoy extended Clan lobbying efforts when he met with the Federated Union of New York which at this time was the largest group of Unions in the world. Not only had New York Unions have a long history of Irish membership at grass-root and leadership levels but like most Unions it had strong anti-imperialist leanings. The Clan's connections with New York Labor Unions would be a lasting one and exist for decades to come. On the eve of the vote of ratifying the treaty on 12 March 1912, Devoy and the Clan had built a formidable wall of opposition that included Irish-Americans, German-Americans, Labor Unions and broader anti-imperial sentiment in the U.S. After a prolonged debate the treaty was rejected. It was a major political and propaganda victory. At the Clan's convention some months later the organization passed a resolution to spend $5,000 on recruitment and reorganization[96].

Prior to the Easter Rising of 1916 the year 1912 was one of the most momentous in Clan na Gael's history. While the election of Woodrow Wilson could certainly be seen as a setback there were a number of other key achievements that the Clan could celebrate. In the successful efforts to defeat the Root-Bryce Treaty the Clan had built a nationwide political alliance with groups such as German-Americans (again) and Labor Unions. The skills and connections made as well as in particular the political skills of lobbying and networking would be of vital importance in the upcoming years when it came to rallying support for the Easter Rising and War of Independence as well as organizing opposition to the ratification of the

96   Golway, Terry. Irish Rebel – John Devoy and America's Fight for Ireland's Freedom. St. Martin's Griffin. New York. 1999. P. 186-188.

Versailles Treaty. Beyond this the Clan received a membership and financial boost that was able to put in place a structure that was so vitally important in bringing about the circumstances that created the 1916 Rising and the political structure so vitally important during the War of Independence that followed.

CHAPTER 10

The Drumbeat of War – 1912–1914

As events in Europe headed inevitably toward the catastrophe that would be World War One Clan na Gael would yet again find itself looking to the scenario of Britain's difficulty being Ireland's opportunity. However, on this occasion the domestic situation in the U.S. and Ireland would prove problematic. Firstly, as previously discussed there existed in the White House during this critical time an administration with Anglophile leanings and at the same time almost no appetite to get involved in any foreign policy venture that would bring it into conflict with Britain. Secondly, on the Irish front the re-emergence of the Home Rule movement proved a major political challenge to the IRB and its attempts to build a broad base of support strong enough to support an armed insurrection. Despite these major obstacles the formation of the Volunteer movement in Ireland offered a major beacon of hope and encouragement for the Clan to continue in its efforts to stoke rebellion in Ireland.

The introduction of the Home Rule Bill in 1912 offered to Ireland greater freedoms within the confines of the British Empire. Under the leadership of John Redmond, the Home Rule movement had reunited and emerged yet again as the largest political movement in Ireland. From the Clan's perspective the Home Rule Bill fell far short of the desired Republic that it demanded. Unlike the era of Parnell and the New Departure Clan na Gael would resist the new Home Rule Bill. Political compromise was no longer part of the Clan's political makeup. For Clan na Gael and the newer younger generation of the Irish Republican Brotherhood Redmond and Home Rule belonged to a bygone era. Home Rule was no longer seen as a short term political compromise but a political sellout.

As it turned out it would be events in Ireland's northern province of Ulster that would turn to the Clan's advantage. Many Irish Americans who were not actual immigrants from Ulster did not fully understand or even ignored the inconvenient fact that the province contained a very large number of Protestant loyalists who were of primarily Scottish ancestry and had a deep political and cultural allegiance to Britain and the monarchy. It could well be argued that that ignorance exists to this very day for a large majority of Irish-Americans. From the passing of the Home Rule Bill in the British parliament in 1912 militant loyalism in Ulster began to organize politically and militarily to resist what they perceived to be a threat to the political union between Ireland and Britain. In 1912 the Ulster Volunteer Force was formed with the financial backing of business and right-wing interests in both Ulster and Britain. In response Irish nationalists formed the Irish Volunteers with the intent "to secure and maintain the rights and liberties common to the whole people of Ireland".

The origins of the Irish Volunteers, the precursor to the future Irish Republican Army, can be traced to the Clan's sister organization, the Irish Republican Brotherhood. In 1913 the IRB in Dublin began drilling secretly. In an attempt to reach out to the broader nationalist movement the IRB requested Bulmer Hobson, who had been a leading member since joining in 1904, to contact The O'Rahilly, a leading nationalist, to act as an inter-mediary to Eoin MacNeill. MacNeill was a well-known academic figure and a leading individual within the Gaelic League and broader Gaelic cultural revival movement. The IRB felt encouraged to make this outreach after MacNeill wrote an article that stated It is evident that the only solution now possible is for the Empire either to make terms with Ireland or to let her go her own way". At a meeting on 11 November 1913, at Wynn's Hotel on Abbey Street in Dublin the IRB met with MacNeill to form a body to be known as the Irish Volunteers. Just two weeks later on 25 November a meeting led my MacNeill was held to start enrolling members into the new organization.

The event proved a major success with 3,000 members signing up on the first evening. The IRB focused on persuading members of Labor Unions such as the Irish Transport and General Workers Union to join. The ITGWU were in midst of the largest labor dispute in Irish history up until that point and were in a particularly militant mood. Two hundred members of the ITGWU arrived to sign up to the Volunteer movement armed with hurley sticks and followed by a pipe band. As a result of the lead taken by the IRB many of its members were to take up leadership roles in the new organization. For the Irish Republican Brotherhood, the Volunteer movement was to be nothing more than a front for a revolutionary army to be used in the overthrow of British rule in Ireland when the time was ripe[97].

The IRB role in the founding of the volunteer movement was critically important on a number of different levels, particularly in the context of its relationship with Clan na Gael. For most of its history the IRB had been very much the junior partner in the transatlantic relationship with the Clan. It was the Clan who provided the life blood of financial assistance as well as pressurizing the IRB into action during critical moments in the history of Irish Republicanism when it verged on the point of irrelevancy. In 1913 it was the IRB who for the first time took action on its own initiative to ferment rebellion in Ireland. The moment also marked a coming of age for the IRB where it would no longer have to take a subservient role to its sister organization in the U.S. From the perspective of the Clan this would have mixed blessings. From a positive perspective it brought the ultimate aim of rebellion much closer to reality which was always the holy grail and raison d'etre for the Clan. From a negative point of view it was the beginning of a lessening of Clan influence within the revolutionary movement in Ireland as a whole which would become most apparent with De Valera's visit to the U.S. in 1920 during the height of the War of independence.

With the real possibility in Ireland of a civil war between the rival volunteer movements in the north and south of the country the Home Rule Bill was due to become law in 1914. As weapons were smuggled to the UVF in the north by sympathizers within the conservative and military establishment in Britain the situation became critical when the British military based in the Curragh Camp refused orders out of sympathy to move against the UVF and the British government already facing the likelihood of war in Europe backed down. The signals were clear to Clan na

---

97   Connell, Joseph. 2013. Founding of the Irish Volunteers. History Ireland. Vol. 21 (Issue 6).

Gael and the IRB, the British establishment would only respond to the threat or direct use of violence.

The outbreak of World War One on 28 July 1914, changed everything and was to have a profound impact on Irish Republicanism, particularly Clan na Gael. The response of John Redmond and the Irish Parliamentary Party was to throw its full support behind the British government in the upcoming war. After British Foreign Secretary, Edward Grey, made his famous "the lamps are going out all over Europe" speech John Redmond intervened in the debate by stating –

> "I say to the government that they may tomorrow withdraw every one of their troops from Ireland. I say that the coast of Ireland will be defended from foreign invasion by her armed sons and for this purpose armed nationalist Catholics in the South will be only too glad to join arms with the armed Ulstermen in the North".

Redmond agreed that the implementation of the Home Rule Bill which was scheduled for 1914 would be delayed until the war ended. The central purpose for the Parliamentary Party in making this commitment was clearly to prevent the outbreak of Civil War in Ireland with Unionist forces in the North as well as a gesture that would provide a foundation for a future political understanding and compromise in a post-World War One Ireland. Although Redmond was roundly applauded and supported in the British House of Commons for his commitment to the British war effort he faced deep hostility and opposition within the leadership ranks of the Volunteer movement. Eoin MacNeill issued the following statement in response to Redmond's commitment – "Mr. Redmond, addressing a body of Irish Volunteers last Sunday, has now announced for the Irish Volunteer's a policy and program fundamentally at variance with their own published and accepted aims and pledges. He has declared it to be the duty of the Irish Volunteers to take foreign service under a government that is not Irish. He has made his announcement without consulting the provisional committee, the Volunteers themselves or the people of Ireland, to whose service alone they are devoted".

The consequence of this division between the argument of joining the British war effort in order to attain Home Rule and the opposing position of an Ireland first policy and the attainment of a Republic brought about an inevitable split within the Volunteer movement. What would be renamed the National Volunteers joined in the British war effort. This branch took the vast majority of members with it, a total of approximately 175,000. The remaining members which stayed under the title of the Irish Volunteers was made up of a total of around 13,500. At first glance the split would seem to have been a major setback for Clan na Gael and the IRB. However, like the Clan na Gael split of the 1890s it would turn out to be much more advantageous. The remaining Volunteer movement were more firmly under the control of militant Republicans in the IRB than ever before. It would be these remaining Volunteers that would provide the backbone to the 1916 Easter Rebellion[98].

The response to events in Ireland was increased efforts to make available every resource possible to the new Irish Volunteers. It was not lost on John Devoy and Joseph McGarrity, as well as others at Clan leadership level, as to the revolutionary potential of the new organization. From the time of Thomas Clarke's arrival in Ireland under the auspice of the Clan sums of money never less than $1,000 at a time reached the Supreme Council of the IRB. As John Redmond and the Irish Parliamentary Party set up a rival fund-raising effort in the U.S. it never amounted to more than $5,000. As well as this the Clan carried out a relentless propaganda campaign to delegitimize Redmond's new Volunteer movement which seems to have had a major impact in fundraising efforts. According to Devoy himself it is estimated in the years leading up to the 1916 Easter Rebellion the Clan contributed an estimated $100,000 to the IRB and emerging Irish Volunteer movement. These funds reached Ireland through a number of different channels. Individual visiting members of the IRB to the U.S. brought sums of money back to Ireland. Eoin MacNeill on one occasion was cabled as much as $5,000.

The largest sums of Clan na Gael money smuggled into Ireland was carried by Tommy O'Connor. O'Connor held a position on one of the White Star steamers that made frequent crossings across the Atlantic as well as trips from Dublin to Liverpool in England. O'Connor's main point

---

98   Connell, E.A, Joseph. 2006. John Redmond's Woodenbridge Speech. History Ireland. Vol. 22 (Issue 5).

of contact was Sean MacDermott. Other Clan messengers came from unexpected backgrounds that helped then avoid the detection of British intelligence. Devoy thought very highly of one Liam O'Donnell who was an ordained priest and made frequent trips back and forth between the Clan and IRB leadership[99].

Although the IRB were very much starting to take the revolutionary lead in Ireland none of this would have been possible without the role of Clan na Gael. The sending of Thomas Clarke as the Clan's leading emissary to Ireland was absolutely critical in the revitalization of the IRB. Clarke proved to be the elder Republican figure around which a new generation of Irish revolutionaries would emerge under his guidance and experience. The financial assistance provided by Clan na Gael at this most critical juncture allowed the IRB to have more full-time organizers that proved so important in the reorganization and expansion of the Republican movement throughout Ireland. On a more direct military level Clan money would prove vital when it came to purchasing weapons and ammunition without which rebellion would have been impossible.

99   Devoy, John. Recollections of an Irish Rebel. Irish University Press. 1969. Shannon. P. 392-393.

CHAPTER II

Clan na Gael and Imperial Germany

As stated earlier Clan na Gael had political connections with German America dating back to the days of the Boer War. As a result of rising tensions internationally between Britain and Germany these connections now extended to Imperial Germany. Early in 1914 John Devoy and Joseph McGarrity formally met with the German consul in New York. The outcome of the meeting was in the words of Clan na Gael a formal alignment of "the Irish-American movement with Germany on behalf of the Irish Republican Brotherhood in Dublin"[100]. As a result of the Clan being out of reach of British intelligence and military interference the logical decision was agreed upon with the IRB that it would be the Clan that would be the main channel of communication to Imperial Germany.

One of the most fascinating figures that rose to prominence within the Irish Republican movement during this time period was Roger Casement. Casement was born in Sandycove near Dublin in 1864. He was born into the Anglo-Irish tradition as the son of a British Army officer. The young Casement would go on to work in the British Consular service for over twenty years where he would make a name for himself internationally by exposing the brutalities of European colonialism, particularly in the Belgian Congo. It would be logical that it was this time period that awoke within Casement a growing anti-colonialism and anti-imperialism that manifested itself into a growing interest and connection to militant Irish nationalism[101].

For a number of years Casement had been in correspondence with Devoy as both men exchanged views and opinions on the current political situation in Ireland and Europe more broadly. While Casement was

---

100   Bornemann, Sara Bethany, "Political activism and resistance in Irish America: The Clan na Gael 1912-1916. 2018. Electronic Thesis and Dissertation. Paper 2940. Retrieved from <https//ir.library.louisville.edu/etd/2940>

101   Inglis, Brian. Roger Casement. Penguin Books. 1973. London. P. 19-151.

well aware of Devoy's leading role in Irish Republican circles, Devoy also followed Casement's career from his days in the Congo. Both men eventually met when Casement visited the U.S. in the Summer of 1914. Both men seemed to have made an immediate connection with a number in the Clan's leadership commenting on "the sincerity of the man" in reference to Casement. It became apparent that Casement's high profile international reputation and ability to avoid suspicion by British authorities would make him a perfect fit to be liaison with the German government[102].

Although Roger Casement would be the leading and one of the most well know figures leading up to the rising, he was not the only contact point between the Clan and imperial Germany. John Kenny, native of County Kildare and leader of the powerful New York branch of Clan na Gael was another important figure. When World War One eventually broke out with Britain declaring war on 4 August 1914, both Casement and Devoy were unable to travel and instead sent John Kenny to negotiate with the Germans. After arranging the meeting in New York with the German consulate Kenny sailed on 14 August, landing in Naples, Italy. From Naples Kenny would make his way to Rome where he went directly to the German embassy. After a long interview with Ambassador Count von Flutow in which Kenny presented him with the Clan's proposal for German arms shipments to Ireland to assist in a proposed uprising, Kenny was given a pass to travel freely in Germany as the government considered the proposal. After receiving no clear commitment from the German government in relation to military assistance Kenny decided to return to the U.S. After what turned out to be a six-week trip Kenny eventually returned to New York. Before doing so he made a short stop in Dublin where he met with his old friends Patrick Pearse, Tom Clarke and Sean MacDermott.

Although the Clan received no direct commitment from the Germans they were at the same time not dismissed directly out of hand and at least a direct channel of communication was now established with the

---

102   Inglis, Brian. Roger Casement. Penguin Books. 1973. London. P. 263-264.

Imperial German government. After a lunch between Kenny and Casement, Casement was encouraged and considered the trip a success[103].

On 31 October 1914, Casement arrived in Berlin where he would meet a few days later with State Secretary for Foreign Affairs, Arthur Zimmerman. It seems that prior to his arrival Casement had come up with the idea of creating an "Irish Brigade" made up of Irish prisoners of war that were captured in the early days of the war fighting in the British army. Casement was harking back to the romantic heyday of Irish regiments who fought in the armies of France, Austria and other nations in the hope of one day fighting against Britain and striking a blow for Irish freedom. The actions of the Irish Boer Brigade a little over a decade earlier would also have been at the forefront of Casement's thinking.

Both Casement and Zimmerman quickly came to the agreement of separating the Irish and British prisoners by establishing a separate camp. By Christmas 1914 over 2,000 Irish prisoners were relocated to Limburg Camp. As the official representative of the Irish Republican movement Casement had the authority to sign any agreement with the German government that furthered the cause of Irish independence. In a signed agreement Casement gave the guarantee that should the Germans be unsuccessful in landing an Irish brigade in Ireland that these same troops could be used in instigating a rebellion in the then British colonial possession of Egypt. While Clan na Gael agreed to the proposal the IRB were totally opposed. Again, this was another example of the growing independence of the IRB from Clan influence and control. Despite these disagreements it all proved in the end irrelevant. When Casement visited the camp in the hope of gaining recruits he was poorly received with only a very small number open to the idea of joining. Most Irish soldiers while having no particular loyalty to Britain and served mostly for economic reasons were still ingrained with the fundamental belief of not turning your back on men whom you have fought side by side with in a war that was ongoing.

103   Christ, Fran. 2013. Former Resident of the Mount, Kilcock, Ran Secret Missions for Clan-na-Gael and IRB. Kildare History Journal. Available online <http://www.kildare.ie/library/ehistory/2013/02/>

In the midst of the back and forth between the Clan and Imperial Germany a major moment occurred that was to provide Irish-American nationalism with one of its greatest propaganda moments and at a time that could not have been more opportune in laying the foundations for open rebellion. The old Fenian warrior, O'Donovan Rossa died on 29th June 1915, in Staten Island, New York. Both John Devoy, and his right-hand man in Ireland, Thomas Clarke, decided early on that the funeral would be a national occasion where the spirit of independence would be re-awoken and where the Irish Volunteers could demonstrate their military discipline and recruit more young men into its ranks. It would be a moment where Irish Republicanism could show itself as a viable option to Home Rule. There was never any doubt that O'Donovan Rossa would be buried in Ireland and laid to rest in the same soil as the pantheon of previous Irish patriots[104].

Clan na Gael took a leading role in Rossa's funeral that is often over-shadowed by Irish Volunteer involvement during the final stages. During the American stage of the journey the Clan organized a procession and virtual lying in state where prominent Irish Americans that included Dr Thomas Addis Emmet, Supreme Court Judge John W. Goff, representative from the New York's Mayor office John Hartigan as well as John Devoy and Jim Larkin among others. Members of the Irish Volunteers and the Ancient Order of Hibernians acted as guards of honor and funeral pallbearers. On a separate front the Clan fought hard to exclude any attempts by John Redmond and the Home Rule movement to interfere in any way in the proceedings. This was achieved early by warning and persuading the Rossa's family of such attempts. The Clan took on all financial costs of the funeral and propaganda events surrounding it[105].

In Ireland a committee called the Wolfe Tone Memorial Association was established to organize the Irish part of Rossa's procession and funeral. Members of the association included what would be many of the future leaders of the Easter Rebellion as well as a future Taoiseach and

---

104   Kenna, Shane. Jeremiah O'Donovan Rossa. Merrion Press. Sallins. 2015. P. 239.
105   Kenna, Shane. Jeremiah O'Donovan Rossa. Merrion Press. Sallins. 2015. P. 240-241.

President – James Connolly, Patrick Pearse, Thomas MacDonagh, John MacBride and Eamon De Valera among others. Thomas McDonagh would oversee the actual funeral procession which included organizations such as the Gaelic Athletic Association, trade unions, the Irish Citizen Army and Irish Volunteers.

On 18 July 1915, Rossa's body would finally return to Ireland. After a long procession to the pro-Cathedral in Dublin in which Requiem mass was held on 28 July. After the service Rossa's body was then moved to City Hall for an opportunity for Irish people to pay their last respects. On 1 August Rossa would finally make his final journey to Glasnevin Cemetery where he would be laid to rest. During the funeral there took place perhaps the most famous funeral oration in Irish history by Patrick Pearse, the man who would be the symbolic face and romantic poet of the upcoming Easter Rebellion. The oration is worth noting in part as it was very much symbolic of the emotional and intellectual basis for the Easter Rising and also the culmination of decades of Clan na Gael efforts to instigate an armed uprising against British rule in Ireland –

> "The Defenders of this Realm have worked well in secret and in the open. They think that they have pacified Ireland. They think that they have purchased half of us and intimidated the other half. They think that they have foreseen everything, think that they have provided against everything; but the fools, the fools, the fools! – they have left us our Fenian dead; and while Ireland holds these graves, Ireland unfree shall never be at peace"[106].

With these final words a past generation of Irish revolutionaries was laid to rest and a new one was about to enter center stage. The emergence of the IRB and the Volunteer movement would not have been possible without the Clan na Gael's organizational drive and large financial injections into what was for years a dormant and inactive Irish revolutionary movement.

Back in the U.S. the Clan carried out a relentless anti-war campaign in an attempt to nullify growing pro-British sentiment in the more mainstream

---

106   Kenna, Shane. Jeremiah O'Donovan Rossa. Merrion Press. Sallins. 2015. P. 247-252.

media. Clan na Gael seems to have taken a page from organized Labor in attempting to make an argument that defense manufacturers were lobbying hard in Washington to force the country into war for reasons of profit. The Clan's Gaelic American was joined by another major Irish publication, The Irish World, in highlighting the undue influence of the British embassy in Washington and attempts to drag the U.S. into a general European War on the side of Ireland's imperial oppressor, the British Empire. The thought of young Irish-American men been forced to fight alongside Britain in maintaining and defending her Empire, which included Ireland, was too much to bear for many Irish-American nationalists. As a result, it had to be resisted at all costs.

Resistance to a British alliance did not just take place in newspapers. Large scale anti-British demonstrations took place throughout 1915. A major trigger for this was President Wilson's authorization of large-scale loans to Britain. One of the largest Clan na Gael orchestrated demonstrations took place alongside German-American groups when a massive demonstration that included upward of 100,000 protestors attended an anti-war event in Madison Square Garden. A major public relations success of the event was the attendance of William Jennings Bryan as a main speaker. Bryan had just recently resigned as Wilson's Secretary of State primarily in opposition to the direction of foreign policy which he feared was leading the country to war.

In attracting such a high-profile speaker to the event the Clan had scored a major public relations success. Their opposition was now not just portrayed as that of disgruntled "Hyphenated-Americans" but as part of a major strain of American political tradition, that of isolationism and non-entanglement in European wars. The heavy press coverage of the event lasted weeks to the deep frustration of the Wilson administration and the British consulate[107].

After the failure to put together an Irish Brigade Casement next turned his attention to gaining military support from German for a planned

---

107 Bornemann, Sara Bethany. "Political activism and resistance in Irish America: The Clan na Gael 1912-1916. 2018. Electronic Thesis and Dissertation. Paper 2940. Retrieved from <https//ir.library.louisville.edu/etd/2940>

uprising. He hoped to gain success and a commitment where John Kenny had previously failed. On 1 March 1916, after a frustrating number of months, word had come from Devoy to the German General Staff that a rebellion was to be launched in Ireland and that weapons were needed immediately. In a meeting General Staff officer Von Haugwitz discussed a proposed plan to transport German arms into Ireland. The German response to Devoy's call for assistance was –

> "Between April 20 and 23rd two or three fishing trawlers could land about 20,000 rifles and 10 machine guns with ammunition and explosives at Fenit Pier in Tralee Bay. Irish pilot boat is to expect trawlers before dusk....at entry to Tralee Bay...unloading has to be effected in a few hours. Please wire whether necessary steps can be arranged secretly in Ireland by Devoy...Nadolny".

Although Casement was in poor health at this point he was suddenly revitalized with a new lease of life on hearing how quickly events were moving. It was quickly arranged that Casement would return secretly to Ireland by German submarine. In Casement's words "the whole project really took my breath away. I had come to discuss the best means of landing arms in Ireland and I found myself confronted with a proposal for a rebellion in Ireland I believed to be wholly futile at the best, and at the worst something I dreaded to think of". Casement now found himself isolated in Germany with deep hesitations as to the success of any proposed rebellion. The Germans refused to hear Casement's concern about the lack of military from direct German assistance and fear that Irish rebels would be left isolated to be eventually picked off and defeated by a militarily superior British army. The German's main concern was to try to alleviate pressure on her western front by distracting British armed forces with an uprising on her own doorstep. The Germans became so irritated with Casement's opposition that they notified Devoy in New York that they were at the point of cancelling the whole operation. Casement felt forced to go along with a rebellion he felt was doomed to failure. As he stated in his diary "In other words I was to be held up to my countrymen in Ireland and America as something far worse than a coward".

A German ship named the Aud was to be used to land the arms shipment in Ireland. Ironically enough the ship was originally built in England

and was named the SS Castro. After being captured in Kiel Canal at the outbreak of the war it was requisitioned into the German navy and renamed Libau. To provide the necessary cover and secrecy the ship masqueraded as a Norwegian vessel called the Aud. The ship set sail from the Baltic port of Lubeck on 6 April 1916, under the command of Karl Spindler with a total crew of twenty-two men.

On 11 April Casement along with two members of the Irish Brigade set sail on the German submarine U-20. It was almost inevitable as a result of the British naval strangle hold around Ireland that on 21 April the Royal Navy intercepted the Aud which Splindler decided to scuttle rather than fall into British hands after his men had surrendered. Casement had been put ashore at this point at Banna Strand in Tralee Bay where he was arrested soon after. Casement would end up being executed for high treason. These events took place just three days before the outbreak of rebellion and were a major factor in moving events forward[108]. Casement would be the last Irish rebel to be executed in the Tower of London, a tradition that went as far back as the sixteenth century.

On Casement's arrest and almost certain death penalty Clan na Gael launched a major propaganda campaign in the U.S. on behalf of Casement and to put pressure on President Wilson to intervene on his behalf and ask for leniency because of his track record on human rights issues in Africa. The Clan's main access to Wilson was through Joseph Tumulty, Private Secretary to the President. Despite their best efforts Wilson refused to intervene in what he saw as an internal British issue. Casement was eventually executed on 3 August 1916.

---

108   Doerries, Reinhard. Prelude to the Easter Rising. Frank Cass. London. 2000. P. 1-25.

CHAPTER 12

The Opening Round

When the insurrection broke out on 24 April Clan na Gael could do little but observe events from a distance. Shortly before mid-day rebels took over key buildings in Dublin city. Most were still under the impression that volunteers outside of Dublin would rise up on the planned date. The plan was to hold Dublin city center until reinforcements from the rest of the country could arrive. Most of the British military establishment was out of the city attending major horse racing events outside of Dublin and were caught completely unaware which meant the rebels took over most of the buildings with ease. It would be Patrick Pearse, the figurehead of the rebellion that would read what would become the famous Proclamation of the Irish Republic from the steps of the General Post Office in Dublin center –

> "IRISHMEN AND IRISHWOMEN: In the name of God and of the dead generations from which she receives her old tradition of nationhood, Ireland, through us, summons her children to her flag and strikes for her freedom.

> Having organized and trained her manhood through her secret revolutionary organization, the Irish Republican Brotherhood, and through her open military organizations, the Irish Volunteers and the Irish Citizen Army, having patiently perfected her discipline, having resolutely waited for the right moment to reveal itself, she now seizes that moment, and supported by her exiled children in America and by gallant allies in Europe, but relying in the first on her own strength, she strikes in full confidence of victory".

The fact that Thomas Clarke, main Clan na Gael emissary to the IRB, was given pride of place as the first signatory of the Declaration of Independence says everything as to the Clan's role in bringing about the Easter Rebellion of 1916. The Proclamation read by Pearse on the steps of the GPO encapsulated the aims and objectives enshrined at the heart of Irish Republicanism ever since the days of the United Irishmen. The moment was all the more poignant for Clan na Gael as it was the shores of the United States that this ambition was kept alive when prospects in Ireland remained at a low ebb for generations with an almost dormant and inactive IRB.

The ease with which Volunteers took over many of the buildings in Dublin city center may have given the younger and more inexperienced members a false sense of a positive outcome while some of the older membership would have known as to what was to come. On 25 April British troops would start arriving in numbers into Dublin with the first major exchange of gunfire taking place in the early hours of the morning with fighting around Saint Stephen's Green. The inexperience of the rebels resulted in a large number of casualties among their ranks. Further setbacks continued throughout the morning with British forces dislodging rebels from City Hall. Most of the casualties inflicted on the British during the initial fighting was as the result of sniper fire from rebels. Rebel forces were able for a while to stem the British advance by relentless and accurate gunfire from the South Dublin Union building. Throughout the first day of fighting arrival of British forces continued and despite partial rebel success in delaying the British advance setbacks continued. By the end of the first day of fighting it was becoming apparent to the rebel leadership that the expected rising in the rest of the country was not materializing and that MacNeill's earlier countermanding order had an effect. With the exception of sporadic attacks in places like Galway, Ashbourne and a few other locations it was becoming apparent that the uprising was almost mostly confined to Dublin.

On 26th April the situation continued to deteriorate from the rebel perspective as the British send the gunship Helga down the Liffey River to bombard the center of Dublin. Accurate rebel sniper fire continued to slow down and in certain areas stop completely the British advance. Late in the evening the situation for the rebels was starting to become so desperate that some started to set fire to buildings to delay British advances being made.

27th April saw continued bloody fighting and a continuation of the tightening of the net around Dublin City center as rebels were now almost completely cut off from outside help and support. The continued British advance was beginning to have the desired effect with more and more of the city center being turned to rubble. Food shortages for both the rebels and civilian population saw many of the stores and shops being forcibly opened up to the public for food distribution. Due to continuing rebel sniper fire the British start tunneling between buildings to reach their objectives. The combination of continued British shelling and the outbreak of fires throughout the city center forced many rebels to abandon their position and to retreat to an ever smaller circle in the city center.

28 April saw fighting reach the very rebel headquarters at the General Post Office as the GOP came under intense artillery fire. By mid-morning all rebel held positions are completely surrounded by British forces. Despite their obviously desperate predicament rebel forces continued to inflict casualties on British forces with the most notable incident being a fierce gun battle between opposing forces on North King Street. The rebel headquarters at the GPO was evacuated when a fire breaks out as a result of intense incendiary shelling. At this stage escape became impossible and for many of the remaining rebels defeat was now inevitable.

Saturday, 29th April, saw the final shots of the uprising and at 3.30 p.m. Pearse formally surrendered. The British command demanded nothing less than unconditional surrender which Pearse is in no position to refuse. Pearse handed over his sword, pistol, ammunition and signed the documents of formal surrender. The rebellion that Clan na Gael had spent decades working toward had now ended in complete defeat. As previously discussed Devoy had deep reservations prior to the outbreak as to its chances of success. In many ways the success of the rising was the very fact that it ever occurred and that it lasted as long as it did against overwhelming odds. Devoy and Clan na Gael now had a foundation to build upon. They would also soon have their martyrs, so important to the psychic of Irish Republicanism and to future political mobilization.

By the time the Rising ended 1,350 people lay dead or wounded. Deaths would include 260 civilians, 126 British soldiers, 82 Irish rebels and 17 members of the Royal Irish Constabulary. Injuries again would affect civilians disproportionately as a result primarily of British shelling on rebel positions. Of the total of 2,600 injured 2,200 were civilians. In the days and weeks after the rebellion a total of 3,430 Irishmen and women were arrested with most being released in the weeks and months following the rising.

As a result of the mass destruction caused by the rising which many Dubliners initially blamed the rebels for and the fact that many working-class women in the city had sons and husbands who were fighting in Europe there was initial hostility shown toward the rebels. As many were marched down the streets of Dublin after the formal surrender many were pelted with a variety of items and had insults hurled at them. Had the British handled the aftermath of the rising in a manner that took advantage of the immediate public reaction and took into consideration history and the political legacy of executed Irish rebels of the past may have been very different.

However, the British acted in a way which was almost unavoidable for an empire that was in the midst of a life or death struggle on the battle fields of Europe against Imperial Germany. The challenge to British imperial rule in Ireland during a time of her greatest need and vulnerability demanded the ultimate response. After quick and secretive military court proceedings sixteen of the main leaders of the uprising were executed by firing squad between 3–12 May. As news of the executions leaked to the Irish public horror and revulsion quickly set in and sympathy for the rebel cause increased. The vision of James Connolly, shot in the ankle during the rising having to be tied to a chair because he could not stand in order to be executed, horrified many. The British apparently learned nothing from the previous 700 years of rule in Ireland. Clan na Gael now had not only their rebellion, they now had their newest generation of martyrs. An organization as adept at propaganda as the Clan now went into full attack mode in the U.S. The biggest obstacle to the Clan's hopes and prospects of furthering the cause of Irish independence continued to lie in growing tensions between the U.S. and Germany and President Wilson's increasing tendency to veer toward a pro-British position in World War One[109].

109   Caulfield, Max. The Easter Rebellion. Gill & MacMillan. Dublin. 1995. P. 1-264.

Aftermath of the Easter Rising in the U.S.

As news of the uprising reached the shores of the U.S. it was largely met with disbelief by most Irish-Americans. Many in the mainstream Irish-American political establishment saw the event as foolhardy and reckless with no hope of success. The New York Council of the United Irish League called an emergency session and passed a resolution denouncing the uprising as "An insane attempt at rebellion". As to be expected it was the conservative Home Rule movement in the U.S. that was most vociferous in its opposition to the rebellion within the Irish-American community. Once initial outrage was voiced against the rebels in Dublin anger began to be directed at Clan na Gael for its role in what was perceived by many as a debacle. Father Peter Gannon in Omaha targeted the Clan directly when he announced in a popular Catholic publication –

> "They certainly stand on a higher plane in public estimation than the contemptible blowhards of New York and other American cities who urged them on. These fools and fakirs can be proud of their work. True Irishmen, loyal to the principle of national liberty have nothing but contempt for men who urge others to entre in a campaign of armed insurrection while they themselves are careful to keep 3,000 miles between them and the scene of the conflict".

While at the same time as condemning the uprising there were some within conservative Irish-American circles who were deeply concerned as to the aftermath of the event. One such individual with a deep understanding of Irish history and psychic was James Gibbons, a leading figure within the Irish American Home Rule movement. He warned the British Ambassador, Sir Cecil Spring Rice about handling the aftershock of the rebellion correctly as there would be a real danger of "manufacturing martyrs".

Just as in Ireland everything began to change when news of the British executions of the leaders of the rising began to reach American shores. For the first time both Irish-American Home Rule supporters and militant supporters of Clan na Gael were unified in their outrage and revulsion at the executions that followed the rising. Public opinion in the U.S. in general was also shocked at British actions after the rising. The Washington Post newspaper called British actions "stupid and vengeful". Even more anglophile leaning publications like the New York Evening Post remarked that "England has given way to her vengeance, England has roused the moral sense of mankind against her.... she has left us who love her cause in the war against despotism without another word to say for her".

The executions in the aftermath of the Easter Rising as a whole led to a radicalizing of Irish- American sentiment not just in terms of Irish nationalism but also in an increased support for an isolationist approach to the war in Europe and resistance to any sort of Anglo-American alliance. An excellent example of this change in sentiment was Boston's William Cardinal O'Connell. The aftermath of the Easter Rising saw O'Connell completely disassociate himself from the Home Rule cause and endorse a fully independent Ireland. O'Connell would take his outrage publicly with articles in the Boston Pilot titles "England arraigned at the Bar of Humanity". The Irish-American backlash was summed up best when other former moderates such as Father John Burke of the Catholic World stated "Whenever the English government has to deal with Ireland, it shows a pitiful, blundering sense of misunderstanding and oftentimes of injustice which shocks the world". Although conservative institutions such as the Catholic Church remained for the most part pro-Home Rule there was now serious dissent and more of an openness in discussing the cause of Irish independence[110].

Outside of the powerful Irish-American Catholic Church other voices were beginning to shape the response to events in Ireland. Ireland's long history of literature and music was one the main avenues through which acts of Irish rebellion and resistance was immortalized and commemorated and so it

---

110   Rowland, Thomas. 1995. The American Catholic Press and the Easter Rebellion. The Catholic Historical Review. Vol. 81, No. 1.

was to be the case of the 1916 Easter rebellion. In the U.S. the leading literary figure who took up that particular aspect of rebellion was Joyce Kilmer. Born in 1886 Kilmer was raised Episcopalian but converted to Catholicism in 1913. Kilmer adopted his new Irish identity in part because of his father's fascination with Irish history and literature. As a result Kilmer grew up with an exposure to everything Irish. His automatic association of Irishness and Catholicism was a major factor in his religious conversion in 1913.

With the typical zeal of a convert Catholicism played a major theme in Kilmer's writing. Kilmer would go on to become a well -known writer and poet and considered by many at the time Catholic America's poet. Kilmer, like many of his generation was also deeply influenced by the romantic nationalist movement that had swept over Europe in the early twentieth century and was also taking root in U.S. society. The potent combination of nationalism and Catholicism that held in particular high esteem the image of martyrdom left Kilmer particularly prone to the emotional impact of the executions that followed the Easter Rising.

Even before the executions were completed Kilmer was memorializing and setting the literary stage for Irish-America and its views and interpretation of events in Ireland. On 7 May 1916, Kilmer published his first written piece in relation to the Easter Rising titled "Poets Marched in the Van of the Irish Revolt". In the article Kilmer described the revolt as "A poetic revolution – indeed, a poet's revolution – that is what has been happening in Ireland during the last two weeks, says Padraic Colum, himself an Irish poet now in New York.". Kilmer would go on to reprint the literary and poetic works of leading figures such as Thomas McDonagh and Roger Casement which gave the Irish-American audience an insight into the aims and motives of those executed and as a result increasing public sympathy.

Ireland leading literary figure of the time, William Butler Yeats, was more critical of the events of Easter week which was reflected in such works as "Easter, 1916" in which the famous last line stated "A terrible beauty is born". While Kilmer was not in the same literary class as the likes of Yeats he was however, not afraid to take on such a literary titan. In a response to Yeats's famous poem Kilmer wrote "Easter Week" which he dedicated to executed rebel leader Joseph Plunkett. It is well worth quoting the poem in its entirety here as it was perhaps the most important literary response to come out of the U.S. from those sympathetic to the rebellion and the wider cause of Irish independence.

Easter Week (In memory of Joseph Plunkett) (Romantic Ireland is dead and gone, it's with O'Leary in the grave") – William Butler Yeats.

"Romantic Ireland is dead and gone, It's with O'Leary in the grave". Then, Yeats, what gave the Easter dawn A hue so radiantly brave? There was a rain of blood that day, Red rain in gay blue April weather. It blessed the earth till it gave birth To valor thick as blooms of heather. By the time of his early death on the battlefield of Europe during World War One at the age of just thirty-two Kilmer had become the unofficial poet of Ireland's exiled children. He would not live long enough to see the outbreak of the war of independence that would come just a year after Kilmer's death.

For the more anglophile political establishment, the 1916 Rising was seen as a major danger to the long growing and developing Anglo-American alliance. Tensions between Clan na Gael and the Wilson administration would escalate rapidly in the aftermath of the Easter Rising. The Clan's dilemma was the fact that Wilson was head of a Democratic administration and Irish-America had a long held loyalty to the party dating back to the 1840s. The major Irish-American urban political machines were Democratic. Wilson took a calculated risk in believing the Irish bond to the Democratic Party to be sufficiently strong as to launch attacks in the months after the rebellion on what he termed "hyphenated Americans" at the beginning of his 1916 re-election campaign. With rising nationalist sentiment in the U.S. as the result of German naval attacks at sea on civilian shipping the Clan was in a very delicate position. The age-old dilemma of being both American and Irish was coming to the fore yet again. Wilson had played his hand deftly and the Irish vote remained loyal to Wilson and he was re-elected for a second term in office. Part of the staunch Irish support was Wilson's re-election promise to "Keep us out of war". Even if Wilson was not in support of an Irish Republic this promise seemed sufficient to most Irish-Americans. As long as this remained the case Clan na Gael would at least remain placated for the short term while still agitating for support of an Irish Republic and planning for a future war built upon the embers of the failed Easter Rising and growing public outrage[111]. Clan na Gael would see its upcoming role as making sure the 1916 Rising would be not

111   Hopkinson, Michael. 1993. Woodrow Wilson and the Irish Question. Studia Hibernica. No. 27. P. 89-92.

just being a once off insurrection but the basis for a full-scale war of independence. In this process it would play an enormously important and historically underappreciated role.

The greatest leader in the history of Clan na Gael. John Devoy would play a prominent role in the movement from his release from prison and arrival in the U.S. in 1871 to the major split in 1920 and eventual death in 1928.

Daniel Coholan was a leading member of Clan na Gael, the major driving force behind
the Friends of Irish Freedom and ally of John Devoy prior to and during the split
of 1920.

After the split in 1920 Joseph McGarrity would become the leader of Clan na Gael up until his death in 1940. He was the main driving force behind the IRA bombing campaign in Britain from 1939-40.

Eamon De Valera on his 1920 tour of the United States. His insistence on direct control of Clan na Gael funds and fundraising efforts split the organization, a division from which the Clan never fully recovered.

Clan na Gael monument at Mount Carmel cemetery in Chicago commemorating
members of the organization killed in the Boer War fighting Britain.

One of the most interesting leading Clan na Gael figures of the twentieth century. Not only was Mike Quill a leading figure within Clan na Gael from the mid-1930s until his death in 1966 but he was also a leading founder of the Transport Workers Union of America and a major civil rights advocate. The crossover in membership between Clan na Gael and the TWU was significant.

George Harrison became a member of Clan na Gael shortly after seeing active service in WW2 serving in the U.S. Army. He was the leading gunrunning liaison to the IRA during the border campaign of 1956–62 and later on to the Provisional IRA throughout the 1970s and early1980s.

CHAPTER 14

Clan na Gael as a Global Revolutionary Model after 1916

The impact of the 1916 Rising and the role played by Clan na Gael was noticed far beyond the shores of Ireland, Britain and the United States. For many years it was accepted thinking within historical circles to see the Russian Revolution of 1917 as the beginning of the anti- imperial and anti-colonial era of the twentieth century. Recent historical research from the National University of Ireland in Galway and by other historians have started to argue that it was the Easter Rising that was the beginning of this era. The role of Clan na Gael as a transnational revolutionary move-ment was also one that was looked upon by other movements as a suc-cessful model in which to base upon.

As a result of the serious doubts John Devoy and others in the lead-ership of Clan na Gael had in relation to the possibility of success of the Easter Rising it could be argued that the event was seen more as an attempt to mobilize popular opinion against British rule in Ireland rather than a realistic aim of militarily overthrowing it. The profoundly anti-imperial message contained within the Proclamation of the Irish Republic stated "the right of the people of Ireland to the ownership of Ireland .... asserting it in arms in the face of the world". This message set a clear framework for all anti-imperial movements not just within the British Empire, but also outside of it[112]. As a result of its long history in the U.S. and ability to mingle freely with other exiled political refugees and movements it was Clan na Gael with its skills in propaganda and growing international connections that truly launched the 1916 Rising from what might well have been a mere once off insurrection to a full-scale rebellion from 1919-21 that would be the

---

112   Lado, Dal, Enrico; Healy, Roisin; Barry, Gearoid. 2018. 1916 in a Global Context – An Anti-Imperial Moment. London. Routledge. P. 3-4.

beginning of the undoing of the British global empire. While the IRB in Ireland was focused entirely on the domestic issue of achieving independence it was Clan na Gael who held a more global anti-imperial vision that would assist not just Irish independence but the long-term destruction of the British Empire in its entirety.

The first major revolutionary movement to see the significance of the Easter Rising were the Bolsheviks. Twenty years after the Rising in a letter to Nora Connolly, daughter of executed leader James Connolly, Leon Trotsky commented "the tragic fate of your courageous father met me in Paris during the war. I bear him faithfully in my remembrance". Lenin himself was a strong defender of the Rising against the criticisms of other Marxists who denounced it as an ill-conceived uprising by "petty-bourgeois" nationalist dreamers. Instead, Lenin defended it as "a blow against the power of English imperialism". When the Bolsheviks came to power just a year later and became established after a bitter civil war, the Easter 1916 Rising began to be reframed within Marxist theory as an anti-colonial struggle which was part of a wider process of decolonizing the world[113].

A more controversial theory held by some historians is the impact of the Easter Rising in bringing about the Russian Revolution itself. In 1917 Lenin wrote in his State of the Revolution that in a revolution subordination to a "small, armed vanguard of the proletariat" is essential to strike the imperial order in a disciplined and efficient manner. The question is could Lenin have been referring to the rebels of the Easter Rising when he talked about this "vanguard"? Some other similarities also exist. Neither the Irish rebels nor the Bolsheviks had a popular mandate supporting their armed uprisings. Both uprisings started with the takeover of public buildings in the main political centers. Just as Pearse read the Proclamation of the Irish Republic from the steps of the GPO so too did Lenin announce to Russia and the world his famous "To all the Citizens of Russia". Both announcements were made to stunned and surprised crowds with the full expectation of severe governmental backlash. While many historians might dismiss the similarities as inevitable coincidences one cannot ignore Lenin's

---

113   Available online <https://www.opendemocracy.net/en/opendemocracyuk/eas ter-rising-and-soviet-union-untold-chapter-in-ireland-s-great-rebellion/>

deep knowledge of the events of the Easter Rising and staunch defense of it just a year prior to critics within the broader Marxist movement[114].

Within the United States itself four groups took particular notice of Clan na Gael. One was the rising African American nationalist movement under the leadership of Marcus Garvey. The second was the Indian revolutionary movement known as the Ghadar Party which sought the violent overthrown of British rule in India and who had a strong exile movement based within the U.S. Thirdly, you had the Zionist movement whose younger more radical membership looked upon Clan na Gael as the perfect model in which to overthrow British rule in Palestine and set up an independent Jewish state. Finally, the Suffragette movement certainly noticed the successful forms of protest undertaken by Clan na Gael. Many Irish-American women who were also members of Clan na Gael found it easy to transition over to the Suffragette cause and bring with them their extensive experience of protest and organization.

Clan na Gael and its struggle for Irish independence came to the attention of Marcus Garvey. Garvey's first up close introduction to the Irish nationalist cause was the time he spent in London between 1912 and 1914 at the height of the Home Rule crisis. His observation of the Curragh Mutiny and the failure of Britain to uphold its promise of Home Rule left Garvey angry at the unfair treatment of Ireland and the view of a strong parallel between the Irish question and the cause of African Americans.

On Garvey's return to the U.S. in 1914 we went about establishing the Universal Negro Improvement Association with the slogan "Africa for the Africans at home and abroad" which was based on the Irish nationalist slogan "The Irish race at home and abroad". Garvey also paid deep attention to Clan na Gael's widespread propaganda campaign which included articles in periodicals as well as large scale protest meeting which brought together thousands and often tens of thousands of supporters. By the time of the 1916 Rising Garvey was already well acquainted with Irish nationalism and in particular Clan na Gael[115].

---

114   Available online <https://www.rbth.com/history/326719-1917-bolshevik-revolut ion-ireland>

115   Available online <http://theconversation.com/the-easter-rising-100-years-on-how-the-irish-revolution-fired-up-american-politics-58586>

It was the events of the 1916 Rising which really captured the imagination not only of Garvey but the broader African American nationalist movement. For Garvey the Rising was nothing less than a strike against colonialism by a people and a culture that were denigrated by centuries of oppression. The parallels to Africa and the example put forward were inescapable for Garvey who just three years later in 1919 expounded "The time has come for the negro race to offer up its martyrs upon the altar of liberty even as the Irish has given a long list, from Robert Emmet to Roger Casement". The up-close view of Clan na Gael as a transatlantic movement and "exiled children of Ireland" providing support and assistance to an armed anti-colonial struggle thousands of miles away provided Garvey with an image of what he aspired the UNIA to eventually become. This was even more apparent in 1919 when he named the headquarters of the movement in Harlem "Liberty Hall" after the destroyed headquarters of the Irish Citizen Army in Dublin during the rising[116].

Outside of Garvyism but still within the broader African American nationalist movement other notable individuals and schools of ideological thought took major notice of the 1916 Easter Rising and the efforts of Clan na Gael in bringing about what was perceived by many as an anti-colonial moment of significance. One important individual was W.E.B Du Bois. Du Bois represented the much smaller but more left leaning intellectual element of African American society. Being of a more socialist persuasion Du Bois viewed the Easter Rising more from a class perspective. As a writer in the monthly magazine "The Crisis", which was the major publication for the organization the National Association for the Advancement Colored People, Du Bois wrote that "The white slums of Dublin represent more bitter depths of human degradation than the black slums of Charleston and New Orleans, and where human oppression exists there the sympathy of all black hearts must go". Just as Garvey had done Du Bois was expressing a solidarity across color lines in a gesture of anti-colonial solidarity. The example of Clan na Gael and its inspiration as a trans-Atlantic and anti-colonial movement was best summed up when Du Bois said "The recent

116   Available online <https://www.anphoblacht.com/contents/26525>

Irish revolt may have been foolish, but would to god some of us had sense enough to be fools"[117].

What exactly were the Clan's attitudes to Garvey and the UNIA? While difficult to assess overall, it can be assumed to have been a mixed reaction. Irish-Americans, like many white ethnic groups in the U.S. at this time were far from racially enlightened. The era of Clan na Gael, from its foundation in 1867 right up to the 1920s and well after, was part of an ethnic group that was, if not openly hostile to African American political aspirations, then at least deaf or apathetic to those demands. The Irish-American working classes who were always sensitive to labor competition and were often openly hostile to African-Americans and many played prominent roles in racially motivated riots in the early twentieth century. While some in the leadership levels of the Clan may have had some sympathy the vast majority would have been on the spectrum of apathetic to hostile to African American political aspirations, even in cases where aims and objectives would have crossed paths.

On a more positive level from the perspective of Clan na Gael was the growing connections between Irish nationalism and the rising Indian revolutionary movement known as the Ghadar Party. Clan na Gael had established links with the exiled Indian nationalist movement in the U.S. up to a decade prior to the Easter Rising. The relationship and interactions really started to take off with the outbreak of World War One in 1914. The location for this initial interaction was New York City where the small Indian population observed a thriving and very politically active Irish American nationalist movement. One leading Indian nationalist figure who observed Clan na Gael and who certainly took notice of the 1916 Rising was Lala Lajpat Rai. Although Rai always felt more at home in the Home Rule wing of Irish nationalism he did see within Clan na Gael and its efforts a model for a transatlantic movement that could assist in Indian independence.

For Clan na Gael a much more fruitful relationship was to be found the newly formed Ghadar Party which emerged on the west coast in California

---

117   Available   online   <https://newrepublic.com/article/132042/irish-rebellion-resonated-harlem>

with its base of power being San Francisco among a strong diasporic community. The major difference between the newly formed Ghadar Party and Lala Lajpat Rai was that the Ghadar Party espoused a much more violent revolutionary philosophy which meant that it gravitated much more toward Clan na Gael in terms of a political alliance. As World War One progressed and the U.S. eventually entered the conflict the revolutionary partnership would eventually become closer to the point of active military assistance by Clan na Gael which will be discussed later[118].

For Clan na Gael it made perfect sense to groom and assist Indian revolutionaries to stir revolution in what was known to many in Britain as the "Jewel of the British Empire". Of course the primary objective was to stretch British imperial resources and therefore assist in Irish independence, but there was also the belief that losing India would stimulate, along with the Easter Rising, uprisings throughout the once invincible imperial monolith.

One individual who best exemplified this Indian-Irish solidarity was Peter Golden, a leading Clan figure from New York. Golden, along with other Clan members regularly attended meetings hosted by the Friends of Indian Freedom whose name incidentally would be based off The Friends of Irish Freedom founded by Clan na Gael as a fundraising body after the 1916 Rising. It would be common to see leading Indian nationalist figures such as Lajpat Rai rubbing shoulders at major fundraising events for both the Indian and Irish nationalist events. Golden went so far in his support of Indian independence as to write a poem that in many ways could have been as easily applied to the cause of Irish independence –

> Rise, Indians, rise from Motherland, Drive out the foul invader, Strike to their death the dastard crew, Who've plundered and betrayed her; Let not this long awaited hour, Go by without your giving, Unstinted all you have in life, To keep your India living[119].

118   Brundage, David. Lala Lajpat, Indian Nationalism and the Irish Revolution – The view from New York, 1914-1920. 1916 In Global Context – An Anti-Imperial Moment. Routledge. 2018. New York. P. 66-68.

119   Herlihy, Jim. Peter Golden – The Voice of Ireland. Peter Golden Commemoration Committee. Cork. 1994. P. 49-52.

The third group that was heavily influenced by the role of Clan na Gael in instigating rebellion against British rule was the emerging Zionist movement. The American based Zionist movement saw strong parallels between the politics of exile, statelessness and centuries of struggle and the Jewish historical experience. The very visible nature of Irish nationalism and effectiveness in terms of propaganda and fundraising acted as a model as to the potential effectiveness of an exiled nationalist movement. This admiration for Irish diasporic nationalism was noted by one Zionist leader when he commented that "No more fervent or devoted nationalists exist today than the Americans of Irish extraction. We cannot take up a newspaper without being convinced that the thoughts of Irish Americans are constantly occupied with their interests and the interests of the country from which they came".

American Zionists took clear note of the radicalization of Irish nationalism during World War One and in particular after the 1916 Rising. A number of leading Zionists and Jewish press outlets openly supported the Irish insurrection. Even moderate Jewish newspapers like the Chicago Sentinel commented after the executions of the leaders of the Rising in 1916 that Ireland could never achieve true freedom within the framework of the British Empire. Some religious figures even went as far as to compere the Irish revolutionaries to the Maccabees from Jewish history who fought against the Seleucid Empire. The inspiration of Clan na Gael's example went even further when in 1917 Zionism adopted the slogan "Zionism for itself alone" which was a version of the Irish nationalist slogan "Ourselves Alone".

The question that must be posed again is just how much did Clan na Gael influence or impact American Zionism? While a difficult question to fully answer we can conclude a number of facts. Many on the more radical wing of Zionism, particularly among the younger membership were attracted to and started to emulate what was seen as unabashed expressions of Irish nationalism, particularly protest tactics. Jewish Americans, like Irish Americans, always had to walk the tightrope of maintaining ethnic identity while as the same time wanting to be perceived and accepted as American. Older more conservative elements with American Jewry wished to keep a low profile and not bring attention to the community for fear to attracting anti-Semitism which had a long history in the United States. The brutal experience of Jewish refugees who fled persecution in Russia and Eastern Europe also played a major role in the mentality. However, a newer Jewish generation born and raised for the most part in the U.S. we're not hindered by such psychological and emotional constraints. The example of Irish nationalists helped make more acceptable a new form of vocal and visible radicalism that was not seen before within American Judaism. The formation of early American Zionism cannot be truly studied or understood without reference to what the movement learned from Clan na Gael[120].

The emerging and increasingly vocal Suffragette movement of the early twentieth century attracted many Irish American women were at the forefront of not just the Suffragette movement but also the cause of Irish nationalism. One such figure was Leonora O'Reilly who easily moved between the worlds of feminist agitation and Irish revolutionary politics. The skills, insights and contacts made within Irish revolutionary circles were easily transferred by O'Reilly and many other Irish American women into the arena of Suffragette politics. Although Suffragettes had been using hunger strikes as a protest strategy as far back as 1909 in Britain the death on hunger strike in Ireland of Republican political prisoner Thomas Ashe in September of 1917 might well have been an influencing factor in Alice Paul's famous hunger strike just one month later in the same year. Ashe's death would have been very well publicized within Irish-American circles.

As Ireland neared its War of independence the role and example of Clan na Gael as a model for a transnational revolutionary movement increased. Other groups such as French Canada, Australia and even the Middle-East were to feel directly and indirectly the ripples of the 1916 Easter Rising setting in motion the upcoming anti-colonial era that would last in some cases into the 1960s. Exiled political movements in the U.S. saw in Clan na Gael a movement which through its organizational ability and fundraising capacity was able to carry the mantle of revolution for decades when prospects domestically seemed distant if not futile. From a safe haven in a distant land revolution now seemed possible to colonial exiles thousands of miles away.

120   Bernstein, Judah. 2017. "The two finest nations in the world": American Zionists and Irish Nationalism, 1897-1922. Journal of American Ethnic History. Vol. 36, No. 3. P. 5-37.

CHAPTER 15

A Struggle on Two Fronts, 1917–1918

Just as 1916 was a year that changed Ireland, 1917 was a year that would prove one of the most challenging domestically for Irish American nationalism. Due to the provocation of unrestricted German submarine warfare which targeted U.S. shipping and killed hundreds of American citizens, as well as the White House's pro-British sympathies, Woodrow Wilson went before Congress on 2 April to ask for a declaration of war against Germany. Just five days later on 7 April Congress gave consent and war was declared. Clan na Gael was now amid one of the most trying moments of its history. As an organization that always proclaimed loyalty to both the U.S. and the establishment of an Irish Republic by armed revolution, it was now confronted with the U.S. in military alliance with Britain during a war at a time when the Clan was laying the groundwork for a revolution against British rule in Ireland. As well as this the Clan had long established links with Imperial Germany going back to the Boer War with the common aims of undermining the British Empire through military assistance for an Irish rebellion.

Since its foundation in 1867 Clan na Gael had played a successful role in walking the tightrope of dual nationality arguing that there was no contradiction in being both Irish and American. Although the Irish were one of the longest established non-Anglo Saxon ethnic groups in the U.S. the cultural and political attachment remained as strong as ever. Assisting in the political struggle for an Irish Republic was not seen merely as an act of charity but instead as a duty and obligation. John Devoy claimed on one occasion that the Irish Americans were more Irish than the Irish themselves. At the forefront of this fervent identity were Irish-American newspapers and other publications. These publications regularly solicited money for the cause of Irish nationalism[121].

---

121   Mulcrone, Michael. 1993. The World War 1 Censorship of the Irish American Press. History PHD. University of. Washington. P. 119-121.

When it came to Irish-American publications Anglophobia was to be the cornerstone of its overall political sentiment. It was through the lens of this Anglophobia that Irish Americans viewed domestic and international issues. Despite being a scattered ethnic community spread over large parts of the U.S. these publications provided a social glue which helped co-ordinate political efforts toward achieving an Irish Republic. Outside of the political arena these publications expressed a collective memory and historical consciousness more than most other ethnic groups would have abandoned such sentiment soon after arriving in the U.S. or at least within one or two generations[122].

For Clan na Gael its most important form of written messaging and propaganda was the newspaper Gaelic American. John Devoy founded the newspaper in 1903 to be an extension of Clan na Gael and to also act as a counterweight to the Irish World newspaper which promoted the cause of constitutional nationalism as espoused by the Home Rule Party in Ireland. Devoy used the Gaelic American to constantly promote the idea of armed revolution in Ireland. Although Daniel Coholan was the chief owner of the publication it was John Devoy that was the driving force behind the messaging. By 1914 the Gaelic American had about 30,000 subscribers. The fundraising efforts launched through the newspaper provided a large part of the funds used to launch the Easter Rising. The newspaper's importance as a propaganda and fundraising tool for Clan na Gael cannot be overstated[123].

Prior to Wilson's declaration of war Clan na Gael's primary focus and energy was directed in building upon the propaganda outcome of the Easter Rising and expanding its fundraising network and political lobbying within the U.S. Wilson's election promise in 1916 to keep the U.S. out of war was something the Clan sought to rely upon. However, when Wilson changed course and brought the U.S. into the war on Britain's side Clan na Gael now had to divide its efforts into opposing the U.S. entry into the war while at the same time portraying itself as patriotic and maintaining revolutionary efforts abroad. These efforts were made even more challenging with

---

122 Mulcrone, Michael. 1993. The World War 1 Censorship of the Irish American Press. History PHD. University of. Washington. P. 62-63.

123 Mulcrone, Michael. 1993. The World War 1 Censorship of the Irish American Press. History PHD. University of. Washington. P. 19-20.

the introduction of laws that were some of the greatest challenges to free speech within the U.S. seen since the Civil War almost half a century earlier.

Once Wilson committed the U.S. to World War One his administration carried out an unprecedented propaganda campaign aiming at building public support for the war effort and at the same time attack and undermine ethnic nationalism within the U.S., particularly those of an anti-war persuasion. Although German-Americans bore the brunt of what became a growing nationalistic hysteria Irish-American nationalists, particularly Clan na Gael, would also come under severe pressure. The Espionage Act passed in June of 1917 made it virtually illegal to criticize the war or government in any way. Wilson wanted to include a provision that would have punished the publishing of any information that the President deemed might be useful to the enemy. Wilson pleaded that press censorship was necessary for national security during a time of war. The provision was defeated by a vote of 184-144 when thirty-six democrats broke with the President on the issue.

What seemed like an initial victory for Clan na Gael turned out to be only a short term reprieve. The final version of the act made it illegal to cause or attempt to cause disloyalty. What "disloyalty" meant would be open to the courts to interpret who during a time of war tended to be historically sympathetic to the government's position. The postmaster general was authorized to exclude from the mails any material in violation of the law[124]. For a publication that relied heavily on the postal service, as the Gaelic American did, to send the paper to their subscribers and who were now deemed to be "unpatriotic" this would prove a devastating blow.

During the heated debate on patriotism within the cauldron of World War One Clan na Gael was involved in a major conspiracy that would end up being used by its enemies within the U.S. as a weapon to condemn the organization as disloyal. What became known as the Indo-German Conspiracy occurred in 1917 when German agents, Indian nationalists in the form of the Ghadar Party and Clan na Gael conspired to send shipments of weapons from California to India to instigate a rebellion against

---

124 Murphy, Paul. *World War One and the Origin of Civil Liberties in the United States*. W.W Norton & Company. New York. 1979. P. 74-199.

British rule. The weapons shipment was initially organized in New York where a ship called the Annie Larsen was supposed to rendezvous with a larger steamship, the Maverick, off the Pacific coast of Mexico at Socorro Island. The Maverick was then supposed to take the shipment of weapons first to the Dutch East Indies and then on to India.

As a result of infiltration by British intelligence, particularly the use of an Irish double agent by the name of Charles Lamb, and a spy within the Ghadar Party by the name of Chandra Kanta Chakravarty, U.S. authorities were able to break up the conspiracy early on. The conspiracy trials took place in San Francisco. The trial would last from November 1917 to April of 1918 and turn out to be one of the most expensive up to that point in U.S. history. The primary involvement of Clan na Gael was of a logistical nature as the organization had a significant and widespread revolutionary network throughout the U.S.

Although Irish-American involvement was evident from early in the trial it was downplayed for political reasons which made sense considering they made a powerful voting block within the U.S. However, this attempt did not prevent the British propaganda machine within the U.S. from attempting to portray Clan na Gael as unpatriotic and disloyal in attempting to aid the enemy of a critical U.S. ally during a time of war. The Gaelic American responded by highlighting no disloyalty to the U.S. but an action designed to end imperial rule in India. The trial focused mainly on the Indo-German aspect of the conspiracy and as a result the Clan were left unscathed despite the British consulate's best efforts. However, despite this element of good fortune which could have been a public relations disaster Clan na Gael continued to face major problems during the war[125].

By early 1918 the Gaelic American had been badly hit. Nearly every issue was banned from the mail. In typical fashion Devoy was not taking the setback sitting down. He attempted to take the offensive. Firstly, the Gaelic American contrasted itself sharply to socialists and communists saying they deserved banning much more so than a loyal publication that sough only the establishment of an Irish Republic along the lines of the U.S. By this

---

125   Plowman, Erin, Matthew. 2003. Irish Republicans and the Indo-German Conspiracy of World War 1. New Hibernia Review, Vol. 7, No. 3. P. 80-95.

time Devoy was firmly on the radar of the Justice Department. Attempts to prosecute Devoy for violation of laws relating to "disloyal" publications failed when U.S. Attorney Francis Caffey decided not to take up the case; "I felt that Devoy was actually doing no harm to the business the Government has in hand .... the contempt proceeding, whether successful or unsuccessful, might play into his hands".

Continuing to defend itself and its actions Devoy reverted on the age-old Irish American argument that the British and anglophiles within the Wilson administration were behind the attacks on the Gaelic America. Devoy stated in the Gaelic America "you are doing more harm to America in this war, Mr Barnes, Mr Ochs, Mr Reid, Mr Pulitzer, Mr Burleson and Mr Gregory by your persecution and misrepresentation .... than ...German spies could do in 100 years...... [you are] making a mockery of President Wilson's Declaration that all people have a right to self-government and self-determination ....and you are doing it to help England hold Ireland down, not to serve America".

As a result of serious restrictions on the newspaper the financial strain began to tell. In mid- July of 1918 the publication issued an urgent appeal for $10,000 to cover operating costs. These requests would be issued every week until, the end of the war. In a setback to the newspaper the U.S. postal system withdrew second class mailing privileges in September. On the eve of the Armistice the Gaelic American was almost financially broke and issued an article calling on Wilson to "call off the dogs". In the article Devoy stated "we are persecuted and our loyalty to American is impeached by Mr Wilson's subordinates at the very time that our race, in larger numbers than ever before, is fighting magnificently for America on the battlefields of France.... (the) persecution is certainly not carried out without Mr Wilson's knowledge, but it is not a question of fixing responsibility, but putting an end to the state of things which works evil for the country".

The gesture by Devoy was in the end futile and the restrictions on the newspaper remained in place long after the end of the war[126]. By the end of the war the number of editorials in the Gaelic American plunged by over 40

---

126   Mulcrone, Michael. 1993. The World War 1 Censorship of the Irish American Press. History PHD. University of. Washington. P. 298-300.

per cent. Even though deeply Anglophobic articles remained Devoy tried in vain to offset any sense of disloyalty by also promoting in the paper ads encouraging the sale of war bonds. More and more the Gaelic American was forced to issue statements of loyalty to the U.S. and was almost entirely on the defensive for the duration of the war. While censorship certainly had a negative effect on Clan na Gael Irish American hostility toward Britain remained undiminished as the community rallied itself for the outbreak of the Irish War of Independence that would break out in 1919. While the Gaelic American never fully recovered it would now be the Friends of Irish Freedom that would become the very powerful fundraising arm of Clan na Gael. However, even the FOIF was to suffer major setbacks during the war.

The early attacks on the FOIF and Daniel Coholan were led by the New York Times. After a speech in 15 August 1917, The Times labeled it "disloyal and seditious" for its apparent "anti- British, anti-American, pro-German" sentiments. The Times even went to far as to attack the New Police Department who protected the public gatherings of the FOIF from "Loyal Americans" and who had a large Irish membership as "coddling Sinn Feinism". Sinn Fein was the emerging political wing of the Volunteer movement, soon to become known as the Irish Republican Army.

The New York Times also used the past connections of Irish-American nationalists to Imperial Germany to further paint the FOIF as being "disloyal". Numerous articles from 1917-18 attempted to paint the organization as seditious rabble rousers who hid behind the protections of freedom of speech to undermine the American war effort. Outside of the New York Times other organizations such as the American Defense Society bitterly attacked the FOIF. The ADS was an American nationalist organization that held pro-ally and pro-interventionist views regarding World War one. The ADS attempted to bring legal action to highlight what they saw as public displays of disloyalty by the FOIF. The argued that the only public meetings that should be allowed were ones that supported the U.S. war effort.

One of the most intense backlashes came against Coholan occurred when details and rumors began to leak from information obtained from the arrest of Wolf von Igel back in 1916. Von Igel was and aide and spy for the German military attaché to the U.S., Franz von Papen. Although the papers obtained from Von Igel's arrest were never made public at the time allegations in the media were made that Coholan was in communication with Imperial Germany at a time when the U.S. was still a neutral nation. Although never charged the mere rumor and allegation was enough to further taint Coholan and the FOIF as disloyal and "un- American".

Further attacks and pressure came from another quarter when the Mayor John Mitchel of New York accused Coholan of attempting to ferment revolution in Ireland and showing disloyalty to the U.S. Coholan was never one to stay silent in the face of accusations and attack. He responded to Mitchel by stating that "The men who are really guilty of disloyalty to our common country are those who are now, for their own selfish purposes, engaged in sowing dissensions and discord among the various racial groups.... instead of working zealously to unite them against the common enemy". Attacks became so common and increasingly virulent that Coholan felt compelled to launch a libel case against the Evening Mail for making unfounded accusations. He won the case and was awarded the sum of $5,000.

The FOIF continued to try to take the offensive. Public appeals supporting Irish independence and arguing against involvement in World War One, particularly the alliance with Britain continued to be made. One such appeal made to Congress and to President Wilson directly stated that "Ireland is a distant nation, deprived of her liberty by force and held in subjection by England by military power alone". The strategy used to attempt to compare Ireland's plight to that of nations such as Belgium who suffered under German occupation. Attempts in seeking broad support were also attempted to hark back to the U. S's past support for Cuba in her anti-colonial struggle against the Spanish. One such petition stated "We earnestly hope that like Cuba, Ireland will be made free by the actions of America".

How much validity was there in Devoy's argument that the Gaelic American was being particularly targeted by pro-British elements within the Wilson administration and the British lobby operating out of its embassy in Washington? At this point it can be safe to assume that as the most vocal and violently anti-British publication in the U.S. that the Gaelic American was certainly on the radar early on of the Wilson administration. By this point it was no secret as to the role played by Clan na Gael in bringing about the Easter Rising and the continued threat that they posed not just to British rule in Ireland but also to its imperial structure globally, particularly after the Annie Larsen Affair and the Irish role more broadly in coordinating globally with exiled revolutionary movements in the U.S.

Despite these attempts to use American anti-imperial and Republican rhetoric to its advantage most of Irish America prioritized support for the U.S. war effort. This position was further enhanced the Catholic Church's position in supporting the allied struggle in Europe. In the case of Irish communities it was common for priests from the altar to highlight the sacrifice being made by Irish regiments in the British Army as well as Irish Americans in the U.S. military. The general message from the pulpit was not to allow hatred of British rule in Ireland to overshadow what was a "just cause" against Imperial Germany.

The mounting pressure on the FOIF began to take its toll and membership and donations began to fall off significantly. For Coholan and the leadership it was seen as necessary to change strategy to accord with the significantly changing attitudes within Irish America. The new campaign would include a strategy steeped in the rhetoric of the American Revolution and comparing Ireland's struggle to that if the U.S. Secondly, the FOIF would use the Irish American sacrifice during the war to gain sympathy more broadly in American society for the cause of Irish independence. Such propaganda literature included statements such as "Let us pay our debt – America! Remember what you owe to Ireland. As you honor the Irish blood shed for American liberty, help the cause of liberty now". On top of these new approaches constant reference was made to Wilson's promise to the rights of self-determination for small nations as promised by President Wilson[127].

The war on two fronts would continue with the situation in Ireland edging closer to war and the political and propaganda campaign raging in the U.S. Clan na Gael and the FOIF never forgave Wilson for what they saw as a betrayal. In the end the Irish American community would be a

---

127   Douglas, Delia, Shanon. 2015. The Rise and Fall of the Friends of Irish Freedom: How America Shaped Irish American Nationalism in the Twentieth Century. History PHD. Union College. Schenectady. P. 38-56.

significant part of an overall alliance within the U.S. that would eventually defeat Wilson's attempt to get the U.S. to become part of the League of Nations. At the Versailles Peace Conference Clan na Gael was at the forefront of Irish-American demands for a hearing demanding Irish independence. At the end of 1918 Clan na Gael helped organize a rally at Madison Square Garden which was attended by 25,000 people demanding Irish self- determination. If the anglophile elements within the Wilson administration and the British Embassy in Washington thought they would have the upper hand at the end of the war they were clearly mistaken. With the defeat of Wilson's attempts for the U.S. to join the League of Nations and a general retreat into isolationism in the years after the war Clan na Gael, and Irish America more broadly, would have its final revenge[128]. Yet again Clan na Gael showed a remarkable resilience in surviving and enduring during a trying time. It would not be long until it would be tested yet again. This time the test would come not from Britain or pro-British elements within the U.S., but from within Irish nationalism itself.

128 Mulcrone, Michael. 1993. The World War 1 Censorship of the Irish American Press. History PHD. University of. Washington. P. 317-319.

CHAPTER 16

Political Situation in Ireland, 1916–1919

In the aftermath of the Easter Rising in Ireland the separatist Republican movement developed from strength to strength. Sinn Fein emerged as the political wing of the emerging struggle while the Volunteer movement, soon to become known as the Irish Republican Army, would emerge as the armed wing of the new movement. The Volunteer movement as well as Sinn Fein branches spread rapidly in the months following the Rising attracting thousands of both young men and women who themselves were products of the Gaelic language, cultural and literary revival that started in the 1890s. This political awakening can be seen as the last, even inevitable, piece of the jigsaw that was necessary for a new revolutionary generation that Clan na Gael had been waiting for generations to emerge and had played such a crucial role in creating.

The impact of the Easter Rising on the increased radicalization of the Republican movement was to be quickly seen with the hunger strike and death of Thomas Ashe, a former participant in the Easter Rising and leading figure in the emerging Volunteer movement. The tactic of hunger strikes would be a feature throughout the Republican struggle right up until the 1980s and had a long cultural meaning dating all the way back to pre-Christian times. The purpose was to highlight an injustice or wrong committed and to shame a stronger adversary in the eyes of society into righting that perceived wrong. The death of Ashe in September of 1917 set off an emotional earthquake in Irish Republican ranks, and no more so than Clan na Gael. Thomas Ashe was a well-known figure to Clan na Gael as he had visited the U.S. back in 1914 as a representative of the Gaelic League. Ashe's popularity among the rank and file of Clan na Gael was seen with his considerable fundraising success not just for the emerging Volunteer movement but also the Gaelic League. The fact that he convinced so many radical Irish- Americans to part with funding for the non-military purpose

of promoting the Irish language says much to his personal charm and powers
of persuasion. When news of Ashe's hunger strike and subsequent death
reached the U.S. the emotional outpouring of grief, anger and the desire
to speed up the day of revolutionary reckoning intensified.

On a political front Sinn Fein was making major gains. The first Sinn
Fein party convention in the aftermath of the Easter Rising took place in
1917 and was the first occasion in which the party openly and publicly
took the position of supporting the establishment of a Republic. The first
major stance in relation to opposition to British rule after the Rising came
with a massive wave of opposition to the British proposal to implement
Conscription to Ireland in April, 1918. The bloodletting on the western
front had caused a severe shortage in manpower within the British military. The severity of the British position was further enhanced when Russia
dropped out of the war because of the Bolshevik takeover and the signing
of the Treaty of Brest- Litovsk on 3 March which meant that Germany
could now divert large amounts of troops from the eastern front to the
west. With this transfer of troops, the Germans launched their second
Spring offensive on 9 April 1918[129].

Recruitment to the British Army in Ireland after 1916 had fallen off dramatically in the aftermath of the 1916 Rising and the pressure to impose conscription on Ireland now proved overwhelming for British Prime Minister,
Lloyd George. There were warning from within the British cabinet as to
the possible consequences of introducing conscription. The Irish Attorney
General, James O'Connor, much nearer the situation than those in London,
warned that conscription would lead inevitably to rebellion, possible resignations within the British administration in Ireland and a coming together
of political forces into a unified opposition.

After the 1914 Home Rule Bill was proposed until the end of the
war it was yet again resurrected as a promise to the Home Rule Party in
the hope that support could be enhanced for conscription. Unknown to
many in London the Home Rule movement was in the process of being
overwhelmed by the rising Sinn Fein as the party of John Redmond no

---

129   Townsend, Charles. The Republic – The Fight for Irish Independence. Penguin
       Books. London 2013. P. 6-14.

longer represented anywhere near the majority of public opinion. The
Conscription Bill passed with overwhelming support in the British parliament. Although the likes of Winston Churchill strongly supported
the move others anticipated a grave coming crisis in Ireland. Not only
the strong possibility of violent opposition to Conscription from Irish
Republicans but growing violent opposition to Home Rule after the end
of the war by Protestant Loyalists in the north of Ireland which brought
the real specter of civil war.

Just as anticipated by many, reaction in Ireland to the passing of the
Conscription Bill was swift and overwhelming. Sinn Fein used the opportunity to enhance its position and public profile to become the face of the
opposition and the Volunteer movement benefited from a huge increase
in recruitment. For one of the first times since the New Departure in the
1870s Irish public opinion, apart from northern loyalists, were unified in
their opposition. Members of the diminishing Home Rule Party were now
mostly either mute of vocally opposed to conscription while Irish Bishops
directed the clergy to celebrate a public mass of intercession to avert the
"scourge" of conscription and to administer pledges at public meetings to
resist conscription "by the most effective means at our disposal". At the
same time Sinn Fein and Labor Unions were organizing and carrying out
large scale street protests which was best exemplified in the General Strike
of 23 April.

In a desperate attempt to delegitimize Sinn Fein and growing separatist
sentiment the British government developed the idea of a "German conspiracy" being behind the emerging Republican movement. On 16 May a
large number of Sinn Fein members were arrested. A total of seventy-three
were deported from Ireland to mainland Britain with more following later.
On fully realizing the power and influence of Clan na Gael in the U.S. the
British attempted to connect the conspiracy allegation across the Atlantic.
A quite astonishing and in some ways desperate telegram was sent to the
British Ambassador in Washington to forward to President Wilson himself. What was asked of Wilson was the publication in the American press
of these conspiracy charges which were to include Clan na Gael. Wilson
refused the request outright for a few reasons. Firstly, he did not want to be
seen to be doing the bidding of the British in suppressing the Republican

movement in Ireland at a time when Irish-American were a vital bulwark of the Democratic Party that was under strain because of World War One. Secondly, British "evidence" was extremely weak and would be hard to sell to the general public. The consequences of these British actions were to further entrench Irish public opinion behind Sinn Fein and the growing calls for independence. Again, the British government seemed to have learned nothing from their experiences in their handling of the aftermath of the Easter Rising.

On 11 November 1918, World War One came to an end with an Allied victory without conscription ever being implemented in Ireland. The consequences of the ill-conceived British actions were to have major long-term repercussions. Firstly, it spelt the virtual end of the Home Rule Party and the end of any conceivable chance of a political resolution that involved remaining within the British Empire at least in the short term. Secondly, Sinn Fein's high profile resistance to conscription laid the foundation for massive political gains later in 1918 during the general elections. Finally, the events of the crisis may also have been a major factor in Lloyd George's heavy-handed approach in attempting to suppress the Irish War of Independence from 1919-21 by seeing Irish Republican actions during World War One as a "Stab in the back"[130].

The general election held in December of 1918 was momentous in many ways. The demise of the Home Rule Party was highlighted by the fact that Sinn Fein ran unopposed in 25 constituencies and ended up winning a sweeping victory of 73 seats out of a total of 101 seats available. Before the election Sinn Fein had held a mere six seats. The Home Rule Party dropped from sixty-seven seats to just six and ominously for the future Ulster Unionists increases from seventeen to twenty-two seats. Sinn Fein benefited enormously from an emerging youth vote for a new and radical generation of voters that now also included young women voters who had just received the right to vote. As well as this the poorest elements of society increased their participation in the voting process. The Easter Rising of 1916, the anti-conscription crisis and growing anti-war sentiment

---

130   Ward, Alan. 1974. Lloyd George and the 1918 Conscription Crisis. The Historical Journal. Cambridge University Press. Vol. 17, March.

all contributed to a more radicalized voter turnout which benefited Sinn Fein enormously.

By the election of 1918 Sinn Fein had become a broad front movement that whose membership was possibly as high as 130,000 members. Although the Catholic Church was no outright supporter of Sinn Fein the fact that both Sinn Fein and the Church shared many similar positions on issues such as anti-Conscription and many of the grass-root clergy were members of cultural and sporting organizations that included many Sinn Fein members as leading organizers contributed toward a greater moral legitimacy for Sinn Fein in the eyes of many voters[131].

With the increased energy and legitimacy now emanating from the sweeping election victory Sinn Fein prepared for its most momentous step, the refusal of all elected members to recognize the legitimacy of the British parliament and the establishment of a rebel parliament in Dublin to be known as Dail Eireann. The Dail met on 21 January 1919 and was outlawed by the British government in September of 1919. The rebel Dail made international news and sparked great hope in Clan na Gael ranks in the U.S. in the hope of not repeating previous errors by acting too quickly and violently the British government held back hoping to just ignore the Dail but at the same time drawing the redline of intervening should the Dail actually start taking up practical government function and undermining functioning British rule in Ireland. Once the Dail began actively undermining British rule by collecting taxes and setting up a competing court system, the military was ordered to forcibly shut down the Dail and arrest all sitting members of the rebel parliament. With advance warning many Sinn Fein members avoided arrest and went underground where the rebel parliament continued to function in large part with the financial assistance from Clan na Gael[132].

On the same day the first Dail was opened on 21 January a small event in the townland of Soloheadbeg in County Tipperary took place that was to mark the beginning of the Irish War of Independence. Irish Volunteers

131   Available online <https://www.irishtimes.com/culture/heritage/fintan-o-toole-the-1918-election-was-an-amazing-moment-for-ireland-1.3719853>

132   Townsend, Charles. The Republic – The Fight for Irish Independence. Penguin Books. London. 2013. P. 32-78

from the 3rd Tipperary Brigade commanded by Seamus Robinson and containing future legendary guerrilla fighters such as Dan Breen, Sean Hogan and Sean Treacy ambushed a consignment of gelignite that was being escorted by members of the Royal Irish Constabulary. Two members of the RIC were killed as the Volunteers commandeered the explosives that would be used in attacking RIC and other government buildings symbolizing British rule in Ireland. From this point onward what would become as the Irish Republican Army would escalate an increasingly violent and successful guerrilla war that would involve Flying Columns in the countryside attacking isolated RIC barracks and forcing them to retreat into the towns and cities while the IRA took over large parts of the countryside. As the situation deteriorated rapidly the British government would later make the fateful decision of sending in what would become known as the notorious Black and Tans and Auxiliaries who used what essentially could be described as terror tactics to subdue the general populace from supporting what was now an open rebellion[133].

From the years 1916 to 1919 one dominating figure emerged that who was to prove enormously consequential not just for the struggle in Ireland but for the relationship of Clan na Gael to the Republican movement in Ireland. Eamon De Valera would continue what Charles Parnell had failed to achieve, gain complete control of the financial resources of Clan na Gael which would prove enormously important in the upcoming war of independence. Unlike Parnell De Valera would prove a much more ruthless and cannier adversary.

---

133   Breen, Dan. My Fight for Irish Freedom. Anvil Books. Tralee. 1975. P. 38-59.

CHAPTER 17

Revival of Clan na Gael and Friends of Irish Freedom

After the end of World War One and prior to the beginning of the Irish War of Independence Clan na Gael prepared for political action on the domestic front in the U.S. and laying the foundation for war in Ireland. The preparation for war had been happening since the 1916 Rising and the Clan played a significant role in turning what could have been a once of insurrection into a full-scale rebellion. As previously mentioned one of the Clan's strongest assets at the outbreak of the Irish War of Independence was The Friends of Irish Freedom which they established in the aftermath of the Easter Rising and as previously mentioned was little more than a front to legally fundraise and lobby for the cause of Irish independence. This would take the function of legal and constitutional lobbying and the subversive funding of the rebel government and Irish Republican Army back in Ireland.

On a domestic front in the U.S. the FOIF were determined to hold Wilson to his promise of freedom to small nations. Father Magennis was the new president of the FOIF declared early on that "the president has said that all people are entitled to self-government and self- determination as that statement applies as much to the Irish as the Czecho-Slovaks. From previous experienced prior to and during World War One the FOIF understood Wilson was more than willing to sacrifice the struggle for Irish independence to build a strong Anglo-American alliance in a post-World War One world order. Clan na Gael and its extension, the FOIF, took a proverbial public relations beating during World War One which had a negative impact on fundraising and membership both of which slackened off significantly after the U. S's entry in World War One. The number one objective at the end of the war was to rebuild the organization by expanding membership, fundraising activity and the propaganda campaign for Irish independence[134].

---

134   Doorley, Michael. Irish-American Diaspora Nationalism – The Friends of Irish Freedom, 1916-1935. Four Courts Press. Dublin. 2005. P. 81-82.

The first steps toward political revival was held just a month after the end of World War One when the FOIF organized what they called "Self-Determination for Ireland Week" with the purpose of bringing the Irish question "back into the public mind". An estimated 25,000 people attended an event in Madison Square Garden on 10 December. The two main speakers included Cardinal O'Connell of Boston and New York Governor Charles Whitman. Both John Devoy and Daniel Coholan make brief speaking appearances as well. A wireless that was sent to President Wilson was read to the gathering "asking that he stand at the peace conference for self-determination for Ireland". In relation to Ireland it was Wilson's Fourteen Points with its repeated reference to self-determination that would come back to haunt his relationship with Irish America. When accessing Wilson's position on the Irish question during these critical years we need to look beyond the words of the Fourteen Points on where exactly Wilson stood when it came to national self-determination of smaller nations[135].

Before World War One ended President Wilson announced to a joint session of Congress among other things "What we demand in this war, therefore, is nothing peculiar to ourselves, is that the world be made fit and safe to live in; and particularly that it be made safe for every peace loving nation which, like our own, wishes to live its own life, determine its own institutions, be assured of justice and fair dealing by other peoples of the world as against force and selfish aggression". These words reverberated throughout the world, especially among the colonial European empires, and none more than Britain's oldest colony, Ireland and particularly her exiled community in the U.S.

While many in the Irish American community were optimistic of the prospects of U.S. support for Irish independence an older more experienced veteran was much more pessimistic. John Devoy, at this point a veteran for half a century in the cause of Irish independence, pointed out what he called "one fatal defect in Wilson's points". Devoy argued that it applied "only to a portion of the world controlled by Germany and her

---

135   Douglas, Delia, Shanon. 2015. The Rise and Fall of the Friends of Irish
       Freedom: How America Shaped Irish American Nationalism in the Twentieth
       Century. History PHD. Union College. Schenectady. P. 57-58.

allies – and utterly ignore the rest". Under the indomitable John Devoy the uncomfortable question was posed of "what about British imperialism?" This uncomfortable question for the Wilson administration would be the basis upon which Clan na Gael would launch its campaign in garnering support for Irish independence. The moment Wilson made his famous Fourteen Points speech Irish America under the leadership and drive of Clan na Gael, mostly through its front organization the FOIF, would commence a relentless campaign to include Ireland under the umbrella of nations whose independence the U.S. should officially support.

The Friends of Irish Freedom, most certainly under the direction of Clan na Gael, who as stated earlier dominated the leadership levels of the organization, played a leading role in ramping up the issue of Irish independence. During Easter week of 1918, in coordination with the second anniversary of the Rising, meetings were held in almost every town and city where any significant Irish community existed in the U.S. making public resolutions calling for the application of Wilson's Fourteen Points to Ireland. The culmination of these efforts came on 18 May with the Second Irish Race Convention in New York where representatives from Irish communities all over the world came together. The high point of the gathering was a resolution by Justice John Goff calling for "the application to Ireland now of President Wilson's noble declaration of the right of every people to self-rule and self-determination ". An appeal was specifically put to Wilson personally to "exert every legitimate and friendly influence in favor of self-determination for the people of Ireland"[136].

Besides the direct appeals to Wilson himself extensive political lobbying of Congress also took place. Irish-American and other more anti-imperial leaning Congressmen introduced resolutions relating to Irish self-determination. In December 1918 the House Committee on Foreign Affairs held a hearing on a resolution put forward by Thomas Gallagher of Illinois. The fingerprints of the FOIF was apparent in the wording which was almost identical to their own official position. The resolution was

136 O'Grady, Joseph. 1963. Irish-Americans, Woodrow Wilson and Self-Determination. American Catholic Historical Society. Vol. 73, No. 3. P. 159-163.

adopted by the committee and stated "the right of Ireland to freedom, independence and self-determination".

With the endorsement of many leading members of the Catholic clergy favoring Irish independence Irish-America was coming together in a unified front at a critical moment leading up to the beginning of open conflict in Ireland. However, all was not as unified as it might have seemed. Some within the Clan began to take issue with the use of the term "Self-determination" as opposed to clearly stating support for a Republic. Devoy defended using the term "self-determination" as it would hold Wilson to account for a term that he constantly used himself and that it was an excellent approach to continue to bear pressure on his stance of supporting small nations struggle for independence. Those who were weary of the term saw it as being too open to interpretation and possibly leaving the door open to applying to a form of Home Rule or other limited form of independence that fell short of a Republic. This issue would be of critical importance at the end of the upcoming War of Independence.

The FOIF went from strength to strength in the years after WWI. From a membership of approximately 2,000 at the end of 1918 it rose to a regular membership of 6,068 by February 1919 with associate membership estimated at 30,000. The single most dominant figure within the FOIF and the one most responsible to its rise to power was Daniel Coholan. Coholan's popularity and organizational ability was highlighted by the fact that neither Devoy nor the rapidly rising figure of Joseph McGarrity challenged his role.

Events were moving so rapidly at this point that it was decided to hold another Irish Race Convention in 1919 in Philadelphia. Through the FOIF it would be Clan na Gael that would set the agenda. From 22–23 February 5,000 delegates discussed a number of issues pertaining to recent political events and future strategy. The central achievement of the Conference, however, was the discussion surrounding the upcoming Paris Peace Conference and the sending of an Irish delegation. The Convention ended up appointing the American Commission on Irish Independence to go to Paris and lobby on behalf of recognition of the Irish Republic. The members of the newly appointed Commission were Frank Walsh, Edward Dunne and Michael Ryan. The two power centers of Clan na Gael were represented with Edward Dunne from Chicago and Michael Ryan from Philadelphia being represented. It was also thought to be of benefit to have legal expertise for the upcoming conference with both Walsh and Dunne having a professional legal background. During the Conference the Irish Victory Fund was established to assist in the establishment of the expected Republic. In some ways the Clan and FOIF expected too much from the conference and this over confidence was to receive a sharp check early on.

At the beginning Irish America saw the Paris Peace Conference through the very narrow prism of gaining recognition for an Irish Republic. President Wilson had a much larger vision of what he hoped would come from this unprecedented coming together of nations in the aftermath of the most destructive conflict the world had ever seen up to that point. Wilson was certainly familiar with the Irish independence struggle but it was far from being a priority during this critical time period. Wilson's dream was of a League of Nations that would act as a preventative measure to future conflicts and would bring peace to all humanity through peaceful negotiation and arbitration. Irish Americans would slowly over the duration of the conference come to see the League of Nations as an instrument through which the U.S. would form an alliance with Britain and maintain the status quo of British imperialism throughout the world, including Ireland[137].

It seems that the first person close to Wilson to truly appreciate the rising power of the FOIF and Irish American sentiment in general was Joseph Tumulty who was secretary and close confidant to Wilson as well having an important insight into Irish American sentiment. In a letter to Wilson Tumulty expressed these concerns – "Your attitude in this matter is fraught with a great deal of danger to both the Democratic Party and to the cause you represent .... Republicans are taking full advantage of this. You know that I am not a professional Irishman but your refusal to see this delegation will simply strengthen the Sinn Fein movement in this country". Although he had not planned to meet the Irish Commission Wilson reluctantly agreed to do so after Tumulty's advice.

---

137   Douglas, Delia, Shanon. 2015. The Rise and Fall of the Friends of Irish Freedom: How America Shaped Irish American Nationalism in the Twentieth Century. History PHD. Union College. Schenectady. P. 59-62.

At this meeting prior to Wilson's departure to Paris tensions were high because of the contemptuous relationship between Coholan and Wilson dating back a number of years. Not only had Coholan opposed Wilson's candidacy from within the New York Democratic machine but Wilson though of Coholan as nothing less than disloyal because of his connections to Imperial Germany during World War One. As a result, Coholan did not attend the meeting hoping it would improve the overall atmosphere. It did not. Wilson stated unequivocally that he could not endorse an Irish Republic in Paris as it was a domestic matter for Britain to deal with. At this point one cannot help but believe that Clan na Gael and the FOIF had now given up completely on winning Wilson over. However, the political struggle in the U.S. continued with a refocus on Congress.

The Gallagher resolution passed the House of Representatives on 4 March which urged the Paris Peace Conference "to favorably consider the claims of Ireland to the right of self- determination". Even though the act was more a statement of support than an actual intention to act it passed overwhelmingly by 216 to 45. The act was an important indicator as to the influence Clan na Gael and the FOIF had in Congress and served a sharp contrast to Wilson's attitude to the Irish question.

The issue of Irish-American opposition to the League of Nations started to become a major issue in the transatlantic relationship. The Republican movement in Ireland was leaning toward a still yet vague support of the concept of the League of Nations and feared that Clan na Gael and FOIF opposition to it would hamper attempts to gain recognition of an Irish Republic at the Paris Peace Conference. Devoy remained adamant that the League was "the most dangerous combination ever formed against Ireland". Devoy criticized Sinn Fein support for the League of Nations further in sup- porting Coholan's efforts and stating he was making "a superb fight against it, you ignore it and want the fight against it dropped. Judged by this acid test which of you is the better friend of the Irish Republic?". This sharp division highlighted as much as anything how different Irish American nationalism was from its counterpart in Ireland. The Clan's American background instilled in it many aspects of a political tradition that was isolationist and more Jeffersonian than its Irish counterpart.

At this point in the deteriorating relationship between the Irish and Irish-American branches of the Republican movement an important and often overlooked figure emerges who was to play a decisive role in the upcoming split in Irish-America. Patrick McCartan was appointed as Sinn Fein representative in the U.S. and was a major factor in shaping the views and strategy of Sinn Fein toward Clan na Gael and the FOIF. McCartan was from Carrickmore in County Tyrone, the same small town as Joseph McGarrity and as a result both men developed an affinity toward each other which developed into a growing political alliance. The rift between the Devoy/Coholan New York branch of Clan na Gael/FOIF and the McGarrity/McCartan faction in Philadelphia was well under way prior to De Valera's famous and controversial visit in June of 1919. Prior to De Valera's visit McCartan had already persuaded him that the best interests of Sinn Fein and the IRA lay in supporting the McGarrity faction in Philadelphia which was much less concerned with broader international issues such as the League of Nations and more concerned with direct and immediate political and financial support of an Irish Republic.

The growing divide between both factions in the U.S. and in the transatlantic relationship was further accentuated using the Victory Fund by the FOIF in their campaign against the League of Nations. McGarrity's growing bitterness was based on his fundamental belief that the fund's sole purpose was its direct contribution toward the independence struggle in Ireland and not in what he really believed to be a domestic political issue in the U.S. Coholan's response to McGarrity's attacks did not help matters when he suggested that "if Mr. McGarrity desired to send money to Ireland, he had better establish another fund as this money was to be used in America". The FOIF, under Cohalan's dominating leadership, had made their position clear – the struggle against the League of Nations would take precedence over the financial needs of Sinn Fein. The battle lines were now clearly drawn[138]. It was now domestic Irish nationalism vs. Irish American nationalism in a competing vision that was a long time coming to a head.

How much was it a deliberate Sinn Fein attempt in sending McCartan to report back on and even actively take part in splitting the Clan and the FOIF to gain control of the fundraising efforts or to what extent was it

---

138   Doorley, Michael. *Irish-American Diaspora Nationalism – The Friends of Irish Freedom, 1916-1935.* Four Courts Press. Dublin. 2005. P. 96-99.

something that evolved over time? The question was hard to assess. What seems clear was that when Coholan stated clearly that he intended on prioritizing resources to the anti-League of Nations campaign then ongoing in the U.S. that Sinn Fein and more hardline elements within Clan na Gael had decided enough was enough. One figure at this time that could have united the movement and develop some sort of compromise was John Devoy. However, at this time he seems to have fallen under the influence of the more outspoken and energetic Daniel Coholan. Devoy could also have realized that a takeover by the Republican movement in Ireland of the Clan's only political leverage, its large financial resources, would mean the elimination of any voice it would have in the independence struggle and what a post independent Ireland would look like. Coholan, by personality and temperament, was not a person to compromise or back down and as shown in his earlier life when he showed himself to have a knack for making enemies. On the other side you had Joseph McGarrity who was as an uncompromising Irish Republican as could be found within the ranks of Clan na Gael. The situation was a powder keg and it would be De Valera that would be the match to set off one of the most momentous moments in Irish-American nationalism and cause a schism from which Clan na Gael and the FOIF would never truly recover. While many historians have dismissed the split within Irish-America prior to and during De Valera's visit as a simple power struggle there were also other factors at play that complicated the issue even further. Relations between the IRB in Ireland and Clan na Gael was often contentious with many in Republican ranks in Ireland resenting the level of control of those living abroad had on the movement in Ireland. The newly invigorated IRB began to assert what it felt to be its moral and rightful authority on strategy and the way forward to achieving an Irish Republic. Another factor which the Clan had to contend with at this pivotal moment in its history was a generational confrontation between the older established order as represented by John Devoy and a newly emerging and militant faction led out of Philadelphia by Joseph McGarrity. McGarrity and others felt it was time for a newer and more energetic leadership to take over control of the Clan as Ireland moved toward open conflict. However, Devoy and his supporters felt McGarrity was too inexperienced and not yet ready for leadership. McGarrity mobilized opposition to the Devoy and Coholan leadership on the argument that the older leadership had in some ways become too Americanized and embroiled in American domestic issues at the expense of the aim of achieving Irish independence. This was not the first time in Clan na Gael history that this argument had come to the fore but on this occasion it was to have major and long-lasting consequences[139].

Despite these emerging divisions it was quite remarkable just how quickly Clan na Gael and the FOIF rebounded back into prominence and importance in the aftermath of World War One. Many Irish-Americans felt it necessary to rally behind the U.S. cause against Imperial Germany so as not to have their loyalty questioned. As a result, many put their Irish nationalism as a secondary issue and in some cases put on hold any overt display of Irishness or "foreign" loyalty. Although John Devoy and Joseph McGarrity played their expected roles in this revival it was Daniel Coholan and his leadership of the FOIF that played a particularly prominent role. Cohalan's organizational abilities, speaking skills and larger than life personality that would turn the FOIF into the most successful Irish-American fundraising organization ever. In many ways it would provide the life blood to the Irish revolution from 1919-21.

139   David, Troy. 2006. Eamon De Valera's Political Education: The American Tour of 1919-20. New Hibernia Review. Vol. 10, No. 1. P. 71.

CHAPTER 18

Eamon De Valera and Irish-America

Eamon De Valera was born on 14 October 1882, in New York City. His mother, Catherine Coll was originally from Bruree, County Limerick. His father, Juan Vivion De Valera, was a Spanish artist from the Basque Country in Spain. They were married in 1881 at Saint Patrick's Church in Jersey City. Circumstances for the family took a major downturn in 1885 when Juan Vivion died. As a result of the trying circumstances the young De Valera was sent to live with his uncle, Ned Coll, back in County Limerick. Some questions surround the beginning of Eamon De Valera's life which historians have debated for years. Not only does a marriage certificate not exist for De Valera's parents but his birth certificate was also altered. The baby De Valera was registered as George but ended up christened as Edward. Both birth certificate and baptismal certificate were altered. These facts have led many to believe that De Valera may have been born out of wedlock, a major stigma during the time period within the framework of Catholic Irish-America.

After the young De Valera moved to Ireland his mother, Kate Coll, eventually remarried giving birth to two more children. De Valera's mother seemingly made no attempt to bring him back to the new home and life she had made for herself in upstate New York. No reason is immediately obvious but one reason may have been that Kate's new husband may not have wanted someone else's child living under his roof.

In Ireland De Valera excelled academically as a youth. At 16 years of age, he won a scholarship and was accepted to Blackrock College in Dublin. After continuing to win further scholarships he obtained a position as a mathematics teacher in Rockwell College, County Tipperary. After graduating in 1904 from the Royal University of Ireland in mathematics De Valera went on to further academic study at Trinity College in Dublin. After doing so De Valera would go on to teach at Belvedere College,

Craysfort Teachers' Training College in Dublin among others during his early academic career. Throughout this stage of his life De Valera contemplated on and off a religious life which in the end became submerged in the upcoming political struggle and later political life although he would always remain deeply connected to the Catholic Church.

De Valera's first tentative steps into the political arena was in the Irish language revival which was taking place as part of the broader Gaelic cultural revival of the late nineteenth and early twentieth century. Having been born abroad and having a non-Irish name such participation may have been part of a process of creating identity and belonging. This early portion of De Valera's life was very unlike that of other Irish revolutionaries from the time period. Living a sheltered academic life in the arena of mathematics contrasted sharply with the likes of John Devoy and Joseph McGarrity. While both Devoy and McGarrity came from small town and rural Ireland and later spent most of their lives deeply rooted in the major Irish American urban centers in the U.S., De Valera in contrast was a distant figure emotionally and, in many cases, physically during the early part of his life and even later in his political career. Although he would himself take up arms De Valera would see himself much more as the intellectual revolutionary compared to the men of action like Devoy and McGarrity.

De Valera, like so many from that generation, evolved from the cultural awakening of the time period to one of increasing political radicalization. In 1913 De Valera joined the Irish Volunteers. Right up to the Easter Rising of 1916 De Valera rose rapidly through the ranks to become commandant of the Third Battalion of the Dublin Brigade. Although not necessarily charismatic or outgoing in manner De Valera did have the bearing of a leader and an intellectual ability to portray himself as a chieftain like figure. As a commander De Valera played a role in the Howth gun-running operation and was soon after sworn into the secret oath bound Irish Republican Brotherhood by Thomas McDonagh. Although the Catholic Church was passionately opposed to all oath bound organizations this did not seem to deter De Valera who like many revolutionary intellectuals of the time such as Patrick Pearse began to equate revolution and religious duty as inseparable.

De Valera's rise to national prominence came with the Easter Rising of 1916. De Valera was given command of Bolan's Mill on Grand Street in

Dublin. After a week of heavy fighting De Valera and the men under his command fought admirably and were among the last to surrender after receiving orders to lay down arms from Patrick Pearse. As a leading commander in the rising it would have been expected that De Valera would have been one of those chosen to be executed. The fact that De Valera was a U.S. citizen seems to have played a part in excluding De Valera from execution. At this point of World War One the British government was trying to gain U.S. participation in the war on the side of the allies. The optics of executing a U.S. citizen fighting in the cause of a Republic against the British Empire would only have provided ammunition to anti-war sentiment, particularly to Clan na Gael. In the aftermath of the rebellion De Valera would become the iconic and highest-ranking leader of the increasingly mythologized rising. The non-execution moment was truly a turning point in De Valera's rise to power and prominence. He now had the revolutionary credentials that could rival even those of John Devoy.

De Valera did not completely escape punishment and was imprisoned firstly in Dartmoor prison in Britain and later moved to Maidstone and Lewes. After being released on a general amnesty in June of 1917 De Valera ran as a Sinn Fein candidate for a by-election in East Clare which he won. In 1918 he ran for a seat in East Mayo and won that also. Inevitably De Valera was elected President of Sinn Fein in 1917. In 1918 Sinn Fein won the large majority of seats in an election landslide. De Valera was arrested with numerous other Sinn Fein members with the British government clampdown on the new Dail and he was sent to Lincoln jail from which he soon escaped in February 1919. De Valera was shortly after chosen as President of Dail Eireann essentially giving him the position of President of the rebel Republic. De Valera soon took the decision that the fight for independence would have to be more than a war waged by arms at home. It would require massive financial assistance and an international campaign of recognition and publicity as to the struggle in Ireland. There could only be one destination under such circumstances, the United States[140].

---

140   Coogan, Pat, Tim. De Valera – Long Fellow, Long Shadow. Arrow Books. London. 1995. P. 1-124.

Before ever arriving in the U.S. Irish-America was already very well acquainted with De Valera. Soon after he escaped execution the Boston Globe referred to De Valera in an article titled "American Led Irish Rebels". In the article De Valera was described a "tall, dark and of remarkable courage". De Valera's family in the U.S. were lobbying hard for his release while he was imprisoned in England with letters and appeals reaching as far as the desk of Joseph Tumulty, secretary to President Wilson. De Valera himself never liked being referred to as American or Irish-American. Another point of resentment for De Valera was the belief that his American citizenship saved him from execution. Years later in his personal documents De Valera wrote "the fact that I was born in America, would not, I am convinced, have saved me". Throughout his long and eventful life De Valera would be consistent in his denials that his American background had any role in saving his life.

Before ever arriving in the U.S. as President of the young fledgling rebel Irish Republic De Valera already had a deeply complicated relationship with the country of his birth. From a purely political perspective it would have made sense had De Valera attempted to embrace and highlight his American roots to connect with Irish-America for propaganda and fundraising purposes. Not only did De Valera never embrace his American background but in many cases he shunned it. His childhood roots hold the key to this attitude and in many ways his later actions during his famous tour to the U.S. from 1919-21. The feeling of maternal abandonment based upon the failure of his mother to take back the young De Valera and questions over the legitimacy of his birth could only have created a deep sense of rejection and anger. No matter how much Irish-America tried to embrace him in later years De Valera always kept an emotional distance build upon a foundation of animosity and rejection. This was highlighted at rejecting the country of his birth as having any role in saving his life in the aftermath of the Easter Rebellion. What De Valera would go on to achieve would be attributed to his Irish characteristics and upbringing[141]. At least some of these factors may have played a psychological role in his future attitude toward Clan na Gael.

---

141   Schmuhl, Robert. Ireland's Exiled Children – America and the Easter Rising. Oxford University Press. Oxford. 2016. P. 119-140.

CHAPTER 19

De Valera and Clan na Gael

On the face of it one can view De Valera's tour of the U.S. at the height of the Irish War of Independence as unusual timing at best and at worst a dereliction of duty during his country's greatest hour of need. To avoid arrest, promote the cause of Irish independence on the doorsteps of the world's most powerful country and to harness the large financial resources of Irish-America was seen and argued successfully by De Valera as essential and that he would serve the cause of independence better in the U.S. during this critical time period. The failure of the Irish delegation to get anywhere in terms of recognition of an Irish Republic during the Paris Peace Conference of 1919 only enhanced and strengthened De Valera's argument.

During the Paris Peace Conference, the Irish delegation was ignored by Wilson, considered irrelevant by the French and treated as nothing less than offensive by the British. With little success being achieved in Paris the delegation went to Ireland where it immediately stirred up controversy. The provocative speeches brought the condemnation of British Prime Minister Lloyd George. References to a "military dictatorship in Ireland" brought responses from conservative British publications such as The Times who described the Delegation as spreading "False and malicious" propaganda and even criticized Lloyd George for even giving permission for their entry into the country. With growing opposition at home to the idea of the League of Nations Wilson was growing in frustration at the efforts of the Irish Delegation. Wilson confided in a close associate "I don't know how long I shall be able to resist telling them what I think of their miserable mischief making. They can see nothing except their own small interests". The intervention of the Irish Question at this critical time only added to the dissension and delay in ratifying what Wilson hoped would be the culmination of his political career and legacy.

A heated meeting took place between Wilson and members of the Irish Delegation in the hope of coming to some sort of agreement. When the Delegation brought the issue of Wilson's promise for the right to self-determination of small nations his response was that he was only referring to nations involved in the war. Wilson was soon beginning to realize that his own words were coming back to haunt him. When Dunne criticized the President for refusing a visit to Ireland to examine conditions himself Wilson grew so angry that he threatened to blame Irish nationalists for the failure. When the meeting was published in the U.S. hostility toward Wilson from the Clan and the FOIF only increased further. In the end, as frustrating and untimely as the Irish question was for Wilson it was just not a priority and as a result the Irish delegation returned in frustration. This major setback on the international front would be the main spur to Eamon De Valera's visit to the U.S.[142].

When De Valera arrived in the U.S. the situation in Clan na Gael was already volatile. As previously mentioned Patrick McCartan, Sinn Fein envoy to the U.S. and particularly to Irish America, played a huge role in shaping De Valera's views and perceptions prior to his arrival in the U.S. McCartan's suspicion and animosity toward the Devoy/Coholan wing of Clan na Gael was transferred to De Valera who began to see both as an opposing powerbase outside the direct control of the rebel Irish government, particularly De Valera's own reach. McCartan's newly developed relationship with the younger more radical wing of the Clan under the leadership of Joseph McGarrity was seen as much more amiable and sympathetic toward direct assistance to the Irish struggle and less involved in domestic American political issues. As a result De Valera was already strongly gravitating toward McGarrity to the exclusion of Devoy and Coholan. The growing divisions were further reinforced when the IRB send their own envoy, Harry Boland, in April of 1919, who also ended up supporting the McGarrity faction of Clan na Gael. As a member of the IRB De Valera would have had McCartan's viewpoints further reinforced by that of Boland's report. Prior to De Valera's arrival he voiced publicly

142   Duff, John. 1968. The Versailles Treaty and the Irish-Americans. The Journey of American History. Vol. 55, No. 3. P. 592-597.

the need for funds raised in the U.S. to go directly to the cause of independence in Ireland. The attempt to bypass both Devoy and Cohalan by taking away their financial and therefore political leverage was clear. The opening shots were fired.

From the beginning the central target from the now pro-De Valera and McGarrity faction in the U.S. was the increasingly successful Victory Fund set up by the FOIF back in February of 1919. De Valera's arrival in the U.S. on 12th June. On De Valera's arrival he was openly welcomed by both factions of Clan na Gael with no discord on display, at least publicly. While De Valera preferred the McGarrity faction of the Clan it does seem by all accounts that he did not wish to see a split in the movement and instead see a change in leadership and policies prioritizing funding directly to Ireland as opposed to American political machinations. It would turn out that because of the strength of personalities involved and deep ideological differences that this would be impossible. Devoy and Coholan viewed De Valera as being inexperienced on the situation in the U.S. and saw his visit as an opportunity to inform and educate him. For Joseph McGarrity De Valera would be the vehicle to catapult him to the leadership of Clan na Gael[143].

De Valera's arrival in the U.S. was truly that of a visiting head of state, although one not recognized as such by the U.S. government. The central aim was not just propaganda purposes but to also organize a massive bond drive that would be used directly for domestic purposes in Ireland. The official launch of the De Valera visit and introduction to the Irish American public did not really come until 23 June when a function was held as the famous Waldorf-Astoria Hotel outside of which was an enormous sign reading "Help the Irish Republic".

With a visit to New York City Hall De Valera would continue his U.S. tour to Boston and hold his first public speech at Fenway Park. The event was a massive success with an estimated 50,000 people in attendance. At the event placards were seen everywhere stating "We demand England withdraw from Ireland" and "England is disqualified and unfit to rule

---

143   Davis, Troy. Eamon De Valera's Political Education: The American Tour of 1919-20. New Hibernia Review. Vol. 10, No. 1. P. 72.

Ireland". The enthusiasm was so intense that a local newspaper in Boston even labelled De Valera "The Irish Lincoln".

The occasions would be repeated in Chicago and many other locations in the coming months. De Valera's attendance in Wrigley Field in Chicago drew an estimated 25,000 supporters[144]. It would become apparent early in that De Valera's tour would be a massive propaganda and financial success. How did the Wilson administration view the De Valera tour? Although at local state level De Valera was feted as a virtual head of state Wilson gave no such federal recognition and did as much as he could to ignore events. However, De Valera would make this as difficult as possible by publishing a long list of demands for U.S. support for Irish independence. Wilson replied to such demands and efforts to undermine the creation of the League of Nations by stating publicly in a speech in Denver "Out of doors, that is to say outside of the legislative halls, there is no organized opposition to the treaty outside the people who tried to defeat the purpose of this government in the war.... Hyphens are the knives that are being stuck into the document and the issue is clearly drawn". The attempt on this occasion to paint groups like Clan na Gael and the FOIF as treasonous did not work as effectively as during the war years. The political environment had changed and momentum was building behind those opposing the League of Nations[145].

The initial exultation of De Valera's tour would not last long enough to cover up the growing tension and division within Clan na Gael's ranks which would soon become more public. As De Valera's speaking and fundraising tour continued Coholan and his supporters began an influencing campaign by writing letters to leading Irish American figures arguing De Valera's ignorance of the situation in the U.S. and how it was damaging the cause for Irish independence. Coholan charged De Valera and McGarrity as being responsible for the growing split within Clan na Gael. De Valera always denied any intention of fracturing the Clan but he could not have been oblivious to the fact that by strongly favoring and

144   Hannigan, Dave. De Valera in America. 2010. Palgrave Macmillan. New York. P. 1-41.

145   Hopkinson, Michael. 1993. Woodrow Wilson and the Irish Question. Studia Hibernica. No. 27. P. 106-107.

supporting the McGarrity faction over the established Devoy/Coholan wing of the Clan that this was exactly what he was doing[146].

McGarrity wrote an article in the Irish press implying Coholan's lack of cooperation on 1 November of 1919 which was to be a start of a rapid increase in tensions. McGarrity wrote "There may be some so-called Irish leaders in the U.S. who have capitalized on Irish support and sympathy for their own selfish ends. He (De Valera) has the right to expect undivided support in the manner he so desires. It is not for any self-appointed leader in the USA to question his appeal or his methods. He alone speaks for the voice of Ireland.

The fading influence of John Devoy at this point was seen in a resolution he promoted within the FOIF urging cooperation with the bond drive. However, the resolution was also a warning shot across the bows of De Valera and McGarrity as it also stated "We respectfully recommend to President De Valera, that the men in charge of this work be instructed to devote their whole attention to it and leave to the Friends of Irish Freedom the work of organizing our people in America to combat English propaganda according to the plans laid down by the Race Convention in Philadelphia last February"[147].

Divisions and ruptures within Clan na Gael continued and in February of 1920 escalated considerably. As De Valera's American tour progressed he campaigned more publicly for U.S. funding to be used expressly for the use of the fledgling rebel government in Ireland. Only an Irish government in Ireland knew how to use such funding to attain independence. To all concerned it was a direct attack on both Coholan and Devoy and was further complicated by the fact that it was the FOIF who provided a loan of $100,000 in order to kick start the Irish Bond Drive started by De Valera. Although the FOIF initially opposed a financial drive outside of their direct control they eventually felt compelled to support one due to public opinion and enthusiasm surrounding De Valera's tour. Despite this input both McGarrity and McCartan continued to accuse Devoy

---

146   David, Troy. 2006. Eamon De Valera's Political Education: The American Tour of 1919-20. New Hibernia Review. Vol.10, No. 1. P. 73.

147   Doorley, Michael. Irish-American Diaspora Nationalism – The Friends of Irish Freedom, 1916-1935. Four Courts Press. Dublin. 2005. P. 15.

and Coholan of impairing efforts for secure even more money for Ireland. Devoy and Coholan were becoming increasingly isolated as De Valera both privately and publicly showed increased deference to the McGarrity faction of Clan na Gael[148].

De Valera threw fuel on the dispute with a controversial interview he held in February of 1920 with the Westminister Gazette. The origin of the controversy was because of a bill introduced to Congress to gain funding for the "salaries of a minister and consuls to the Republic of Ireland". The bill was defeated based on it being a threat to Britain who was America's loyal ally in the recent war. De Valera got involved by asking the question "Why doesn't Britain do with Ireland as the United States did with Cuba? Why doesn't Britain declare a Monroe Doctrine for her neighboring island? The people of Ireland, so far from objecting, would cooperate with their whole soul".

De Valera's comments represented a major disconnect to Irish America for a number of reasons. Firstly, De Valera displayed a startling lack of knowledge as to Irish America's anti- imperialism, particularly in relation to the Spanish American war fought a little over twenty years prior when U.S. expansion beyond continental U.S. was opposed on the basis that it was replicating British imperial expansion that Ireland had existed under for centuries. Secondly, De Valera misunderstood or ignored the fact that the Platt Amendment represented an indirect yet stifling restriction on actual Cuban independence leaving the country as little more than a dependency on its overwhelmingly more powerful neighbor. Finally, the Monroe Doctrine for many Irish Americans was seen as little more than a legal tool to defend American expansionism much in the same way as the British Empire used the idea if spreading "civilization" and "Christian" values to racially "inferior" peoples. De Valera failed to understand that Irish American nationalism went beyond just the case of Irish independence and British imperialism but over the centuries had evolved into a global

---

148   Douglas, Delia, Shanon. 2015. The Rise and Fall of the Friends of Irish Freedom: How America Shaped Irish American Nationalism in the Twentieth Century. History PHD. Union College. Schenectady. P. 72-73.

anti-imperial vision that opposed all forms of imperialism that included both British, American as well as others.

De Valera's interview provided the FOIF and the Coholan/Devoy faction more broadly an opportunity to portray De Valera as out of touch with Irish America. Elements of the Irish American media launched stinging attacks on De Valera which brought the increasingly ugly dispute into the public arena. De Valera was temporarily put on the defensive and felt compelled to explain his position and at the same time denounce the Coholan/Devoy faction publicly for the first time. In an editorial De Valera wrote "One of Ireland's greatest afflictions at the moment is the behavior of the Coholan group in America. It is all dished up here in the daily papers to break the poor people's hearts. What a time they have chosen, these Friends of Irish Freedom, to round on us. We are being dragooned and shot like wild animals". The dispute and split had now reached the point of no return[149].

De Valera communicated back to Ireland the threat he now saw as being posed by the Devoy/Coholan faction of Clan na Gael and FOIF. In a communication to Arthur Griffith, a leading figure in Sinn Fein, De Valera stated serious consequences "from a movement now on foot here. At this distance the enemy and mischief makers could create such trouble as would make it impossible to do effective work....to ease the mind of everybody I want you to know that at all times that I never in public or private do or say anything here which is not thoroughly consistent with my attitude at home as you have known it. That will enable you to judge whether anything I may by newspapers be reported to have said is true or false. Never forget that the press is the instrument used by the enemy – garbled statements, misleading statements, etc." The regular use of the word "enemy" indicated just how bitter the split was becoming.

De Valera wanted to highlight that the Devoy/Coholan faction was beyond redemption and that any outreach or show of charity was no longer possible – "It is time for plain speaking now. A deadly attempt to ruin our chances for the bonds and for everything we came here to accomplish is being made. If I am asked for the ulterior motives, I can only guess that

149   Doorley, Michael. Irish-American Diaspora Nationalism – The Friends of Irish Freedom, 1916-1935. Four Courts Press. Dublin. 2005. P. 116-117.

they are 1. to drive me home – jealousy, envy, resentment of a rival – some devilish cause I do not know what prompts or 2. To compel me to rubber stamp for somebody. The position I have held is the following – 1. No American has a right to dictate policy to the Irish people. 2. We are here with a definite objective – Americans banded under the trade name.... Friends of Irish Freedom – ought to help us attain that objective if they are truly what their name applies. De Valera's growing bitterness can be clearly seen in referencing his opponents as "Americans" as opposed to Irish or Irish Americans. His belief was clear for all to see – De Valera no longer saw his opponents as even Irish, they were fully Americanized to the point of being out of touch completely with the cause of Irish independence and at worse being detrimental to the entire effort.

It is interesting that De Valera seems to have identified Coholan as his primary opponent and the main force driving Devoy's opposition. There may have been some lingering admiration and sympathy for the old Fenian warrior as opposed to the American born product of the corrupt Democratic political machine of Tammany Hall. De Valera wrote a scathing letter to Coholan at the height of the growing split – "I have decided that to continue to ignore the articles in the Gaelic American would result in injury to the cause I have been sent here to promote. The articles themselves are of course the least matter. It is the evident purpose behind them, and the general attitude of mind they reveal that is the menace –

> "I am answerable to the Irish people for the proper execution of the trust of which I have been charged. I am definitely responsible to them, and I alone am responsible. It is my obvious duty to select such instruments as may be available for the task set me. It is my duty to superintend every important step in the execution of that task. I may not blindly delegate these duties to anyone whatsoever. I cannot divest myself of my responsibilities.

The Friends of Irish Freedom organization is an association of American citizens, founded to assist the Irish people desire...You are the officer of the Friends of Irish Freedom, who, de facto, wields unchallenged the executive power of that organization. You are the officer through whom its several resources are in the main applied. You are the officer who has accepted its most important commission and spoken not merely in its name, but in the name of the whole Irish race in America. It is vital that I know exactly how you stand in this matter[150]".

De Valera's attack on the loyalty of the FOIF brought a quick response from Coholan – "Are you not in great danger of making a grave mistake when you talk in your communication of selecting "instruments" in this country and of "levers" and "power end" and "other end of the lever" through which you hope to accomplish your purpose here? Do you really think for a moment that American public opinion will permit any citizen of another country to interfere as you suggest in American affairs? Do you think that any self-respecting American will permit himself to be used in such a manner by you?".

Coholan had reached his limit with De Valera and his challenge to his authority over the FOIF. In an extraordinary meeting called by Coholan in the Park Avenue Hotel in New York on 19 March the leadership of the FOIF came together to discuss De Valera's conduct and to demand his immediate departure back to Ireland. In a surprising turn of events De Valera, who was not invited to the event, crashed the meeting along with McGarrity and Harry Boland. In a dramatic moment emotions and pent-up tensions exploded in acrimony with De Valera declaring that there was no room in the country for both himself and Coholan. In essence, De Valera was laying down a clear choice to all those in attendance that they had to make a choice, it was either the elected President of the rebel Irish Republic or Cohalan. Eight hours of heated discussion and disagreement followed in what we can only imagine was a cauldron of emotions and a moment when Irish American nationalism came head-to-head with Irish nationalism. As the two competing visions went back and forth passions were so intense that individuals had to retire from the room for short periods of recuperation before returning to join the battle. In the end a compromise was reached. De Valera promised not to intervene in matters that were of Irish American concern only while Coholan guaranteed not to intervene in matters that were of purely Irish concern. Although a temporary agreement was reached there could have been little doubt to those who attended the heated meeting that any hope of a true reconciliation was highly unlikely.

---

150   Douglas, Delia, Shanon. 2015. The Rise and Fall of the Friends of Irish Freedom: How America Shaped Irish American Nationalism in the Twentieth Century. History PHD. Union College. Schenectady. P. 75-76.

CHAPTER 20

A Divide Too Great – the Split of 1920

The truce between Coholan and De Valera was never destined to last. As the Victory Fund drive gathered momentum De Valera's desire to see the money go the fledgling rebel government in Ireland started to conflict increasingly with Coholan's desire to see the money stay in the U.S. to agitate for Irish independence, counter British propaganda and more broadly defend and promote American global anti-imperialism. This position began to isolate Coholan from the mainstream Irish leadership. The fact that during this time period most of the press releases from the FOIF focused more on defeating Wilson's League of Nations proposals and on promoting Isolationism just highlighted the incompatibility of both competing visions.

The two distinct and competing factions set up their powerbases in different parts of the country. De Valera opened offices and established himself in Chicago while the Coholan/Devoy faction centered their efforts in New York. The division in Irish ranks was at this point very public with De Valera in particular having to walk a fine line in not seeming to interfere in internal U.S. matters as a foreign, although not recognized, head of state. De Valera tried to avoid public mention of division as did Coholan to denied there was "division and dissension in the ranks of Americans interested in the independence of Ireland". In the Summer of 1920 there were very good reasons for continuing the public image of unity[151].

In 1920 war raged in Ireland with the conflict getting increasingly bitter and violent. At this point the IRA was in the process of driving the Royal Irish Constabulary from rural outposts into towns and other major urban centers leaving the countryside increasingly under the control of the Republican military forces and judiciary. In cities such as Dublin and

---

151   Cronin, Sean. The McGarrity Papers. Anvil Books. Tralee. 1972. P. 81-82.

Cork the IRA had established a very successful intelligence and counter-intelligence networks that was crippling the British governmental structure. The British response was to unleash a reign of terror with the introduction of what became known as the Black and Tans who were made up mostly of demobilized British veterans from World War One. They introduced a level of torture and extrajudicial killings not seen since the great Irish rebellion of 1798. The IRA responded in kind with successful ambushes of British forces at locations such as Kilmichael where the legendary 3rd West Cork Brigade under the leadership of the IRA's most successful guerilla commander, Tom Barry, killed seventeen British soldiers. This growing intensity was felt across the Atlantic by both sides of the growing divide.

De Valera now saw the time of reckoning quickly arriving as the war in Ireland raged and saw the need as urgent as ever to gain full control of the FOIF. James O'Mara, who was the De Valera's bond drive manager, demanded from Diarmuid Lynch, who was the sitting Secretary of the FOIF, in April the full amount of the Irish Victory Fund. O'Mara stated that such money morally belonged to Ireland. The demand was denied formally and the position restated that such money was to be used for "educating American public opinion". Coholan continued in his attempts to lobby hard for official recognition of the Irish Republic to not just further the nationalist cause but to undermine De Valera's position.

Coholan's position was becoming increasingly untenable. The early 1920s saw the increasing growth of nativism and a corresponding hostile climate to foreign entanglements. The ruling Republican Party did not want to leave itself open to hostile attacks from the pro-British media in the U.S. with its constant reminders of alliance during World War One. Coholan's desperate attempt to get a resolution adopted by the Republican Party at their convention in Chicago passed initially but was soon dropped after the confusion of contradictions between the demands of Coholan and De Valera's intervention. De Valera demanded the unconditional and immediate recognition of the Irish Republic which ran visibly counter to Coholan's more flexible and less clear demand for a form of self-determination. The countering demands left many leading Republicans feeling that the Irish did not know what they wanted and as a result dropped the resolution entirely. Coholan was furious to say the least at De Valera's intervention as what he saw as his personal political domain. Recriminations and blame flowed for days and weeks afterward[152].

The year 1920 posed other challenges to the FOIF. It was the year of the Red Scare where foreign independence and anti-colonial movements were tainted with allegations of pro- communist sympathies. In 1917 the Irish Progressive League was formed for the purpose of supporting the mayoral candidacy of Morris Hillquit. Hillquilt was a founding member of the Socialist Party and received a high level of support from sections of the heavily pro-Union Irish American working-class community. As a result, there was inevitably a significant crossover in membership[153]. This association with a radical leftist organization was problematic by itself but was complicated even further by the fact that the Irish Progressive League was very supportive of De Valera. Cohalan and the FOIF acted quickly to consolidate the threat to the organization and expelled all members of the League. The result was the FOIF had alienated itself further from mainstream Irish America by being attacked by the Irish Progressive League publicly as well as the continuing onslaught from pro-De Valera supporters and media.

De Valera now felt the moment opportune to intensify the attacks on the FOIF. Irish American newspapers sympathetic to De Valera began to urge the FOIF to oust what they called the "Coholan Americans" from leadership of the organization. De Valera himself began to make contacts with individuals belonging to and close to the FOIF to discuss ways to 'democratize" the organization, the term being just another way of demanding a change in leadership. When it became known to the leadership of the FOIF that De Valera was proposing to abolish the Coholan controlled executive the likes of John Devoy became further infuriated. Devoy stated to Coholan that De Valera was "out to smash us, and he is nibbling away at the ramparts all the time. He is the most malignant man in all Irish history".

A critically important meeting of the FOIF was scheduled for 17 September. Devoy was convinced that De Valera and his supporters would use the occasion to push through changes to the FOIF's constitution that

---

152   Doorley, Michael. Irish-American Diaspora Nationalism – The Friends of Irish Freedom, 1916-1935. Four Courts Press. Dublin. 2005. P. 128-130.
153   Nelson, Bruce. Irish Nationalists and the Making of the Irish Race. Princeton University Press. Princeton. 2012. P. 16.

would put in under no less than the full control of the rebel President. The meeting just like the previous one was dramatic. When De Valera appeared uninvited attempts were made to physically prevent him from doing so. With Harry Boland at his shoulder both men forced their way in where bitter arguments and recriminations followed. De Valera's suggestions for reforms were soundly defeated and in the words of a staunch Coholan loyalist, Mayor Grace of Charleston, South Carolina "the Friends of Irish Freedom would not seek dictation from a foreign potentate". De Valera staged a dramatic walkout, not the last one in his political career. What final bonds that might have existed were now finally broken and De Valera now fully realized that there was no hope of taking control of the FOIF. The only alternative at this point was to compete directly with Coholan and Devoy with a rival organization[154].

With the assistance of wealthy oil magnate Edward L. Donehy, De Valera established the American Association for the Recognition of the Irish Republic. The fighting back in Ireland was escalating between the IRA and the British military and De Valera felt the urgency and pressure to send back to Ireland the large sums of money required to fund the rebel underground government as well as arming and maintaining the IRA military campaign. De Valera's name recognition and popularity in the U.S. along with the support of the Joseph McGarrity wing of Clan na Gael resulted in a severe falling off in membership of the FOIF. At its peak the FOIF had an estimated 100,000 members and by 1921 that number had fallen off dramatically to a mere 20,000 members.

There were a number of reasons for the success of the AARIR and the decline of the FOIF and the Devoy/Coholan wing of Clan na Gael. At the end of the day De Valera was the elected head of the long-awaited rebel Irish Republic, a position which for most Irish-American gave an authority that superseded that of any Irish-American political figure when it came to the cause of Irish independence. The atrocities being carried out by the British military, particularly the notorious Black and Tans, was being reported in the American press and gave a sense of urgency to De Valera's appeals for

---

154   Doorley, Michael. Irish-American Diaspora Nationalism – The Friends of Irish
          Freedom, 1916-1935. Four Courts Press. Dublin. 2005. P. 131-133.

financial assistance. For many Irish-Americans the idea promoted by the likes of Coholan of playing the long game of political lobbying and agitation was no longer relevant during this critical moment of the Irish War of Independence. Urgent appeals for money to be sent directly to Ireland was now seen as the priority.

Further reasons included attacks by De Valera and others that the FOIF had become too American and that they had lost touch with the reality of the political situation in Ireland which was exemplified in the prioritizing of political lobbying in Congress and other political maneuverings instead of focusing on the struggle in Ireland. The split when it came would mean that Clan na Gael and the FOIF would never attain the same level of political influence and power as it did between 1916-19. In terms of broader public perceptions, the image in public displays of feuding Irish factions only played into negative stereotypes of the Irish being volatile, prone to factionalism and lacking unity. The FOIF would linger on into the 1930s with decreasing effectiveness while the split in Clan na Gael meant the movement would never again reach the levels of influence within Irish nationalism that it once held[155].

155   Douglas, Delia, Shanon. 2015. The Rise and Fall of the Friends of Irish Freedom: How America Shaped Irish American Nationalism in the Twentieth Century. History PHD. Union College. Schenectady. P. 79-81.

CHAPTER 21

Clan na Gael and the Irish Civil War

The war in Ireland came to an end when a truce was announced for 11 July 1921. By this point most of the executive of Clan na Gael still supported John Devoy. The tensions with the IRB back in Ireland had reached such a level that the IRB under the direction of Harry Boland disassociated itself from the Clan. Attempts by the IRB to oust Devoy from leadership of Clan na Gael had no effect. Despite this association the McGarrity wing of the Clan based primarily in Philadelphia maintained contact with the IRB back in Ireland. One can only assume that the IRB held out hope of McGarrity at some point taking over leadership of the Clan from the aging Devoy. With this recognition McGarrity made a total split from the Clan to form a new organization to be known as the Re-organized Clan na Gael. As to be expected Devoy refused to recognize the new organization and operated as before. Devoy also condemned the continued use of the name Clan na Gael by McGarrity for his new organization.

After the truce came into place rumors began to circulate quickly of a prospective treaty between Britain and a new Irish State. Initially the Republican movement in Ireland showed a united front as it prepared to face some of the most experienced diplomats the British Empire had at its disposal. De Valera braced the nation for the treaty negotiation by stating in his Easter message to the nation in 1921 "Our cause is just and we will surely triumph". He went on to declare "Let us finish the fight finally this time in order that it will not recur for our children and children's children. The sacrifices we must make will be great, but the peace they will bring will be worth the price".

During the war and immediately after it Michael Collins came to be a major figure not just within the IRA and IRB but also within the political wing of the Republican movement, Sinn Fein. Collins's exploits during the counter-intelligence war against Britain had by now made him into a legendary figure with his fame spreading across the Atlantic among Irish-Americans. His name was the only other one that could even rival that of De Valera. The media played a major role in Collin's rise to prominence in creating a Scarlet Pimpernel type figure to ride around Dublin on a bicycle coordinating an assassination campaign against British inform-ants and intelligence officers. This image created a larger-than-life figure. Collins provided a sharp contrast to the more austere and distant figure of De Valera as he was much more among the thick of the fighting and com-manded a deep loyalty not just from the men who fought under him but a deep admiration from the broader public in general within Ireland. Up until his untimely death Collins never lost his common touch and ability to communicate to and connect with the average Irish person[156].

The makeup of the Irish delegation that would negotiate with the British were Arthur Griffith, Michael Collins, Robert Barton, Eamon Duggan and George Gavan Duffy. While the Irish team lacked anyone of diplomatic experience the British team contained arguably the most experienced diplomatic team the Empire could have assembled. It con-tained Prime Minister David Lloyd George, Lord Birkenhead, Austen Chamberlain, Winston Churchill, Sir Laming Worthington-Evans, Sir Gordon Hewart and Sir Hamar Greenwood. In terms of experience and negotiation skills it was in many ways boys against men. Also, the British still held overwhelming military superiority and the possible threat of flooding Ireland with British troops should negotiations fail which Lloyd George brought up during tense negotiations.

Although the Irish team entered negotiations with the primary aim of achieving a united Irish Republic it soon became apparent that the British were never going to accept this. The issue of national security was always of primary concern to Britain and the presence of an independent nation to its western flank that could provide a steppingstone to future invasions or threats to British shipping was never going to be acceptable. Also, there was the issue of Protestant Loyalists in the north of Ireland who were never going to accept being part of a Catholic dominated Irish Republic or for that matter any sort of independent state.

---

156   Coogan, Pat, Tim. Michael Collins. Arrow Books. London. P. 3-157.

When one looks at the Irish negotiation team it is hard not to notice the absence of the elected head of state for the rebel Irish Republic, Eamon De Valera. De Valera's choice of not joining the negotiation team has created many questions and criticisms in the years and decades following. After a preliminary meeting in London on 12 July to discuss upcoming negotiations ended inconclusively it has been speculated that De Valera sensed that obtaining a Republic was never on the cards and as a result he physically distanced himself from later negotiations in anticipation of what he believed would be well short of full independence. By doing so De Valera could denounce any agreement reached that was short of a Republic and simply put the blame on the negotiation team. Pressure was put on Michael Collins by De Valera to be part of the negotiations which he very reluctantly agreed. Collins always saw himself as primarily a soldier and less a politician. By this point De Valera saw Collins as a rival political figure and resented his popularity among the general Irish population. Was this an attempt to deliberately hurt Collins's reputation politically by having him part of a potentially failed negotiation team? One can only speculate. Judging by De Valera's actions during his tour of the U.S. it is not beyond reasonable deduction to see him as destroying political rivals who threatened his position of power.

During the treaty negotiations the Irish team were in many ways completely outmaneuvered by the much more experienced British negotiation team. The objective of achieving a Republic became a non-starter from very early on the discussions. What independence Ireland was to achieve would be along the model of Canada or Australia within the framework of the British Commonwealth. Such an arrangement would include an oath of allegiance to the British monarchy for all elected members of the Irish parliament. Not only did this become apparent but also the fact that a growing and violent opposition within the six counties of the north of Ireland was portraying a real potential for civil war. An alliance quickly formed between northern unionists and the British Conservative Party in support of the idea of a separate Protestant controlled state that would have its own separate parliament. The issue with such a state would was that almost a third of the population would be made up of Irish Catholics with nationalist aspirations and provide a powder keg for future conflict.

By the end of the negotiations the Irish delegation, with threats from Lloyd George of a full scale military action should they not sign the treaty the position was dire was dire. Time to bring back the treaty to Ireland for discussion was denied. In the end the treaty was signed at 2.20 a.m. on 6 December 1921. The main terms of the agreement was the establishment of an Irish Free State that would contain twenty-six counties, a Governor General would be in Dublin to act as the representative of the British government and all elected members to the Irish parliament would have to swear an oath of allegiance to the British Crown. A separate state known as Northern Ireland which would contain the six counties in the northwest of the country and would contain its own elected parliament.

Throughout the treaty negotiations Joseph McGarrity was kept updated on proceedings through communications with Eamon De Valera, both of whose relationship was growing ever closer. In contrast Devoy and Coholan were kept very much out of the loop and had only information from the newspaper to keep them up to speed. Considering Devoy's almost half a century commitment to the cause of Irish independence this had to have been a particularly frustrating period. When news of the signing of the treaty began to emerge to the general Irish public heated discussion and passions were quick to flare. Political battle lines that would soon turn into military lines were drawn as De Valera and his supporters regarding the treaty as a total betrayal of the Republican cause and vowing never to pledge allegiance to any foreign monarch. Michael Collins and Arthur Griffith supported the treaty arguing that it was a stepping stone toward eventual full independence and would buy the breathing space needed to recover from the destruction of the war of independence[157].

The division and animosity in Ireland over the treaty was quickly being reflected with the two wings of Clan na Gael. Joseph McGarrity and his breakaway organization were quick to condemn the treaty and fall in behind De Valera and his opposition to it while Devoy and Coholan gave their support to Collins and Griffith in supporting it. After De Valera's role in splitting Clan na Gael and diminishing the power of the FOIF one

---

157   Townsend, Charles. The Republic – The Fight for Irish Independence. Penguin
       Books. London. 2013. P. 111-221.

cannot help but feel that Devoy and Coholan saw this as an opportunity at striking a blow against De Valera and possibly limiting his power and damaging his image within the broader Irish Republican movement. This was seen by the fact that initially Devoy and Coholan opposed the treaty because they thought De Valera would support it and only changed their position when De Valera came out in opposition to it.

Further splits were becoming evident within the ranks of Irish America. Within two months of the signing of the treaty the AARIR came out in opposition to it and gave its support to De Valera. With growing divisions and the growing potential of a civil war efforts were made for reconciliation both in Ireland and among Irish American factions of Clan na Gael. In Ireland a short lived and ultimately failed effort was made in what became known as the Collins-De Valera Pact which attempted to create a national coalition of pro and anti-treaty candidates of Sinn Fein to run in upcoming elections. Divisions, however, were too deep for such a coalition to last and it fell apart soon after being agreed upon.

In the U.S. Michael Collins send his trusted confidant and leading figure within the IRB to America to attempt to heal the deep divisions and come to some sort of understanding that would avoid further division and possible conflict. In March 1922 Denis McCullough arrived in the U.S. with instruction to "make peace" between the rival factions. The severity of the situation was indicated by McCullough's title of "Special Commissioner" with the main purpose of "the organizing of friendly relations between our separated groups in America". McCullough worked closely with the Irish government's special envoy, Professor Timothy A. Smiddy.

From December 1921 to into January 1922 the Dail witnessed heated debate arguing for and against the ratification of the agreement signed in London. In total there were 124 elected members in the Dail and when the eventual day arrived for the vote the result was close. Sixty- four members voted for ratification, fifty-seven against and three abstentions. Those who supported the treaty argued on behalf of a war weary electorate who saw the treaty as a stepping stone to full independence. Those opposing the treaty saw it as a betrayal of the Republic for which they fought for and a wasted sacrifice of those who died for the cause. The ratification of the treaty by the Dail on 7 January of 1922 only resulted in rising tensions. As

the British Army began withdrawing from the twenty-six counties a race
began between pro and anti-Treaty factions of the IRA to occupy the military barracks being evacuated. Elections held in June 1922 strengthened
the position of pro-treaty candidates leaving the anti-treaty forces more
backed into a corner of having to rely on eventual armed resistance to prevent the implementation of the treaty.

The U.S. was also an important battlefield in which the treaty debates
took place. Gavan Duffy, minister of foreign affairs for the Irish government, suggested to McCullough "the principle upon which unity can best
be founded is the principle of acquiescence by the Irish beyond the seas
in the wishes of the Irish people as constitutionally expressed, involving
support to the Irish government....and abstention from Irish party politics
and from taking sides as between Irish political parties". Smiddy welcomed
McCullough's arrival in New York on 31 March 1922 as tensions were rising
in Ireland. Smiddy had informed McCullough that while Irish American
opinion greatly desired Irish unity there was substantial support for De
Valera. At the same time Smiddy and McCullough were careful to keep their
distance from the FOIF even though the organization was heavily in support of the treaty but whose reputation was damaged during the feud with
De Valera and its policy approach during the Irish War of Independence.

On 14 April McCullough visited Philadelphia to meet with Joseph
McGarrity and the anti-Treaty wing of Clan na Gael which were a separate
organization at this point. The meeting brought very little positive results
as McCullough quickly concluded afterward that it would be impossible to
bring about unity on the treaty between the rival factions in the U.S. The
best that McCullough hoped for was to attempt to de-escalate tensions
by reducing personal and vicious attacks that both branches of the Clan
were launching against each other through Devoy's Gaelic American and
McGarrity's rival Irish Press.

In meeting both factions of Clan na Gael it is noteworthy that
McCullough found himself more favorable toward McGarrity and his
anti-Treaty supporters as opposed to Devoy and Coholan whom he viewed
as being more motivated in their intentions by hatred of De Valera as opposed to logical political thinking. McCullough himself was a Belfast man
and may have seen in McGarrity a kindred Ulster spirit and personality.

Although both men disagreed over the treaty neither could have been happy to see their native counties and homes left partitioned from the rest of the country and part of what eventually would become a vicious Protestant controlled sectarian state. From the pro-Treaty perspective McCullough was left in the dilemma of seeing neither side as being conducive to bring about unity within Irish American. As a result the strategy of attempting to create unity was abandoned in favor of shoring up support for the treaty in the U.S.[158].

By June 1922 the situation in Ireland was a powder keg. Anti-Treaty forces had taken over the Four Courts building in Dublin city center back in April and had essentially been using it as the headquarters for a rival military to that of the official Irish government. From April until June the government essentially ignored the anti-treaty occupation hoping that a peaceful negotiation could eventually be arranged. Britain for the most part was willing to let the Irish resolve the issue themselves. However, this all changed with the assassination in London of General Sir Henry Wilson on 22 June of 1922. Wilson was the main security advisor to the Northern Ireland government and was responsible for coordinating a vicious sectarian campaign and brutal suppression of the Republican movement in the north. Two IRA men, Reginald Dunne and Joseph O'Sullivan shot Wilson dead outside his home. Both men were eventually captured and executed. Although the anti-Treaty IRA were immediately blamed for the action many have speculated on the possible role of Michael Collins in authorizing the operation. Collins was one of the few men at this point who still had good relations with members at leadership levels of the anti-Treaty IRA and ongoing communication with the northern branches of the IRA who were taking heavy casualties under the repression of Wilson and northern loyalists

Whoever was ultimately to blame for Wilson's assassination it was the anti-Treaty forces operating out of the Four Courts who were ultimately blamed for authorizing the killing. For the British government this was the last straw. They put unbearable pressure on the new Free State

158   Davis, Troy. 2014. Irish Americans and the Treaty: The View from the Irish Free
       State. New Hibernia Review. Vol. 18, No. 2. P. 85-90.

government to take action to oust the anti-Treaty forces from the Four
Courts threatening that if they did not do so the British government would
take action themselves. In June the bombardment by Free State forces took
place against the Anti-Treaty forces in the Four Courts. This marked the
beginning of a short but vicious civil war that tore apart the very fabric of
Irish society and turned former comrades against each other. Although
the conflict lasted less than a year it would cause scars that lasted for generations with atrocities carried out by both sides[159].

The immediate objectives of the Free State representatives in the U.S.
was to counter the propaganda of the anti-Treaty and pro-De Valera establishment now being clearly led by Joseph McGarrity. The first part in
delegitimizing the anti-Treaty forces in Ireland was the constant reference
to them as "Irregulars". They were no longer referred to as Republicans
by the Free State media and their supporters. A central objective of both
Smiddy and McCullough was to monitor fundraising and potential gunrunning operations in support of the "Irregulars" in Ireland. This went so
far as hiring private detectives to monitor the actions of leading anti- Treaty
voices in the U.S.[160].

These concerns turned out to be well founded. McGarrity already
had been involved in gunrunning operations to Ireland during the War
of Independence and had a well-established fundraising network in the
U.S. headquartered out of Philadelphia. McGarrity kept in regular contact
both with De Valera and the main military leader of the anti-Treaty forces,
Liam Lynch. Lynch was requesting significant funding in order to purchase
artillery, ammunition and Thompson sub-machineguns. McGarrity went
immediately into action with time being at a premium as the military fortunes of anti-Treaty forces in Ireland were in the process of taking a major
downward turn. Sean Moylan was the major liaison between McGarrity's
Clan na Gael and the anti-Treaty forces in Ireland and both men launched
a major fundraising drive for the war effort. McGarrity already had $35,000
on hand planned to raise a further $50,000 throughout major cities mostly

159   Younger, Calton. Ireland's Civil War. London. 1986. P. 50-420.
160   Davis, Troy. 2014. Irish Americans and the Treaty: The View from the Irish Free
      State. New Hibernia Review. Vol. 18, No. 2. P. 91.

on the eastern seaboard and Midwest where the Irish community was strongest. A Clan secret agent with the codename "Blackman" was to arrange the chartering of a boat and the hiring of weapons experts to train the anti-Treaty forces in the use of artillery and heavy weapons.

Despite the massive effort on McGarrity's part the situation for the anti-Treaty forces began to deteriorate rapidly with their forces being pushed out of major parts of the country and eventually being confined mainly to the province of Munster in the south. Events moved faster than McGarrity could keep up with. After naval landings behind anti-Treaty lines tightened the noose to such an extent that organized resistance collapsed and the remaining diehards turned to guerrilla warfare. The death of Liam Lynch in a running gun battle on the Knockmealdown Mountains on 10 April 1923, marked the end of the conflict to all intents and purposes. On 27 April De Valera as head of the rebel Republican government signed a proclamation ordering the "suspension of all offensive operations....as from noon, Monday, April 30". It is highly unlikely that even if McGarrity's arms smuggling operation had succeeded that it would have affected the eventual outcome of the war. The Free State forces far exceeded the Irregulars in manpower and ironically thanks to British supplied weapons, in firepower as well. The short but bitterest of Civil wars had ended. It would cost the country the lives of great leaders such as Michael Collins, untold physical damage, the death of an estimated 1,300 and lasting political hatreds and divisions that would continue for generations[161].

Peter Golden would travel to Ireland in the role of an unofficial Clan na Gael representative in an attempt to act as an intermediary to end the conflict. His reports and poetry from his visit perhaps best epitomize the Irish American disillusionment and heart-breaking tragedy of what was unfolding –

> "Those who has fought unitedly and with such splendid results against the common enemy were now arrayed against each other, and a vendetta was being created, the end of which no man could or indeed would care to foresee."

---

161   Cronin, Sean. The McGarrity Papers. Anvil Books. Tralee. 1972. P. 130-136.

Golden's poem "A Prayer for Ireland" overflows with frustration and tragedy as he sees Ireland fall into a pit of violence and despair in a war that no longer carried the romantic and righteous cause of fighting against the foreign oppressor but one where brother fought against brother –

There is brooding horror here, Is no eye clear to mark its trend? Have men gone mad that they but say, From day to day – 'Fight to the end'.

The end of what? And who shall gain? Those who are slain – Can Ireland lose? Almighty father, give them light. That they may right and just may choose.

And lift this nation in Thy Name, Up from the shame of civil woe, Bring back again in peace and love, The glory of a year ago[162].

Although the focus of Clan na Gael's actions during the Civil War have been focused on the McGarrity wing of the movement which was now a totally separate organization the actions of the Devoy/Coholan Clan needs to be briefly assessed. As a life-long ardent revolutionary it is hard to believe that the partition of Ireland and the remaining oath of allegiance could have sat well with Devoy. The establishment of the Irish Free State must have been a bittersweet moment. It did not provide him with his long hoped for Republic but like many who supported the treaty he believed it was a significant step forward in achieving the aim of full independence. As ardent a revolutionary as Devoy was this was part of a life-long pattern of showing, when the occasion would arise, the ability to foster political and ideological flexibility to advance the greater cause. At the same time, it cannot be ignored that Devoy and Coholan's deep animosity toward De Valera played a role in supporting the Free State during the Civil War as well.

In the end, the Civil War in Ireland proved a major watershed event in the course of Irish American nationalism, and in particular for Clan na Gael. The organization would never again reach the same levels of power and influence either in the U.S. or in Irish politics. It was in many ways a division that was growing for years prior to 1920 and the later Civil War

162   Herlihy, Jim. Peter Golden – The Voice of Ireland. Peter Golden Commemoration
        Committee. Cork. 1994. P. 66.

from 1922-23. The Devoy and Coholan wing of Clan na Gael very much saw as an integral part of Irish- American identity the desire for acceptance into mainstream American society and the ability for upward social mobility which came with that. A natural outcome of this was the emphasis on working within American political institutions and local urban political machines to the benefit of achieving Irish independence. While never shying away from revolutionary conspiracy there was always a deep sensibility to make sure that it never ran counter to American interests and therefore jeopardizing Irish American identity within the broader framework of mainstream U.S. society. This could often mean the slow and seemingly un- revolutionary process of political lobbying and the idea of playing the "long game" and waiting for the right moment for revolution.

On the other hand, you had a section of Irish American nationalism as represented by Joseph McGarrity which had its roots much closer to Ireland and was less deeply connected to American politics and political tradition and was far less willing to play the "long game". This tradition focused much more on outright revolutionary conspiracy and direct contact and influence to events in Ireland. Little concern would have been given to Anglo-American relations, views on international events were narrowly focused and the emphasis on armed militancy far outweighed political considerations and in many cases the reality of the situation in Ireland.

From 1924 onward it would be Joseph McGarrity and his Clan na Gael that would take over the role of revolutionary Irish-America when the Devoy and Coholan faction voted to disband and John Devoy himself passed away just four years later in 1928. By 1928 membership of the FOIF would fall to a mere 654 members. The organization would continue on until 1935 fundraising for the new Irish Free State until forced to close due to litigation concerning whether the funds should go to De Valera's anti-Treaty movement or the existing Free State government. McGarrity' Clan an Gael would keep ongoing links with the remaining IRA in Ireland who at this point were devastated by the Civil War defeat and driven deep underground. Clan na Gael's focus from this point on did not involve continuing the bitterly divisive war against the Irish Free State government but instead rebuilding the organization for a future struggle to end partition in Ireland and push out the remaining British presence. This was politically astute as it was something that could unite Irish-America as opposed to a conflict involving Irishmen killing Irishmen. However, there would be a number of factors in the U.S. throughout the 1920s that would prove major obstacles to achieving anything close to the once powerful Clan that existed prior to the split in 1920.

CHAPTER 22

The Decline of Clan na Gael during the 1920s

Irish American nationalism and support for Clan na Gael took a major downturn in the years following the end of the Irish War of Independence and the Civil War which followed. There were a number of reasons both internal and specific to Clan na Gael and the broader Irish community in the U.S. as well as factors that were external to both in broader American society and political scene of the 1920s.

When looking at internal factors within Clan na Gael there is little doubt that the major infighting and divisions within the ranks of the organization played a role in causing disenchantment and a falloff in support from the general Irish American public. This would have been further exacerbated by the fact that the infighting was taking place in the midst of the bitter fighting back in Ireland when the expectation was that all of nationalist Ireland and Irish America should have been united during this ultimate test of will which was the culmination of centuries of Irish American efforts to bring about and support the cause of independence in Ireland. The very public displays of hostility and competing visions over strategy and what an independent Ireland would actually look like among Clan na Gael ranks further hampered the ability to gain support in Congress for an Irish Republic. The Clan lost support rapidly in Congress as the result of the bitter infighting within organization's ranks as well as the short but bitter Civil War which followed in Ireland.

The death of John Devoy in 1928, even though by this point he and Coholan had dissolved their wing of Clan na Gael, marked the passing of what can only be described as a monumental figure of Irish American nationalism. Although McGarrity would take over as leader of the remnants of Clan na Gael he never succeeded in making the organization the influential and broad mass movement that Devoy had managed to build. While Devoy very much created Clan na Gael as an organization that was not only an Irish American revolutionary movement but also, an effective political force in American politics in other ways. Under Devoy the Clan lobbied Congress and organized and pressured Irish American politicians within major urban political machines to take a public stand on Irish independence therefore keeping the issue of a Republic always at the forefront of Irish American aspirations and Anglo-American relations.

This strategy was completely overhauled when McGarrity took over the leadership by taking Clan na Gael more away from the center of American political life and creating a smaller more revolutionary clandestine organization focused entirely on influencing revolutionary events in Ireland. Such a movement required less public exposure in order to avoid prying eyes, particularly from organizations such as the Federal Bureau of Investigation. McGarrity and the new Clan would essentially change the organization from being a uniquely Irish American movement to merely an Irish revolutionary movement based in the U.S.

This change in orientation of Clan na Gael and its intentional extraction from mainstream American life would leave it open more than ever to being a "foreign" organization based in the U.S. Instead of now being seen as part of the long-standing American tradition of anti- imperialism the Clan would start to be seen more as an "alien" organization posing a threat to American foreign policy interests. This turning away from American mainstream politics was the result of loss of political clout but also a belief that such involvement both diluted and distracted from the main cause of Irish nationalism. This deep cynicism was also a product of the split within Irish Republicanism during the civil war when a major section of Irish Republicanism turned to constitutional politics and accepting not only partition but a continued political connection to Britain that would remain technically in place until 1949 when the Free State was abolished and a Republic established in southern Ireland.

External factors outside the direct control of Clan na Gael also played a role in the decline of Irish American nationalism. From the beginning of World War One Irish America underwent a rapid process of assimilation into mainstream American life. An inevitable outcome of this process was the gradual breakdown in the attachment between Ireland and Irish America. While strong cultural links remained, many began to lose political interest to events in Ireland which would not re-emerge until the Northern Ireland conflict exploded on the Irish American scene in the late 1960s. Another factor which played into the process of assimilation was the fall off in Irish immigration to the U.S. of those with a searing anti-British sentiment. The end of the Land Lord system and influential Anglo-Irish aristocracy which marked the setting up of the Irish Free State meant that most Irish and Irish American focus was given almost exclusively to economic concerns and social mobility[163].

Looking at external factors outside of Clan na Gael that contributed to the decline of Irish American nationalism one needs to look also at the growth of U.S. isolationism throughout the 1920s. Although the U.S. was only involved in World War One for a short period it suffered 116,516 deaths and approximately 320,000 injured. The mass devastation of the war and the feeling of being forced to fight a war of Europe's own creation left many Americans resentful and skeptical of international entanglements. This was further reflected in the Congressional rejection of U.S. membership of the League of Nations and growing restrictions on immigration. In 1921 Congress passed the Emergency Quota Act which set quotas on the number of immigrants coming into the U.S. This was replaced in 1924 by the Johnson-Reed Act which further reduced those immigrants eligible for entry into the U.S. Irish Americans felt the broader pressure of withdrawing from political involvement in the new Free State which was further enhanced by the deep divisions and conduct of Clan na Gael during the Irish War of Independence[164].

Another major challenge to Irish American nationalism during the 1920s was the rise of anti- immigrant and anti-Catholic sentiment that naturally targeted such overt displays as showing loyalty to a foreign country and political cause ahead of that of the United States. At the forefront of this growing sentiment was the re-emergence of the Ku Klux Klan. Although the Klan was founded back in the aftermath of the Civil War

163   Wipf, Jacob. Clan na Gael and the Decline of Irish American Nationalism, 1900-1921. School of Historical, Philosophical and Religious Studies. Arizona State University. Tempe.

164   Available online <https://online.norwich.edu/academic-programs/resources/isolationism-and-us-foreign-policy-after-world-war-i>

during Reconstruction its original purpose was almost entirely the subju-
gation of freed African American slaves to second class citizens and the
suppression of their voting rights. Although eventually suppressed by the
Federal authorities the KKK reemerged in the 1920s with a message that
not only targeted African Americans but that was also virulently anti-
immigrant and anti-Catholic. After decades many in the Anglo-Saxon
Protestant establishment feared the changing face of life and culture within
the U.S. as millions of Eastern Europeans, Italians and Irish immigrated
into the major urban centers bringing with them their own languages,
culture and religion.

Arguably one of the most visible, vocal and politically powerful of
these groups was Irish- Americans. Unlike many of the other groups Irish
immigrants did not leave their culture or political allegiances behind them
in the "old country" but instead attempted to integrate into mainstream
American life. This was seen by many nativists, particularly the KKK, as
perverse to allegiance to the United States. The very public displays of Irish
political protest on the streets, in publications and activities in Congress
only made the group a particular target of ire for the likes of the KKK and
other anti-immigrant groups.

The Irish Question and Clan na Gael's struggle for Irish independence cut deeply into the struggle for immigrant integration into mainstream U.S. society and more generally Catholic-Protestant relations. When
one adds the split of 1920 within Clan na Gael and the bloody Civil War
which followed Irish American nationalism, particularly militant Irish
Republicanism, the organization was in poor overall standing to stand up
to the onslaught. On top of this when you consider that the Democratic
Party at this stage was still very much the party of racism with many Klan
members also being members of the party it affected the willingness of
many elected leaders to be vociferous on the Irish Question as they once
had been[165].

The new Clan that emerged in the aftermath of the civil war in Ireland
under the leadership McGarrity faced many challenges on the domestic

165   Cuddy, Edward. 1981. The Irish Question and the Revival of Anti-Catholicism in
       the 1920s. The Catholic Historical Review, Vol. 67, No. 2. P. 236-255.

American front as well as a defeated and greatly weakened IRA back in Ireland. However, it did have some advantages over its sister organization in Ireland. The biggest advantage was that the Clan did not have to face the severe security clampdowns experienced by the IRA in the Free State and Northern Ireland. This relative freedom of movement did give the room for the Clan to recover and rebuilt and eventually give a haven for IRA exiles after the civil war defeat. Secondly, at least for a number of years, the Clan's stronger position compared to the IRA in Ireland gave it a certain increased ability to influence overall policy of the Republican movement. This was best exemplified in McGarrity's role in organizing the IRA bombing campaign of Britain from 1939- 40. Despite these positives Clan na Gael would have to adjust to a new reality in the 1920s which would involve a much smaller membership, less financial resources than it was used to and generally a less influential voice in the broader Irish American community.

CHAPTER 23

Rebuilding the Clan

Although the 1920s was a decade of splits and decline it was not without its bright points for McGarrity's new leadership. The aftermath of the Civil War in Ireland brought thousands of hardline and diehard IRA activists to American shores who refused to live under the new Free State and in other instances sought fresh economic opportunities from an economy devastated during years of fighting. McGarrity and Clan na Gael sought to use this new influx as the backbone on which to rebuild the organization into the force that it had once been.

One example of this infusion of Republican refugees that arrived in the U.S. after the Civil War and who was to play a major role in the decades to come was Mike Quill. Quill was born in in the village of Kilgarvan, County Kerry, on 18 September 1905. From the very young age of just 14 years old Quill acted as a dispatch rider for the Kerry 3rd Brigade of the IRA during the War of Independence. Republicanism ran strong in the Quill family with his uncle's house being a focal point of IRA meetings and activity at the height of the conflict. At a very early age Quill showed a proclivity toward organization and leadership as he formed an IRA youth group in the local area which drilled secretly several times a week.

When the Civil War broke out the Quill family took the anti-Treaty side of the IRA. It is said that the young Mike Quill was involved in a bank robbery to acquire funding for the local IRA in the conflict against government forces. The Civil War in Kerry saw some of the worst fighting and atrocities of the entire conflict and took a deep emotional toll on Quill himself. One of the worst of these was what became known as the Ballyseedy Massacre when eight Republican prisoners were tied to a landmine which was detonated killing all the prisoners. Quill's mother died in 1923 but Mike and his brother were refused amnesty to attend the funeral on account of the Church's condemnation of the anti-Treaty IRA and overt support for the new Free State government. The bitter experience of seeing Irishmen fight each other in bitter conflict as well as the treatment by the church toward his family was to play a major role in shaping a very socialist Republican outlook that would be a feature of Quill and many other exiles in the years to come.

Quill attempted to rebuild his life after the war and worked in a sawmill in Kenmare. After a sit-in strike he and his brother were blacklisted from further employment in the area which was an event which furthered his left-wing leanings. With the Irish economy in a generally depressed state in the 1920s and a Free State government heavily monitoring former, and in some cases continued, subversives from the Civil War Mike Quill decided to emigrate to the U.S. and arrived in New York on 16 March 1926. Like many of the political and economic refugees arriving in the U.S. in the years after 1923 Quill was fortunate to already have an established family network and lived with his aunt for a while in East Harlem[166].

The military defeat of the Civil War forced Clan na Gael into refocusing its strategy on becoming even more closely aligned with De Valera and the now alternative strategy of a politically undermining the Free State and bringing about a unified Republic. Clan na Gael would continue its fundraising efforts with the intention of supporting the electoral prospects of Sinn Fein back in Ireland. The pro-Treaty wing of the Republican movement had reformulated itself into a new political party called Cumann na nGaedheal. As during the Civil War Sean Moylan would be the main liaison between Clan na Gael and Sinn Fein in Ireland. By this point many IRA members remained languishing in military prisons or had become so disenchanted with the entire political situation that they permanently laid down arms. Dan Breen reported to McGarrity in early 1924 that there were still approximately 2,000 IRA prisoners in jail. Military prospects for the immediate future were non-existent.

What had originally been military funds were now funneled into the Sinn Fein election Efforts with the end of the military campaign. A total

166   Kelly, Augustine, Joseph. The Labor Philosophy of Michael J. Quill. 1967. Master's Thesis. Loyola University Chicago. P. 3-4. Available online <https://core.ac.uk/download/pdf/48603736.pdf>

sum of $100,000 was sent to Ireland for election purposes. The election of 1923 was one that should have given Clan na Gael great hope and encouragement. Sinn Fein won 63 of the 143 seats available. However, following the policy of abstentionism the seats remained vacant as a protest against the recognition of the Free State and the Treaty which created the state of Northern Ireland. What this tactic essentially resulted in was handing over the reins of political power to the pro-treaty Cumann na nGaedheal to further reinforce the terms of the treaty without any parliamentary opposition. It was hard to see how the policy of voting for political representatives not to take their seats in a parliament which went on about its business without opposition would continue to garner political support for a prolonged period[167].

At this time Frank Aiken was essentially acting as De Valera's second in command in Ireland and would become the last Chief of Staff of the anti-Treaty IRA. Aiken carried great political clout and personal respect from McGarrity and the Clan in the U.S. Both men kept in close contact after the end of the conflict. In a letter sent on 1 October 1923, Aiken compared Clan na Gael and the American Association for the Recognition of an Irish Republic (AARIR) as the American equivalent of the IRA and Sinn Fein in Ireland. This was essentially Aiken's attempt to highlight to McGarrity the ongoing importance of the Clan to the continuing efforts to create an Irish Republic as well as an attempt to motivate and reinvigorate a movement itself scarred and divided from the Civil War. The aim was also to close Republican ranks and create a new united front. This would be more essential than ever as the Clan would no longer have the political support in the U.S. that it once had under Devoy's leadership and would also have to face political enemies in the form of the Free State government, the newly formed and deeply sectarian Northern Ireland government backed up by the British imperial parliament in London.

The pattern of the domestic Republican movement in Ireland of not always fully grasping the political dynamics within her sister organization in the U.S. manifested itself again with Republican movement in Ireland

167   Wilk, Gavin. *Transatlantic Defiance – The Militant Irish Republican Movement in America, 1923-45.* Manchester University Press. Manchester. 2014. P. 13-15.

not fully comprehending the tensions that existed between the Clan and AARIR. These tensions became apparent in 1925 during a fundraising speaking tour by Mary MacSwiney, widow of Sinn Fein mayor of Cork who died on hunger strike in an English prison in 1920. Although both the Clan and AAIRA both sponsored the tour many Clan members began to question the motives of the AAIRA and see it as a rival organization. Accusations by AAIRA members questioned whether Clan funds were actually reaching the IRA back in Ireland. Although both organizations continued their fundraising efforts the relationship would remain strained in the coming years.

Prior to MacSwiney's arrival in the U.S. and growing tensions with the AAIRA McGarrity had to face the difficult task in September of 1924 of facing the Clan na Gael membership at their convention in Atlantic City. It was for McGarrity a trying moment in the aftermath of defeat in the Civil War, the partition of Ireland, the failure to achieve a Republic and the continued mass incarceration of many Republicans back in Ireland where the IRA was largely crippled and driven deeply underground. For McGarrity it was a moment where the Clan had to face up to some harsh realities and his personal obligation to provide an honest assessment of immediate prospects but also a path forward in the long term. He acknowledged publicly "the imprisonment and death of so many of the leaders, the desire to place blame for failure, the foolish gossiping of many individual workers" and "defeatist feeling". In many ways McGarrity felt it necessary to set expectations at a realistic level and to prevent another potential split from elements of the Clan membership who were seeking more immediate military actions.

What came out of the Atlantic City Conference was a very reluctant and loose commitment to the political process but also a continued dedication to the militant Republican cause when the circumstances saw fit. The Clan was establishing itself as the most militant wing of the broader Republican movement in Ireland and abroad. It was also becoming apparent that while De Valera and the Republican movement in Ireland continued to see Clan na Gael as the mere fundraising wing of the movement the Clan themselves were starting to view itself as the true inheritors of the militant Republican tradition of the United Irishmen, the Young Irelanders and the rebels of 1916 and the Civil War. The Clan viewed themselves as an equal to the movement in Ireland and not just a diminished fundraising body with no political input.

At the time of the 1924 convention the Clan treasury contained less than $5,000. With the demand from De Valera in Ireland for up to $100,000 to contest upcoming elections the immediate priorities of Clan na Gael were dedicated to fundraising activities. This in many ways helped focus the organization and gave little time for internal dissension to manifest. However, it was not long before the reality of the post-Civil War Irish-America set in. Unlike previous years fundraising proved largely a miserable failure achieving nowhere near the $100,000 target. This failure along with McGarrity's growing disenchantment in the belief that there was a political path to achieving a Republic saw the beginning of the Clan's slow drift toward a purely militant organization. Future funds would go directly to armed campaigns and away from the political activities of Sinn Fein.

Although McGarrity's loyalty to De Valera remained strong in the years after the Civil War tensions did begin to manifest. While De Valera started down the road to entering constitutional politics within the newly established Irish Free State McGarrity, during the Atlantic City Clan na Gael Conference in 1924 reaffirmed the organization's dedication to physical force in achieving a Republic. McGarrity stated unequivocally on behalf of the Clan and with their full support –

> "It is the opinion of the Delegates assembled at this Convention that no-good purpose can be achieved in taking further part in the election in Ireland and we are of the opinion that the money spend for election purposes can be more effectively be spent in preparing the Army of the Republic for the fight that must be fought before the final goal is achieved"[168].

McGarrity's uncompromising position on continued support for a thirty-two county Irish Republic through the use of armed revolutionary violence made his ultimate split with De Valera inevitable. McGarrity rededicated the Clan's support for what remained of the IRA in Ireland and

168 Tarpey, Veronica, Marie. The Role of Joseph McGarrity in the Struggle for Irish Independence. Arno press. New York. 1976. P. 212-213.

went so far as to invite the IRA Chief of Staff, Andy Cooney, in 1926, in order to dedicate Clan support in the form of fundraising, weapons purchase and building general support in the U.S. for the movement.

At this point in history, it is very easy to see militant Irish Republicanism at an extremely low ebb and even possibly on the verge of future near extinction. In Ireland the IRA, as stated earlier, was a movement crippled in both the north and south of Ireland by strict anti-terrorism laws and close monitoring by both the northern and southern governments. Effective membership, while difficult to measure, may well have been as low as a few thousand. Despite this, the movement in the U.S. did give some grounds for hope in the future.

Despite being now a smaller organization and the recent history of splits and divisions, most recently with De Valera, McGarrity did have a number of advantages. With a smaller more coordinated organization dedicated toward the single cause of a unified Irish Republic with McGarrity as undisputed head, it made the Clan a much easier organization to control with less disputing factions and infighting. While the Clan became less part of mainstream American society it continued to remain deep within the fabric of Irish-American communities. As stated earlier the Clan set up a nationwide network in the U.S. that welcomed fleeing Republicans from the recently ended Civil War in Ireland. This assistance would take many forms.

One of the most basic forms of assistance was setting up many former IRA men in jobs and housing for those few who did not already have family members in the U.S. Some of these members, such as Martin Lavan from Kiltimagh in County Mayo, was actively on the run for shooting dead an Irish Free State officer during the Civil War. Such individuals were provided with such items as false passports and other fake forms of identification[169].

For many IRA immigrants fleeing to the U.S. the adjustment was a difficult one. Many of these young men came mostly from small, tightly knit rural communities and now found themselves in vast and sprawling cities such as New York and Boston. The attraction of an organization like

---

169   Wilk, Gavin. Transatlantic Defiance – The Militant Irish Republican Movement in America, 1923-45. Manchester University Press. Manchester. 2014. P. 34-35.

Clan na Gael proved irresistible. Connections were provided with like-minded Republicans from Ireland as well as from the Clan's point of view providing a ready pool of new and highly dedicated recruits that would provide a hardcore membership in the decades to come.

According to research carried out in Gavin Wink's "Transatlantic Defiance" the majority of newly arrived IRA veterans settled in New York resulting in a movement away from McGarrity's powerbase in Philadelphia. Going forward it would now be the New York Clan that would be the most influential while McGarrity remained at the helm. The earlier mentioned Michael Quill would eventually become the leading figure among Irish Republicans in New York but would not emerge to prominent leadership until after McGarrity's death avoiding any internal power struggles that so crippled the Clan in the past.

Outside of purely political and economic matters the Clan also involved itself in organizing many social events that included numerous dances. These events gave opportunities for Irish immigrants to meet and make social, economic and political connections that in many cases would last lifetimes. It was also an excellent opportunity for the Clan to recruit new members. For many Irish Republicans and political dissidents, the Clan offered a sharp contrast to the almost defunct and seemingly hapless IRA back in Ireland who were in no position to help former members in the aftermath of defeat. Although IRA members in the U.S. formed the IRA Foreign Reserve as an organization to work in cooperation with the Clan in the U.S. they essentially became one of the same with the Clan very much in the leadership role. IRA clubs made up of veterans from the War of Independence and Civil War were established in many cities with agendas and constitutions virtually identical to that of the Clan and crossover membership between both organizations became overwhelmingly common.

Contrary to the account of most historians that the Irish Republican movement was in major decline and mostly moribund in the years 1923–30 the U.S. proved a very different scenario and has been often overlooked. Once former IRA veterans found their feet in the U.S., linked up with the Clan and became economically stable many became reinvigorated after the bitter disappointment of defeat in the Civil War and began to re-establish links with the Republican movement back in Ireland. These exiled veterans from Ireland gave the Clan access to local IRA networks back in Ireland. One example of this was Michael Shanahan, former commander of the County Clare Brigade of the IRA, who moved to the U.S. after the Civil War and was requested by the Clan to re-establish contact with what remained of the IRA back in Clare. The rising importance of the Clan in the U.S. for the IRA back in Ireland was highlighted in the fact that according to IRA veteran Michael Flannery the movement in Ireland tried to organize the immigration of certain leading Republicans that would help in the cause in the U.S. At this point it could be ascertained that the IRA in Ireland saw the future survival of the militant Republican cause as being inextricably linked with the Clan in the U.S. which only goes to highlight the poor state of the movement in Ireland.

Once the process of re-establishing links to the IRA back in Ireland had begun the next natural step was fundraising as this would be necessary for the survival and re-emergence of the movement in Ireland going forward. It was not long before the IRA in Ireland began making formal requests for funding. One of the first significant transfer of funds was for $6,000 sent by the Clan to the IRA back in Ireland. The fact that the funds came from an estimated 5,000 donors showed a significant movement away from big Irish-American donors from the period 1916-21. The requests from the IRA for funding showed the dire state of the movement in Ireland. Requests for sums as small as $300 to $350 were deemed as vital just to keep basic administration running. The response of the Clan, and in particular Joseph McGarrity himself, was indeed impressive. The Clan raised a total of $29,000 over a relatively short period of time to meet basic IRA needs back in Ireland. McGarrity believed the effort to have been 'a wonderful financial return for our very small membership'.

The growing popularity of Fianna Fail back in Ireland and its drawing away of former IRA members into the arena of constitutional politics certainly had a detrimental effect on the IRA in both Ireland and the U.S. De Valera still very much held the aura of the rebel commander of the 1916 Rising as well as the rebel President of the War of Independence. His newly formed political party, Fianna Fail, claimed the label of the legitimate voice of Irish Republicanism and seen by many as the best option for achieving a united Irish Republic. Many in the higher echelons of Irish America society and the political establishment tended to agree and directed much funds and political support to what they hoped would be the first internationally recognized leader of a united Irish Republic.

Even with the onset of the great financial crisis in 1929 and the beginning of the Great Depression the Clan continued to show its fundraising abilities which proved vital for the continued, though very limited, role of militant Republicanism back in Ireland. The restructuring and rebuilding of Clan na Gael in the aftermath of the defeat during the Civil War was a remarkable achievement indeed considering how its sister organization back in Ireland, the IRA, had largely been driven underground and was forced ever more to the fringe of mainstream Irish society. Credit for this must be largely given to Joseph McGarrity and his dauntless and relentless efforts to persevere during some of the lowest points in the history of Clan na Gael. Although in the aftermath of the Irish Civil War the Clan would move away from mainstream American society and from the political lobbying and maneuverings seen under the Devoy and Coholan leadership, the newly formed Clan would totally immerse itself within the Irish American community and provide an exiled community a secure base from which the IRA could operate securely outside of the oppressive governments of the Irish Free State and Northern loyalist government. The tradition dating back to the United Irishmen of 1798 was very much kept alive[170].

---

170   Wilk, Gavin. Transatlantic Defiance – The Militant Irish Republican Movement in America, 1923-45. Manchester University Press. Manchester. 2014. P. 37-70.

CHAPTER 24

The 1930s

Unlike the IRA back in Ireland, Clan na Gael could look upon its efforts of consolidating and rebuilding the Republican movement in the U.S. with a level of success. However, the political situation in Ireland was anything but positive for the cause of militant Republicanism. At this point the primary focus of attention was toward ending partition for armed means and hoping that the south of Ireland would eventually establish a Republic through political means. The year 1932 would see the formation of the first Fianna Fail government with the constitutional political agenda of establishing a Republic and ending partition. However, De Valera's insistence on non-recognition of the Northern Ireland state did little to further the cause of unification as did the IRA's political wing, Sinn Fein, refusal to take their seats in either the Free State or Northern Ireland parliaments.

Clan na Gael started off the new decade with a convention that lasted from 30 August to 1 September in New York City. The choice of New York was no coincidence as it was by this time the choice of settlement of the majority of IRA members who left Ireland in the year's after the Civil War. By 1930 economic conditions had deteriorated internationally with the onset of the Great Depression and the Clan's fundraising efforts were beginning to feel it's impact. McGarrity reported to the membership the failure to raise the expected $100,000 which was targeted for the previous year. Many Clan members, including McGarrity, were resentful of the fact that in 1930 De Valera had carried out a tour of Irish America fundraising for a new Fianna Fail newspaper. Inevitably, both Fianna Fail and the Clan were competing for the same donors. With De Valera's political prospects being very much on the up he inevitably gained the upper hand when it came to fundraising.

During the course of the conference McGarrity never swayed from his aim of armed revolutionary violence. He advocated for the revival of the Irish Republican Brotherhood which had disbanded in the aftermath of the establishment of the Free State. He saw it acting as a secret auxiliary to the IRA. Nothing during the course of the conference advocated or supported any aspect of constitutional Republicanism as espoused by De Valera and Fianna Fail. Despite these very open tensions McGarrity by 1930 could still envision a united Irish Republic under the leadership of De Valera. This balancing act of seeing any political compromise on a Republic or unification as tantamount to treason while at the same time envisioning and recognizing a constitutional political leader in the form of De Valera who operated within the political constraints of the Free State was destined to eventually and inevitably fall apart[171].

McGarrity still held to the romantic vision of the revolutionary De Valera as commander during the 1916 Rising and the rebel president of the War of Independence long after when he stepped into constitutional political arena. While Republicanism in Ireland underwent internal dialog, evolved and adapted to the flow of domestic events the Clan's geographic distance was also tantamount to its psychological separation. While this ideological and cultural separation was not unique in the history of Irish American nationalism it did gather pace within Clan na Gael in the years and decades after the Civil War. As the movement lost its status and influence outside of Irish-American circles and to a lesser extent within Irish-America it became a more insular movement where internal debate and discussion was essentially non-existent or seen as borderline treasonous. In some respect it might have been this hardened mindset that helped the Clan survive through the barren years that lay ahead in terms of political success.

During the early part of the 1930s Clan na Gael began to develop a close, informal and almost invisible relationship with the Transport Workers Union in New York City. While Irish America had been at the forefront of the Labor Union struggle going all the way back to the post-Civil War era the unions provided not just economic benefits but also a political base from

---

171   Tarpey, Veronica, Marie. The Role of Joseph McGarrity in the Struggle for Irish Independence. Arno press. New York. 1976. P. 216-266-268.

which to lobby and agitate not just at a local level but also at national level for the nationalist cause in Ireland. During the Irish War of Independence labor unions with heavy Irish influence often refused to handle goods coming from or going to Britain. Irish run unions would also lobby local Democratic elected officials to condemn British actions and occupation of Ireland. Older more established transport unions in New York had such as Railway workers could have as many as a third of their entire membership made of up a combination of Irish born and Irish American membership. The usual tradition for established Irish members in such unions was to provide any job openings to newly arrived family members from Ireland therefore maintaining Irish domination of the union[172]. The fact that Unions were naturally left leaning and included strong anti-imperial sentiment also lent itself as being naturally attractive to Irish revolutionaries over the decades.

The Transport Workers Union was founded in New York in 1934 by rising Clan na Gael figure Michael Quill. Quill brought the political radicalism of his earlier life in Ireland into the TWU with his militant approach to organizing. Such tactics included sit-ins which Quill used to bring New York leading businesses to its knees. The tactic was seen as necessary by its members during the terrible economic plight of the Great Depression. Such tactics not only achieved many of its stated aims such as better pay and working conditions but also helped spread and expand the union well outside of New York City to make it one of the largest and most important unions in the country[173].

Clan na Gael connections to the TWU was evident from its founding and not just through the prominent figure of Mike Quill. Thomas Humphrey O'Shea was an IRA veteran from Cobh in County Cork during the bloody time period of 1917 to 1924 who had the reputation as an explosives expert who used his skills to blow up police stations. On his arrival in the U.S. in 1927 O'Shea became a turnstile mechanic and rose rapidly through the ranks of the Inter-borough Rapid Transit Company. O'Shea was perhaps

172   Freeman, Joshua. In Transit – The Transport Workers Union in New York City, 1933-1966. Oxford University Press. New York. 1989. P. 28-29.

173   Freeman, Joshua. In Transit – The Transport Workers Union in New York City, 1933-1966. Oxford University Press. New York. 1989. P. 39-45.

one of the most prominent members of the TWU who was also a leading
Clan member. O'Shea's positioning within the Union provided the union
with access to the radical Irish Republican movement in New York[174].

Other prominent Clan figures from this period in the TWU included
Jack Teahan and Connie Lynch. From the mid-1930s Quill never differ-
entiated between his American and global leftist political leanings and
that of the militant Irish Republican cause back home. The relationship
between the Clan and TWU was a mutually beneficial one in the years to
come. For Quill the Clan members provided him with access to what was
fondly referred to as the "Irish Republican Transit" which were leading Clan
members in other labor unions who had the vital organizational abilities
and contacts essential in the eventual formation of the TWU. For the Clan
Quill provided the bridge between a mass of Irish conservative working
class who were apolitical or who had drifted away from the Irish Republican
cause back in Ireland. Also, Quill provided connections with radical leftist
elements in the New York primary of which was the Communist Party[175].

This association to far-left elements in New York City and the U.S.
more widely speaking from a revolutionary movement made up mostly of
Catholic conservative Irish Americans is not as strange as it may initially
seem. During the course of the Irish Civil War the Catholic Church took
the side of the Free State government and heavily condemned the anti-
Treaty IRA. Threats of excommunication and condemnation of IRA hunger
strikers in 1923 left a deep animosity by exiled Irish Republicans in the U.S.
On top of this there was also the attraction of international Communism's
deep commitment to anti-imperialism and anti-colonialism which Irish
Republicanism easily applied to Ireland.

The situation of militant Irish Republicanism in the U.S. offered a
stark contrast to the state of Sinn Fein and the IRA back in Ireland. The
election victory of Fianna Fail in 1932 did much to undermine the IRA case
for armed conflict. Many Irish people of Republican sympathies threw in
their lot with Fianna Fail and choose the constitutional road. After years

---

174   Freeman, Joshua. In Transit – The Transport Workers Union in New York City,
       1933-1966. Oxford University Press. New York. 1989. P. 55.
175   Freeman, Joshua. In Transit – The Transport Workers Union in New York City,
       1933-1966. Oxford University Press. New York. 1989. P. 56-57.

of bitter conflict the majority of Irish people put at least temporarily the issue of partition on the backburner and focused more on peacefully undermining many of the other more short-term and achievable aspects of the Anglo-Irish Treaty they viewed as limiting Irish independence. The achievements of Fianna Fail offered a contrast to the continuing abstentionism of Sinn Fein from both the Free State and Northern Ireland parliaments. For many people voting for Sinn Fein and the IRA was a "lost" vote. The figure of De Valera still loomed large and attracted many previous Sinn Fein voters to the newly emerging political powerhouse of Fianna Fail who in the decades to come would emerge as one of the most successful political parties in western Europe.

The IRA, at least temporarily, were willing to accept De Valera's approach to undermining the Anglo-Irish treaty through constitutional means. Fianna Fail, now in power and needing to emphasize its constitutional credentials, attempted to pressurize the IRA to accept publicly the full terms of the 1923 ceasefire which ended the civil war. Most of the IRA, while they laid down arms, did not fully accept the terms that ended the conflict. In order to help the process, former IRA commander and now Minister of Defense under the new Fianna Fail government, Frank Aiken, spoke with imprisoned IRA leaders in Arbour Hill. Although no formal agreement was reached prisoners were released the next day.

With a clear majority in the Dail and a strong political mandate De Valera kept his word and quickly began to attack and undermine the Anglo-Irish treaty. The Oath of Allegiance to the British Crown that had to be given by every elected member of the Dail was abolished. The Governor-General's power was drastically reduced to the point of being meaningless. Through this period of political success De Valera and Fianna Fail began to distance itself more and more from the IRA to the point of even refusing to consult with the movement on any political decisions.

On its own initiative the IRA pursued a boycott campaign on British goods coming into Ireland which involved the stopping of trains and trucks and widespread destruction. Also, the early 1930s saw the rise of the fascist Blue Shirt movement made of mostly of former Free State military members who were avowedly anti-IRA. Street violence became common as public marches and counter-marches brought both groups in to bloody confrontations. The result of these events where that De Valera was faced with a major law and order issue.

Joseph McGarrity and Clan na Gael as expected were observing events closely in Ireland. McGarrity wrote a letter to De Valera which gives an interesting insight into how the Clan saw the role of the IRA during this time period. In the letter McGarrity stated that the IRA "can do the things that you will not care to do or cannot do in the face of public criticism, while the IRA pay no heed to public clamor so long as they feel they are doing a national duty. You both profess to desire the same goal. Why in God's name do you hesitate to sit down and try to find a working agreement? It is the extreme, the fanatical thing as the English call it that frightens them and causes them to seek for peace". McGarrity would go on to urge cooperation between De Valera and the IRA and stated that he would strongly encourage the IRA Chief of Staff Moss Twomey to reach out in cooperation with the Fianna Fail government.

In McGarrity's attempt to push Twomey toward something looking like a broad Republican front that included Clan na Gael, Fianna Fail and the IRA it became apparent that not only was the IRA leadership turning against Fianna Fail but that De Valera himself was pushing toward forcing the IRA to disband. In De Valera's response to McGarrity's letter he stated "you talked about coming to an understanding with the IRA. You talk of the influence it would have here and abroad. You talk as if we were fools and didn't realize all this. My God! Do you know that ever since 1921 the main purpose in everything I have done has been to try to secure a basis for national unity. How can you imagine for one moment that I don't realize what division in the Republican ranks means at a time like this". The knife to McGarrity's hopes came when De Valera declared "are we to abandon all this in order to satisfy a group who have not given the slightest evidence of any ability to lead our people anywhere except back in the morass". De Valera concluded this most uncompromising of letters by stating "We will not allow any group or any individuals to prevent this from being carried out. Those who are barring our path now are doing exactly what Coholan and Co. did from 1919 to 1921".

It now had to have become apparent to McGarrity that any sort of broad front alliance between Clan na Gael, the IRA and Fianna Fail was out of the question. Making an indirect comparison between McGarrity's Clan na Gael and the earlier Coholan faction of previous years had to have both hurt and angered McGarrity. De Valera, as displayed during the period 1919-21, showed a ruthless streak when it came to having complete control and being undisputed leader of Irish Republicanism. He did not share that mantle with John Devoy and he certainly was not going to dilute his control by any partnership or alliance with the Clan or the IRA. De Valera's growing contempt for Irish Republicanism outside of Fianna Fail and his direct control was highlighted when he referred to the IRA as "too stupid, or too pigheaded' to follow his leadership[176].

De Valera had now made the full transition from uncompromising violent revolutionary to a peaceful constitutional leader. For this transformation to take root he had to distance himself completely from the remaining violent wing of Irish Republicanism. Also, De Valera's continuing links to the IRA and Clan na Gael were used in political attacks by opposition in the Dail. For Clan na Gael and the IRA what was occurring was nothing short of a total betrayal of Republican revolutionary principles and an acceptance of the British occupation in the north of Ireland. The relationship was doomed to end.

Continuing violent confrontations between the IRA and the Fascist Blueshirt movement, the murder of a landlord agent, continuing bank robberies and a shootout with the Gardai during a strike with Dublin tramway workers led to De Valera banning the IRA in 1936. IRA support declined further when De Valera's government introduced a new constitution in 1937 which abolished the Oath of Allegiance to the British Crown and laid territorial claim over the Northern Ireland state. Public support for the IRA faded as many would be supporters gravitated toward De Valera's Fianna Fail who for many had achieved more undermining British rule and the hated Treaty than the IRA had in the thirteen years since the end of the Civil War[177].

---

176   Cronin, Sean. The McGarrity Papers. Anvil Books. Tralee. 1972. P. 156-158.
177   Coogan, Pat, Tim. De Valera – Long Fellow, Long Shadow. Arrow Books. London. 1995. P. 486-490.

As the 1930s progressed the fortunes of the IRA in Ireland was very much mirrored to that of Clan na Gael in the U.S. During the 1930s the Clan was constantly urging the IRA to attack the Northern Ireland state and drive out the last bastion of the British presence on the island. The constant reports of violent IRA confrontation with the Fascist Blueshirts was seen by the Clan as merely distracting from the main issue of undermining the new Northern Ireland state. The loss of support to Fianna Fail was also keenly felt within Clan na Gael ranks. Clan na Gael newspaper sales began to drop as the pro-Fianna Fail publication Irish World increased in sales and circulation. Leading Clan member, J.T Ryan, resigned from the organization after being criticized for an article he wrote in the Irish World as being too pro-De Valera.

Back in Ireland matters became further complicated by a split in the IRA in 1934. Leading left-wing IRA members split from the organization in frustration at the lack of any political progress. The new party was called the Republican Congress. The new party focused more on economic and social issues as well as achieving a united Ireland which many saw as not happening anytime soon. By focusing on social issues there was at least the prospect of achieving something successful and relatively immediate. The Republican Congress failed to have any impact and by 1935 collapsed.

A major factor in hampering Clan na Gael efforts to fundraise in the U.S. was that it was by no means alone or unchallenged in the arena of Irish-American nationalist organizations who we're undertaking fundraising among Irish-Americans. Most prominent among these competing organizations were the continuing remnants of the Friends of Irish Freedom and the pro-Fianna Fail American Association for the Recognition of an Irish Republic. Also, changes in the social makeup of the Clan's membership also contributed to declining fundraising success. The majority of Clan na Gael's membership were becoming more working and lower middle-class while the higher social echelons of Irish America either drifted into mainstream American life or became attracted to the more mainstream Irish-American organizations such as the AARIR[178].

---

178   Hanley, Brian. The IRA – 1926-1936. Four Courts Press. Dublin. 2002. P. 167.

As the 1930s progressed the IRA in Ireland along with Clan na Gael in the U.S. began to take a very much leftward political turn. There were a number of reasons for this. Irish Republicanism was undergoing a crisis that involved the complete lack of any political prospects of achieving a united Ireland, the domination of Fianna Fail on the Republican spectrum of domestic politics and continuing falling numerical and financial support. As a result, many left leaning IRA and Clan members began to look to other avenues for political expression and success. In Ireland it would be the Spanish Civil War that ignited an idealistic cause for which to fight for and focus their revolutionary energy. Under the leadership of Frank Ryan IRA members formed what became known as the Connolly Column and would go on to fight with distinction in a conflict that in the end would see defeat to Franco's Fascist forces.

In the U.S. Clan na Gael was undergoing a similar experience. The main concentration of left leaning Clan members were contained primarily within the James Connolly Club of the Clan in New York City. Leading figures included Gerald O'Reilly, Charles McGinnitty and Mike Quill. Both Quill and McGinnitty were responsible for the printing and distribution of An Phoblacht and the more communist Irish Worker's Voice. With the IRA split in 1934 many of these left leaning Clan members gravitated toward the newly formed Republican Congress. George Gilmore, a leading member of the Republican Congress came to the U.S. in late 1934 in the hope of gaining financial support. He would end up leaving bitterly disappointed at the poor financial situation of the Clan and his mission proved a bitter let down.

Throughout its history Clan na Gael had always been a vocal anti-colonial movement. While much of this was directed against the British Empire it did also, though less vocally, criticize what they saw as examples of U.S. imperialism. This view found further expression and meaning with the increased leftward leanings of the movement during the 1930s which highlighted not just U.S. aggression abroad but also racial injustice domestically. The main Clan na Gael publication, An Phoblacht, was vocal in its criticism of such controversial cases as the Sacco and Vanzeni and the Scottsboro Boys cases. Criticism of U.S. actions in Nicaragua where the paper went as far as to compare U.S. marines as "America's Black and Tans". This level of criticism would have been unthinkable just ten years earlier.

Despite the efforts of Clan na Gael to remain a relevant factor within Irish-America and Irish nationalism nothing could disguise its continued decline. IRA Chief of Staff Moss Twomey sums up this sentiment when he commented that the Clan seemed to have "ceased to exist outside of New York". The rapid decline in the sales for An Phoblacht further compounded the decline[179].

In 1936 IRA Chief of Staff Moss Twomey was arrested and he would spend the next two years in an internment camp in Ireland. Throughout his imprisonment Clan an Gael provided financial support for his struggling family during the two years of Twomey's confinement. The IRA under the new leadership of Sean Russell would enter one of the most controversial periods of its long history. Inevitably, Clan na Gael would follow the same path. However, because of a very different domestic situation in the U.S. it would be the Clan that would perhaps pay the greater price for its participation with its most controversial international ally.

179   Hanley, Brian. The IRA – 1926-1936. Four Courts Press. Dublin. 2002. P. 169-170.

CHAPTER 25

WW2, the Nazi Connection and the S-Plan

The ascension of Russell to the Chief of Staff of the IRA would mark a sharp right turn politically with the renewal yet again of violent confrontation to British rule in Ireland. It would also be the catalyst for a renewal of the right-wing of Clan na Gael under the indomitable leadership of Joseph McGarrity. Together McGarrity and Russell sought to renew the centuries long Irish Republican belief that "Britain's difficulty was Ireland's opportunity".

Elections in 1932 saw the ascendency of the Nazi Party that would see the beginning of World War Two just seven years later with the German invasion of Poland. Anglo-German antagonism had long predated the outbreak of World War Two and whose beginnings could be traced as far back as German unification in 1871. British fears of a dominant power on mainland Europe dictated its policy of alliances which sought to contain German continental and worldwide imperial ambitions. German resentment of the British policy saw the country assist the Boers during the Boer War and attempted assistance to Irish nationalists prior to the outbreak of the 1916 Rising. Clan na Gael's connections to Germany dated back to the days of the combined effort by German-Americans and Irish-American nationalists to keep the United States out of World War 1 and in the defeat of President Wilson's efforts to join the League of Nations. However, the Germany of the pre-World War and World War 1 era would be a much different nation than the one following the election of Hitler and the Nazi Party in 1933 and a Clan na Gael alliance a much more controversial issue.

As stated earlier the ascension of Sean Russell to Chief of Staff of the IRA in Ireland marked a sharp right turn politically that would see the movement become much more confrontational and urging for direct military action. This gave McGarrity, himself a violent more right-leaning Clan leader, the opportunity he had been waiting for. Russell and McGarrity were very similar in many ways. Russell's violent revolutionary credentials were beyond question, a fact that always appealed to McGarrity. Russell led the Dublin Brigade's 2nd Battalion during the 1916 Easter Rising. During the War of Independence which followed be became the IRA Director of Munitions. When the IRA split over the treaty he took the anti-Treaty side. In the aftermath of the Civil War he was interned but escaped in 1925 in a prison break he helped organize.

Russell would prove willing to take any military assistance from whatever quarter was willing to offer it regardless of political ideology. In 1926 he travelled as part of an IRA delegation to the Soviet Union on a weapons buying mission. With a rising reputation he was appointed IRA Quarter Master General in 1927. Throughout the early and mid-1930s Russell stood apart from internal IRA political debates and factionalism with his total focus being trying to organize armed action against British rule in Ireland. This lack of ideological baggage beyond straight forward militant Republicanism left Russell as a natural ally to Joseph McGarrity[180]. On a visit to the United States Russell and McGarrity met for the first time and a fateful alliance was formed as to coordinating a bombing campaign in Britain in order to force a withdrawal from the north of Ireland at a time when the British were in a life-or-death struggle against Nazi Germany.

The new direction of Clan na Gael in the later part of the 1930s was clearly stated when McGarrity noted in his diary on September of that year that "I most strongly advise that, if a fight is to take place in Ireland it must be to free the northeast six counties with a perfected organization in all parts of England to harass the real enemy". This new strategy was to predate a later Provisional IRA bombing campaign in England by over thirty years and was the first time that such a tactic was to be used since the Clan na Gael inspired bombing campaign of the 1880s[181].

From late 1935 to the early part of 1936 McGarrity spent time in Ireland renewing old acquaintance within the IRA and well as cultivating new relationships. It was during this time period that the relationship between

180   Available online <https://peoplepill.com/people/sean-russell/>
181   Tarpey, Veronica, Marie. The Role of Joseph McGarrity in the Struggle for Irish Independence. Arno press. New York. 1976. P. 305.

Russell and McGarrity began. The relationship seems to have taken deep root primarily as a result of both men's traditional violent Republican outlook and immediate desire for armed action against Britain. This relationship was further reinforced when Russell was invited to New York where he arrived on 21 July 1936. Although the initial visit was all about fundraising for the families of IRA prisoners back in Ireland it soon took on a very different meaning. What was supposed to be a relatively minor visit was turned into a major event when Russell gave a newspaper interview. Russell announced that the IRA was planning "To rain bombs on England in a do-or-die attempt to overthrow De Valera and obtain complete independence from Britain". He gave further details of the IRA "drilling in different parts of the British Isles" and having "stores of ammunition hidden in both Ireland and England". He also claimed that the main purpose of his visit was "to raise a million-dollar fund to finance the Republican forces".

The newspaper interview by Russell had a number of consequences. Firstly, he most certainly exaggerated the fighting potential and abilities of the IRA during this time period. As would be soon demonstrated the IRA's military abilities would be limited to bombing campaign carried out by a small number of IRA volunteers. Secondly, although no record exists of McGarrity's reaction to Russell's interview, he could hardly have been happy with this public display of IRA and Clan na Gael intentions in advance of a bombing campaign that required the upmost secrecy. The British embassy, the F.B.I as well as pro-British elements within the Roosevelt administration would have been put on alert. From the late 1930s onward President Roosevelt was already taking a strong pro-British stance with the growing threat of Nazism in Europe. Did Russell get caught up in the spur of the moment during the interview or was it a carefully pre- planned maneuver with the intention of arousing Clan na Gael and broader Irish American support? It seems more likely that Russell inadvertently jeopardized future plans with his public pronouncements and he may also have overestimated Irish-American support more broadly[182].

---

182 Wilk, Gavin. Transatlantic Defiance – The Militant Irish Republican Movement in America, 1923-45. Manchester University Press. Manchester. 2014. P. 124-126.

When Russell returned to Ireland in October of 1936 McGarrity made a futile effort to form some sort of coalition with the De Valera government and the Northern Ireland government under hardline Unionist James Craig. John Harte acted as the Clan emissary to Ireland and made contact with Ms. Edith Ellis, a close friend of De Valera, to communicate the plan. The idea was almost immediately shot down. The efforts to create this coalition was greatly undermined by De Valera's introduction of the 1936 Constitution which among other things removed any mention of a British monarch and abolished the Office of Governor General. Although this was far from what Irish Republicans wanted it was seen as a major stepping stone toward a Republic and greatly undermined any broad support for a renewed armed campaign against British rule in the north of Ireland. The fact that Ireland would remain part of the British Commonwealth and that partition would remain in place left McGarrity with the belief that militant Republicanism was now the only option left to end partition and break the last links to Britain[183].

This failed outreach by Clan na Gael must be looked at in more detail. McGarrity's disconnect from the political situation is starkly highlighted. Not only was it unrealistic to think De Valera would agree to a coalition with Clan na Gael, noting his earlier comments and viewpoints on the Clan, but to think that James Craig, the Protestant fundamentalist hardline leader of the Unionist state in Northern Ireland would ever have anything to do with McGarrity was completely impractical to say the least. Instead of reassessing the situation and adapting politically the Clan under McGarrity retreated more behind the ramparts of militant Irish Republicanism and took on the approach of "going it alone" as the "last soldiers of the Republic". As McGarrity had said to De Valera back in 1933 he very much believed in the power of "the fanatical thing" to frighten the English political establishment[184].

Russell's reckless and unauthorized actions during his U.S. visit resulted in his court martial on his return to Ireland. Although McGarrity continued

---

183   Tarpey, Veronica, Marie. The Role of Joseph McGarrity in the Struggle for Irish Independence. Arno press. New York. 1976. P. 308-313.

184   Cronin, Sean. The McGarrity Papers. Anvil Books. Tralee. 1972. P. 162.

in his support, Russell was subsequently suspended from the IRA for three months. The action held the potential of completely upending McGarrity long term objective of launching attacks in Britain. However, what actually ended up happening was that it provided Clan na Gael with a major opportunity. For most of the 1930s the IRA had been drifting leftward politically and the start of the Spanish Civil War in the 1930s further accentuated the divide with more traditional physical force Republicans within the IRA. With Russell's suspension the most traditional conservative Republicans coalesced around Russell giving McGarrity and the Clan a foothold within the IRA that they had been lacking for most of the decade.

Russell was not the only major point of contact for Clan na Gael to the IRA during this time period. Peter Kearney was in regular contact with McGarrity and Tom McGill toured the country supporting Russell and his physical force agenda. Although McGarrity was firmly in support of the Russell faction of the IRA he also voiced deep frustration at the lack of unity within the movement. Despite having a major foothold within the Republican movement in Ireland McGarrity still realized that major obstacles confronted the Clan without the full cooperation of the Army Council.

With continuing political maneuvering in Ireland, the Clan also upped its efforts in the U.S. to gain broad support for a military campaign in Britain. McGarrity travelled to California in March of 1937 to address a public meeting in San Francisco. Contact was also made with the American Association for the Recognition of an Irish Republic in Los Angeles. This particular branch of the AARIR disassociated itself from the main national body in protest to De Valera's outlawing of the IRA the previous year. The campaign in the U.S. was further escalated with the arrival of Sean Russell in June. The west coast, particularly California, seems to have been the center of focus of Clan efforts. With Clan na Gael assistance Russell moved extensively on speaking engagements and publicity tours in California as the group hoped to take advantage of Irish-American disgruntlement toward the De Valera government in Ireland.

The efforts of Clan na Gael in both the U.S. and Ireland was beginning to have practical results on the ground. During a British royal visit to Belfast in July 1937 a bomb was detonated a few streets away from the event. That same summer elements of the IRA attacked border customs posts with gunshots and setting fire to a number of others near Clones in County Monaghan. Attacks on the railroads between Dundalk and Belfast were also launched. McGarrity was quick to realize that events were starting to progress toward a major escalation in operations. In McGarrity's own words the attacks "gave the world to understand that neither British kings nor British borders will be tolerated in Ireland". By the end of 1937 the fortunes of Clan na Gael was improving as military efforts in Ireland started to show results and fundraising in the US began to increase. Four new Clan na Gael clubs were also formed in Pittsburg, Cincinnati, Detroit and Los Angeles[185].

It was the IRA under the direction of Clan that made the first contacts with Nazi Germany. As early as 1936 leading IRA figure Andy Cooney travelled to Germany with his wife and was the first to suggest collaboration between Irish Republicans and the Nazi regime against Britain[186]. Sean Russell soon followed this initial contact in October 1936 when he wrote to the German ambassador in the U.S. showing a willingness for future cooperation should any conflict arise between Germany and Britain. McGarrity played a major role in facilitating this contact and indicates that the Clan have been in very early contact with the Nazi regime, possibly even before Conney's trip to Germany in 1936[187].

Oscar Phaus, journalist and founder of the German Bund in America was approached by the Abwehr, the German military intelligence service, to establish links between the IRA and Ireland. On a visit to Ireland in February 1938 to meet with leading IRA figures Phaus became acquainted with Seamus O'Donovan, a leading IRA explosives expert. Both men struck up a relationship and from that point onward O'Donovan became the main contact point for the Nazi regime in Ireland. Although O'Donovan would visit Germany from April to August of 1939 and make a request for arms

185 Wilk, Gavin. Transatlantic Defiance – The Militant Irish Republican Movement in America, 1923-45. Manchester University Press. Manchester. 2014. P. 127-129.

186 O'Donoghue, David. The Devil's Deal – The IRA, Nazi Germany, and the Double Life of Jim O'Donovan. New Island publishers. Dublin. 2010. P. 112.

187 Hanley, Brian. 2005. "Oh here's to Adolph Hitler"? The IRA and the Nazis. History Ireland. Vol. 13 (Issue 3).

in October no arms shipments would be forthcoming. The thinking at the highest levels of the German government was that if they were seen to be sending arms to the IRA it may jeopardize Irish neutrality and even bring Britain into the war earlier that the Nazis were planning. It was becoming apparent that Clan na Gael and the IRA were not going to get what they needed from the Nazi relationship and that Germany was beginning to see the IRA as little more than a nuisance factor that would barely distract Britain in its upcoming confrontation in Europe and not worth the overall efforts in assisting in any meaningful way[188]. In the upcoming bombing campaign, it would be the IRA and Clan na Gael very much by themselves.

The growing influence of the Russell faction and the successful support of Clan na Gael meant that by the 1938 IRA Convention the militant wing held the majority on the Executive. Russell's reinstatement as Chief of Staff saw a collapse of opposition within the IRA as some members left the organization or just refused to recognize his authority. Although this is some ways weakened the IRA is had also had the advantage from Clan na Gael's perspective of making the organization, with lack of internal opposition, more cohesive behind the upcoming campaign. McGarrity astute political maneuvering brought to fruition his plan of gaining control through Russell of IRA policy and direction. On 7 May 1938, Russell reported to the Clan leadership – "We are now in a position to say that we are getting right down to our work. exception of Cork, parts of Kerry, and one of the Dublin units, the whole organization is working smoothly. Moss and Jack McNeela have just returned from an inspection of units in Britain and have made a first-class job there. In two weeks, we are sending Jack McNeela to take complete charge".

In an undated letter, probably in the later part of 1938, Russell wrote a letter to McGarrity stating "unless something unforeseen turns up we shall start our working according to date and plan. We have now three men whole time in Britain as there is much work to be done". The wheels were now set in motion for a bombing campaign that would mark the last major controlling influence that the Clan would have on militant Irish Republicanism[189].

188   Coogan, Pat, Tim. The IRA. London. Harper/Collins publisher. 1995. P. 212-214.
189   Cronin, Sean. The McGarrity Papers. Anvil Books. Tralee. 1972. P. 165.

The launch date for what would become known as the "S-Plan" began on 12 January 1939. Precise instructions were issued to IRA units involved. These instructions revolved around the type of targets which included public transport utilities, armament factories, newspaper organizations, commercial premises and specific industrial plants. Interestingly enough no attacks were to take place in Northern Ireland with the intention that such actions may antagonize public opinion[190].

There were some initial advantages the IRA campaign would have had at the beginning of their campaign. Ample funding from Clan na Gael in the U.S. would certainly have facilitated the organizational aspect of the upcoming campaign providing transport, bomb materials and housing for those involved. Although Russell's public pronouncements a few years earlier on the upcoming campaign British intelligence services would have been stretched to maximum capacity monitoring German infiltration and focusing on intelligence gathering in Europe on the Nazi threat. As a result, their resources would certainly have been stretched with the IRA being of comparatively low priority. The IRA units involved would have been able to have moved relatively freely and without suspicion among the wider British populace. The presence of Irish immigrants in Britain had been a common feature for generations as many sought employment in England's major industrial centers. In some cases, certain IRA members may have even been able to feign English accents to disguise their Irish identity completely while also using fake names and documents. Despite these initial advantages the overall estimation of the IRA during this period was of an organization with a loose structure, lack of training and of rudimentary military capability[191]. If added to this was a lack of political support in Ireland and within Irish public opinion, while certainly not pro-British, was in no way inclined to alliances with a fascist foreign power.

On 12 January the IRA Army Council sent an ultimatum to the British Foreign Secretary which stated – "I have the honor to inform you that the government of the Irish Republic, having as its first duty towards its people

---

190   McKenna, Joseph. The IRA Bombing Campaign Against Britain, 1939-1940. McFarland & Company. Jefferson. 2016. P. 20.
191   Smith, M.L.R. Fighting for Ireland – The Military strategy of the Irish Republican Movement. Routledge. London. 1997. P. 63.

the establishment and maintenance of peace and order here, demand the withdrawal of all British armed forces stationed in Ireland. The occupation of our territory by troops of another nation and the persistent subvention here of activities directly against the expressed national will and in the interests of a foreign power, prevent the expansion and development of our institution in consonance with our social needs and purposes, and must cease.

The Government of the Irish Republic believe that a period of four days is sufficient notice for your government to signify its intentions in the matter of the military evacuation and for the issue of your Declaration of Abdication in respect of our country. Our government reserves the right of appropriate action without further notice if upon the expiration of this period of grace these conditions remain unfulfilled"[192].

The fact that Joseph McGarrity wrote the proclamation indicated the central role he and Clan na Gael had played in bringing the campaign to this point. In reading the declaration Clan na Gael and the IRA never really believed in a voluntary British withdrawal and fully expected the bombing campaign to commence on the pre-planned date. The time given of four days to even discuss the IRA ultimatum with the British government preparing for what many saw as the inevitable upcoming war against Germany was also never realistic. The entire document seemed little more than a "polite' formality.

The Clan na Gael leadership under McGarrity's influence were fully prepared for the inevitable British response to the ultimatum. In actuality the British government choose to ignore it altogether and did not even respond. When the first news started to arrive on 16 January of five bomb attacks in London and three attacks in Manchester, targeting such things as a power station and principal water mains, McGarrity was delighted with the news. He fully intended that while the campaign continued in Britain that Clan na Gael would not remain idle in the U.S. With media outlets attributing the attacks in Britain to communists McGarrity was quick to correct such mistakes by informing media outlets that it was the IRA that was responsible along with its Irish-American support network.

192   Bell, Bowyer. The Secret Army – The IRA. Routledge. London. 2017. P. 166.

As the IRA bombing campaign continued into July of 1939 with attacks on infrastructure targets such as public transport, electricity supply, gas mains as well as arson attacks on economic targets such as department stores the British government decided to take draconian action. At this point Britain had given an ultimatum to Germany in relation to Polish security and vowed war should Hitler invade. World War two was just weeks away and Britain intended to eliminate the IRA threat as soon as possible. In February, as a result of a raid on the home of IRA member Michael O'Shea, the British government discovered documents showing the full outline and extent of the S-Plan. The British parliament passed what became known as the Prevention of Violence Bill which gave the British Police and intelligence services wide powers to arrest and detain IRA suspects[193].

As British intelligence ramped up their efforts along with increased coordination with local police forces arrests and disruption of IRA operations began to mount. Increased monitoring of Irish communities in Britain as well as strict controls of movement of people between Britain and Ireland was put in place. Even those who were merely suspected of IRA connections without actual evidence were issued expulsion orders. As a result of this approach a total of 119 people were deported and 14 people prevented from entering Britain at all.

Increased infiltration of the IRA as well as British government coordination with the De Valera government also began to have an impact on the IRA campaign. One prime example of these intelligence successes were when in a single night the entire Liverpool unit was arrested in one large, coordinated police swoop[194]. The Irish government were beginning to take the IRA threat seriously. The main reason was the expected outbreak of World War 2 in Europe and the threat the bombing campaign would have on Irish neutrality. Release of classified documents showed De Valera as accepting assistance from the British government in smearing Sean Russell as a communist agent[195]. The IRA had no longer a safe haven

193   Tarpey, Veronica, Marie. The Role of Joseph McGarrity in the Struggle for Irish Independence. Arno press. New York. 1976. P. 328-330.
194   McKenna, Joseph. The IRA Bombing Campaign Against Britain, 1939-1940. McFarland & Company. Jefferson. 2016. P. 82.
195   Available Online <https://www.bbc.com/news/world-12848272>

in Ireland from which to operate with the introduction of internment under the Emergency Powers Act of 1939. Under the act the Irish government was also given power to implement censorship of the press and mail service. These factors did a great deal to hamper communication between IRA units in Britain and headquarters back in Ireland[196].

Remarkably, considering that a major bombing campaign was in progress in Britain, the IRA Chief of Staff, Sean Russell decided on 8 April to conduct a propaganda and fundraising tour of the U.S. under the guidance and support of Clan na Gael. On 6 May Russell spoke at the Clan na Gael Convention. Russell was presented to the audience as "responsible for a resurgent Irish army in history's annals.... which has made a page of history so glorious that, in history's annals, it is possibly unmatched".

McGarrity personally accompanied Russell on his tour of the U.S. which included even west coast cities as far afield as San Francisco. Throughout the tour both men were under the constant surveillance of the FBI at the request of Scotland Yard in Britain. The growing links between the Roosevelt administration and the British government in the face of Nazi Germany starts to become ever more apparent in these increased monitoring the activities of Clan na Gael. FBI intelligence indicated that the main purpose of the visit to San Francisco was to link up with prominent east coast Germans with Nazi links. The main purpose of such a meeting was apparently to discuss the following – 1. Assassination of visiting British Royalty. 2. Sabotage campaign of British shipping docking at U.S. ports on the west coast. 3. Launching a coordinated anti-British campaign in the U.S. detrimental to American foreign policy interests.

As the Russell tour continued it was becoming more apparent that the Roosevelt administration was becoming more hostile to the visit based on its impact on Anglo-American relations and on the rising danger of Nazi Germany. This came to a head when in September of 1939, Russell was issued with an expulsion order which stated he had to "depart from the United States to any country of his choice". With the almost certainty of being arrested and interred on his return to Ireland Russell decided to

---

196   Coogan, Pat, Tim. De Valera – Long Fellow, Long Shadow. Arrow Books. London. 1995. P. 522-526.

leave for Germany. With the invasion of Britain being an early Nazi plan on the outbreak of WW2 Russell was seen as a potential asset and therefore allowed entry into the country[197].

Before returning to events in Ireland one must ask as to why Russell choose this critical point of the bombing campaign to be out of contact with operations in Britain where leadership and direction was in desperate need? Defenders of Russell argue that being out of Ireland removed him from the danger of being arrested and that his presence in the U.S. was essential for propaganda and fundraising efforts in order to prolong the campaign and to maximize the propaganda results. Detractors of Russell's absence during this time period argue that as Chief of Staff he at least symbolically needed to be seen at the forefront directing operations as IRA men risked death and long imprisonments during active operations. The reality was that Russell's presence in Ireland during this period would have had little practical impact on the outcome of the campaign. His presence in the U.S., which the Clan hoped to produce a fundraising boost which indeed it did, also bought down the political wrath of the Roosevelt administration and FBI upon the Clan who were to be monitored closely for the duration of World War Two therefore hampering any efforts to impact events in Ireland at least in the short term.

During the course of the Russell saga in the U.S. the situation was deteriorating rapidly for any prospects for success for the IRA and Clan na Gael's bombing campaign in Britain. The situation became inextricably worse with a disastrous bomb attack in Coventry on 25 August 1939. On that day the IRA carried out a bomb attack on economic targets in the city one of which was the busy shopping center at the heart of the city. At 2.32 p.m. a bomb was detonated which ended up killing five civilians and causing major damage of nearby businesses. The attack was particularly callous with no advance warning and seemingly with the intend of causing maximum casualties considering where the attack took place[198].

---

197   Tarpey, Veronica, Marie. The Role of Joseph McGarrity in the Struggle for Irish Independence. Arno press. New York. 1976. P. 331-334.

198   McKenna, Joseph. The IRA Bombing Campaign Against Britain, 1939-1940. McFarland & Company. Jefferson. 2016. P. 92.

In the days, weeks and months prior to the Coventry attack the British police and security services was starting to have real successes in dismantling the IRA infrastructure in Britain. Arrests and raids over the time period resulted in increased intelligence on IRA movements and operations within the country. The police were quick to pick up the IRA members involved in the attack in Coventry. On 5 September all four IRA operatives involved were charged and trials began 11 December 1939. The trial lasted a mere four days, with witnesses and police intelligence reports giving pretty conclusive evidence against those involved[199]. Of the five IRA members tried only two ended up being convicted of murder, James McCormack and Peter Barnes. Both men were sentenced to death and subsequently hanged on 7 February 1940. The remaining three were convicted as abetting in the attack and received long prison sentences.

Prior to the executions of Barnes and McCormack Clan na Gael commenced a public campaign to pressure the US government to appeal to Britain for a reprieve for both men. During this time McGarrity had close personal contact with Congressman James McGranery who was the Clan's access to President Roosevelt. Roosevelt responded with apprehension in getting involved in such an emotionally charged case and believed the issue "too hot a matter to touch". Roosevelt was still walking the tightrope of building a close alliance with Britain in the now inevitable upcoming war in Europe as well as not trying to antagonize the isolationist Irish-American vote in the U.S.

With no forthcoming support from Roosevelt the Clan turned their attention to Congress where they commenced a letter writing campaign to members. McGarrity voiced to the Clan executive Con O'Brien "even if one or two get up in the house and voice a protest it is bound to have a good effect". The letter writing campaign as well as public protests ended in producing a resolution introduced by Democratic Congressman Thomas A. Flaherty requesting that President Roosevelt appeal to the British government to commute the two death sentences. Roosevelt at this point was under growing pressure to maintain the balance in his increasingly

---

199   McKenna, Joseph. The IRA Bombing Campaign Against Britain, 1939-1940. McFarland & Company. Jefferson. 2016. P. 99-129.

pro- British relationship as well as the crucial Irish-American base of his own party. As a result Roosevelt sent a letter to the British ambassador in London requesting a reprieve of six months to look further at the case. In his communication with the ambassador Roosevelt stated his concern as to the effect of the executions on Irish groups in the US and what effect this may have on a future alliance with the growing threat of Nazi Germany. The official British response to Roosevelt's request came from the Home Secretary, John Anderson. He stated simply "Commutation would not be justifiable". British public outrage was just too great. Just one day later on 7 February, both Barnes and McCormack were executed.

As word reached the U.S. of the executions the Clan already had plans in place for wide scale mobilization. Along with other Irish-American organizations the Clan helped organize a gathering at the New York's Irish Pavilion of the World's Fair. Both executed IRA men were commemorated with the Irish flag being lowered to half-mast. The fact that a mere one hundred people attended the event showed a major decline in the Clan's influence to mobilize and garner Irish American support. Although other Clan na Gael protests took place in other cities such as San Francisco it never reached the level of mass mobilization as that seen in the aftermath of the 1916 Rising and the ensuing executions.

The aftermath of the executions saw continued IRA bombings in Birmingham and London with the final attack taking place on 18 March 1940, with a bomb going off at a rubbish dumb in London. It was in many ways a fitting end to a campaign that achieved nothing in bringing about the expulsion of Britain from the north of Ireland. In total the campaign involved 300 explosions, 10 deaths and 96 injuries[200]. A total of 67 IRA members were convicted to lengthy prison terms. Those who evaded arrest made their ways back to Ireland to find themselves in many cases under government surveillance or interned for the duration of World War Two. The Irish Free State was to prove almost as hostile to the IRA as mainland Britain or Northern Ireland[201].

---

200   McKenna, Joseph. The IRA Bombing Campaign Against Britain, 1939-1940. McFarland & Company. Jefferson. 2016. P. 138-143.

201   Tarpey, Veronica, Marie. The Role of Joseph McGarrity in the Struggle for Irish Independence. Arno press. New York. 1976. P. 338.

The failure of the bombing campaign, however, did not have the impact of forcing McGarrity and Russell to change strategy and look at other, if any, options that were available. By May 1940 Russell had made his way to Germany to cooperate with the intelligence wing of the German military, the Abwehr, for possible assistance to an IRA campaign in Ireland aimed against Northern Ireland. The entire plan was nipped in the bud early on when German agent Hermann Goertz was discovered only days after parachuting into Ireland and promptly arrested. In his possession was found a wireless transmitter, $20,000 and documents of what was described by authorities as being of a "military character".

In January 1940, as a part of the overall plan, McGarrity made his way to Italy where he met with German consular officials in Genoa. During the course of the meeting McGarrity managed to persuade the Germans to secretly transport Russell to the U.S. and from there to Ireland, in order to increase pressure on the Germans McGarrity lied to them by falsely claiming that Russell still had a valid U.S. passport that was about to expire. After lengthy internal debate the German Abwehr and Foreign Ministry they agreed to transport Russell to the U.S. For McGarrity it was imperative to have Russell back in Ireland because it was through Russell that McGarrity and Clan na Gael could exercise the most influence on the IRA. Once Russell reached New York it was a relatively easy matter through the Clan's extensive network that included the Maritime Union to get Russell hired as a fireman on the SS Washington. In late April Russell left for Ireland[202].

As the plan progressed with the Clan's hope of revitalizing the IRA in Ireland McGarrity's health took a turn for the worse. McGarrity was suffering from incurable cancer of the throat. In a letter written in February 1940 to a close friend McGarrity confided "The doctor gives me a very adverse report". Just a month later he admitted to James Brisbane, the Secretary of the Executive of Clan na Gael, that his condition was "very, very sad, a condition that forces me to abandon all activities, even that which is

202 ǀ Wilk, Gavin. Transatlantic Defiance – The Militant Irish Republican Movement in America, 1923-45. Manchester University Press. Manchester. 2014. P162-166.

dearest to my heart, the struggle for the independence of our loved Ireland".
Joseph McGarrity died at his home in Philadelphia on 5 August 1940[203].

Just nine days after McGarrity's death Sean Russell died. While being
transported on a German U-boat back to Ireland Russell had complained of
severe stomach pains and died suddenly. According to Russell's brother he
had suffered from severe stomach issues for years and most likely died of a
burst gastric ulcer. Russell was buried at sea and the operation abandoned[204].

The death of both men, particularly McGarrity, marked the end of
an era for Clan na Gael. Never again would Clan na Gael have such direct
control of events in Ireland or such a level of control over the actions of
the IRA. McGarrity was a monumental figure in the Clan, second only
to John Devoy. His death marked a loss of a driving force that would be
particularly noticeable for the remainder of World War Two up and until
the mid to late 1960s when the Clan struggled to find any voice or role for
itself within Irish Republicanism. It did not help that the IRA in Ireland
was a spent force in the aftermath of the failed bombing campaign and suffered severe repression both in the Irish Free State and Northern Ireland.

The situation in the U.S. was not much better for Clan na Gael. The
U.S. entry into World War Two in the aftermath of the attack on Pearl
Harbor and the subsequent declaration of War by Germany forced Clan
na Gael into facing a new wave of American patriotism that challenged
then Clan's trans-Atlantic allegiance to an armed struggle against a major
U.S. ally in the form of Britain. For some of the older members of the organization it must have seemed in many ways a repeat of World War One.

As a consequence of U.S. entry into World War Two Clan na Gael had
to curtail their revolutionary activity to such an extent that during their national convention in 1943 the Executive of the organization FBI, who more
closely monitored Clan activities after 1941 stated that the Clan "dropped
much of its militant, anti-British attitude". Such close surveillance by the
FBI, a growing alliance with Britain in the war against Nazi Germany and
an increase in public pro-British sentiment as well as a crippled IRA back

---

203   Tarpey, Veronica, Marie. The Role of Joseph McGarrity in the Struggle for Irish
      Independence. Arno press. New York. 1976. P. 337-340.

204   Coogan, Pat, Tim. The IRA. London. Harper/Collins publisher. 1995. P. 211.

in Ireland left the Clan almost completely handicapped for the duration of the War. As the war progressed and Nazi atrocities became more publicly known the Clan made no further attempt to renew contacts for any operations in Ireland for fear of public outcry and in some cases as a result of moral compunction.

The only flurry of activity that occurred during World War Two was the sentencing to death of six IRA members for the shooting dead of Royal Ulster Constabulary officer in Dungannon, County Tyrone in the Summer of 1942. The Clan jumped at the opportunity at making itself once again relevant to events in Ireland and within the broader Irish American community. Organized protests occurred in the forms of letter writing campaign to elected officials and to other Irish American organizations. The Clan's significant efforts to make outreach and alliances with other Irish American organizations such as the Ancient Order of Hibernians and the American Association for the recognition of an Irish Republic in many ways was a recognition that Clan na Gael was no longer the organization that is once was and needed to build and be part of a broader coalition in order to have any impact on events in Ireland.

The U.S. State Department indicated concern over the handling of the issue that it would create "very wide and unquestionably undesirable publicity". The concern was so great that Secretary of State Sumner Welles expressed to the American ambassador in London "urgent hope that that the death penalty be commuted to imprisonment", and that the U.S. government should intercede. The Irish Minister in Washington Robert Brennan also communicated to the U.S. State Department the very real likelihood of "serious trouble" should the executions proceed.

The year 1942 was a year of great danger for the Allies in Europe. The Soviet Union was in a life and death struggle with the Nazis in Eastern Europe and the Siege of Leningrad was on a knife edge. With the real possibility of a Soviet defeat and the Germans being able to move their eastern armies back west would mean that an invasion, or least a full-scale siege, of Britain was a real possibility. Under such circumstances the growing Anglo-American alliance, particularly for the British, became vitally important. As a result, the British relented in the cases of the impending IRA executions by commuting the death sentence of five of the six. The execution of

Thomas Williams was the only one that would proceed. On 2 September Williams was executed at Crumlin Road jail in Belfast. Very little protest followed in the aftermath. Although the IRA threatened retaliation nothing ever materialized. Many Catholics benefited from the war time economy, although widespread and institutionalized discrimination confined most to low paying employment. Also, fear of sectarian backlash and a return of sectarian pogroms of the early 1920s kept many nationalists from expressing themselves politically through visible protest[205].

FBI pressure intensified on Clan na Gael as the war progressed. A particular focus of their attentions were Connie Neenan. Neenan was a leading IRA figure from the War of Independence and on the anti-Treaty side during the Civil War which followed. He relocated to the U.S. in 1926 where he became an active member within Clan na Gael[206]. It was discovered that Neenan operated under the alias of Con Collins in many of the Clan's communications which only increased the FBI's interest even further, particular that of J. Edgar Hoover. On 23 April 1943, knowing he was on the FBI's radar and possibly facing the real possibility of deportation Neenan offered himself up to the FBI. During the course of the interview Neenan offered to fully cooperate with the FBI by providing "information concerning his activities or activities of the Irish organizations in New York City. Neenan had essentially turned into an FBI informant on Clan na Gael internal workings.

J. Edgar Hoover would describe Neenan as a "highly confidential source which in the past has proved accurate and reliable" although never mentioning his name. The insight given by Neenan in the following years was to be the most comprehensive look into the operations and ideology of Clan na Gael ever seen by the U.S. government. A detailed structure of the Clan as well as its relationship with the IRA, fund raising operations and gun running operations over the years gave the FBI an account of an organization that ran a transatlantic revolutionary operation for decades right under the nose of the U.S. government. Although Neenan gave a lot

---

205   Wilk, Gavin. Transatlantic Defiance – The Militant Irish Republican Movement in America, 1923-45. Manchester University Press. Manchester. 2014. P. 174-176.

206   Wilk, Gavin. Transatlantic Defiance – The Militant Irish Republican Movement in America, 1923-45. Manchester University Press. Manchester. 2014. P. 32.

of technical details of operations and historical information he did not give any details or information implicating existing members of the Clan. A State Department official went so far as to say Neenan's information contained "very little that was new or of special interest". In some ways Neenan seems to have played the FBI by seeming to cooperate while at the same time doing little of any harm to Clan na Gael in the U.S. One wonders in some ways if the entire exercise was orchestrated in advance by Clan leadership in order to deflect increasing FBI pressure on the organization. After all, Neenan left out many critical details concerning the Clan's relationship and interactions with Nazi Germany[207].

The World War Two era ended with Clan na Gael in a much weaker position that it had entered the period. The disastrous partnership with the IRA in the bombing campaign in Britain was highlighted by the fact that not only was it a total failure but the movement was so decimated by arrests and political repression in Ireland and Britain that it would be almost sixteen years before the IRA would be in a position to launch another armed campaign. The death of Joseph McGarrity was also a major blow. The movement in the aftermath of his death now lacked the direction and driving force that McGarrity's personality and sheer willpower brought to Clan na Gael. World War Two brought to the organization the attention of the State Department and the FBI in a way never seen before. Prior to World War Two Clan na Gael was seen more as an internal political lobbying organization. It was not, however, regarded as an active threat to national security. The Clan's willingness to cooperate with a regime as extreme and as anti-American as Nazi Germany changed that perception. From that point onward the FBI would have the organization on its radar making such operations in the past such as fundraising and arms smuggling much more difficult.

Another feature of World War Two which is often overlooked during this time period in relation to the decline of Clan na Gael and Trans-Atlantic Irish nationalism in general is the role the conflict played in the greater integration of Irish-Americans into mainstream U.S. society.

---

207 Wilk, Gavin. *Transatlantic Defiance – The Militant Irish Republican Movement in America, 1923-45*. Manchester University Press. Manchester. 2014. P. 176-181.

Many Irish-Americans fought in World War Two both in the Pacific and in Europe. Just like in World War One this led to greater acceptance within the American mainstream both culturally and economically. Two major events relating directly to Ireland also increased American identity for many Irish Americans, Irish neutrality and De Valera's letter of condolence to Germany after the death of Hitler.

Although the Irish Free State was officially neutral in World War Two and refused to allow British use of its ports during the war De Valera and his government most certainly showed favoritism to Britain during the conflict. Such examples included the arrests and internments of German spies and downed pilots. The German embassy was also under close observation. At the same time British pilots were returned to Britain and intelligence was freely exchanged between both nations. In the U.S. this was not widely known among Irish Americans who viewed Irish neutrality as contrary to American security and national interests.

Much more damaging to Irish-American connections to Ireland was De Valera's unprecedented visit to the German Minister in Dublin and his offering of condolence on behalf of the Irish nation to the German people on the news of the death of Adolph Hitler. For De Valera this was a reassertion of Irish independence and a deliberate and intentional insult toward Britain. De Valera's Anglophobia was well known and predated by many years the Irish War of independence. Despite his intentions the move was a disastrous public relations exercise. By the end of World War Two the genocidal nature of Hitler's Nazi regime was well known and reported, especially in the U.S. In the European theatre American forces suffered a total of 552,117 casualties which included 104,812 killed. Irish neutrality during the war and De Valera's condolences on Hitler's death alienated many Irish Americans and highlighted a deepening disconnection to the U.S. at the expense of political connections to Irish nationalism.

Other social factors played a role in diminishing the role and power of Irish American nationalism during and in the years after World War Two. For much of the history of Irish America the social status of most was that of working class and unskilled laborers with a large Irish presence in the police force of many northern cities such as New York and Boston. World War Two offered many economic opportunities for Irish Americans to improve their financial status and move out of ethnic enclaves into more suburban neighborhoods. For Clan na Gael this resulted in a loss of power and influence on the Irish American vote as other ethnic groups moved in. The diminishing once powerful Irish urban political machines were becoming a thing of the past as was the Clan's ability to exert political influence at the highest levels of American society.

As a final point and perhaps as important as any previously mentioned was the Anglo- American relationship during and after World War Two. At the end of World War Two the U.S. and Britain would form a political and military alliance based not just on the shared experience of fighting together in the war but also in the emergence of the Cold War and the growing threat of the Soviet Union. Both countries formed bonds that would last until the end of the century and beyond. The issue of Northern Ireland that would emerge periodically within Irish American nationalism would be confined to the arena of "an internal British matter" until Bill Clinton's involvement in the Good Friday Agreement in 1998. World War Two led to the further disengagement of many Irish Americans from the issue of partition in Ireland and what Clan na Gael considered the unresolved national question. The immediate years ahead looked bleak indeed from the Clan's political perspective[208].

208 Tully, Day, John. Ireland and Irish Americans, 1932-1945. Irish Academic Press. Dublin. 2010. P. 134-40.

CHAPTER 26

1945–1968 – Political Wilderness

At this point it is important to look more closely at Northern Ireland whose destruction as a political entity separate from the Irish Republic Clan na Gael was to dedicate itself to. It will also go far in explaining the IRA Border Campaign of 1956-62 and the explosion of violence that would result in the IRA's twenty-eight-year guerilla insurgency from 1969 to 1997 which Clan would play an important yet historically underappreciated role in.

The Northern Ireland parliament was established in 1921 as a result of the Government of Ireland Act passed in the previous year. Although part of the United Kingdom the new state would have a large amount of control of such things as local government and policing. In the years and decades that followed the British government in London largely ignored events in the province leaving almost all matters to the newly established parliament. As a result, little oversight over events and conditions that followed was ever provided leaving many on mainland Britain almost totally ignorant of growing and eventually violent Catholic nationalist discontent.

The early years of the Northern Ireland state saw nothing less that the establishment of a government apparatus of political suppression of the native Catholic minority as well as wide scale discrimination in employment and housing. The old Royal Irish Constabulary was abolished and replaced with the new Royal Ulster Constabulary and part-time B-Specials which were made up almost entirely of Protestant loyalists. In many cases there was a significant overlap in membership in the deeply sectarian Orange Order whose central purpose was to protect the supremacy of the Protestant establishment over what they saw as the racially and religiously inferior local Catholic population. Most Catholics either refused or were not allowed to join the new force that would act as the main instrument of the Parliament in Belfast in minimizing the social and political threat of Catholic opposition to the new state.

As the years passed many Catholics began to accept the reality of their situation and began to participate in the political process. However, major obstacles were put in place to minimize their voice in the new state. Primary among these barriers was the process of Gerrymandering which drew up electoral boundaries to favor the Protestant majority at the expense of the Catholic minority. A prime example of this process was seen in Derry City where although it held a significant Catholic majority most of the city council was made up of Protestant loyalists. Also, the ability to vote depended on one being a property owner or a primary tenant. This disproportionately affected the native Catholic population as they made up the majority of renters as many were too economically disadvantaged to own their own homes.

When it came to employment a similar policy of exclusion existed. Preferential treatment in hiring and promotions were given to Protestant loyalists while the lower skilled and lower paid employment was mainly confined to Catholics. In the area of public housing preferential treatment was also given to Protestants while Catholics in places such as the Bogside in Derry and in West Belfast were confined to what amounted to ghetto communities where amenities such as indoor plumbing was poor to nonexistent. By the 1940s the pattern of what amounted to a virtual one-party state was well entrenched with the RUC and B-Specials providing the armed wing of political enforcement[209].

The first stirrings of Irish nationalism both in Ireland and the U.S. in the aftermath of World War Two came with the Anti-Partition Campaign of 1948-51. De Valera used the opportunity of being out of power during the time period to visit the U.S. and promote what would become the long-standing Irish Republican belief that the six counties of Northern Ireland had been taken away unjustly from the rest of Ireland and that partition was in itself illegal as it was never consented to by popular vote[210].

---

209   Bardon, Jonathan. A History of Ulster. The Blackstaff Press. Belfast. 2005. P. 466-552.
210   Available online <https://journals.openedition.org/etudesirlandaises/2348>

By March 1948 when De Valera arrived in New York on the first stage of a world tour he no longer held the same aura as the young rebel President who toured the U.S. during the Irish War of Independence. Journalists who followed his nationwide tour never forgot Ireland's neutrality during World War Two as well as his extremely ill-advised visit of condolence to the German minister in Dublin in the aftermath of Hitler's suicide. As well as this the U.S. government was heading into the era of the Cold War with Britain being a central and important ally in the upcoming struggle with the Soviet Union.

Observations made by the British consulate in the U.S. during De Valera's tour are also quite telling. British diplomat David Gray observed that while he was apprehensive as to the possible impact of De Valera's visit to the U.S. "Well, I know believe it is negligible and will remain so while Britain is following the line she is pursuing". It was also observed that De Valera's tour received more media attention in Ireland than it did in the U.S. The idea of starting the world tour in the U.S. was that it was supposed to be the high point and gain world attention laying the foundation for a successful tour overall. The fact that the campaign never really took off in the very country that had the largest Irish population in the world outside of Ireland indicated a major decline in the political interest in partition and the Irish situation in general. Although many Irish Americans maintained cultural interest and contacts to their native home their political interests and allegiances were becoming ever more American. Clan na Gael played a periphery role overall during De Valera's visit. The split of earlier years still very much remained in the memories of both parties. The Clan's involvement would be nothing more than propagating and reinforcing the same message of anti-partition as De Valera espoused while at the same time having no direct involvement in the nationwide tour. This was a far cry from the revolutionary heyday of 1916-21. Eventually De Valera would end the anti-partition campaign in 1951 with no progress made toward a united Ireland[211].

---

211   Rogers, Silas, James; O'Brien, J., Matthew. After the Flood – Irish America, 1945-1960. Irish Academic Press. Dublin. 2009. P. 38-49.

For Clan na Gael and the IRA one overwhelming message came out of De Valera's ultimately futile attempt to end partition was that constitutional Republicanism would not achieve the end of partition and the violent revolution was as necessary as ever. The years 1951 to 1956 saw the IRA in Ireland start to reorganize and reemerge yet again as a force. A new influx of membership who were "young, dedicated and single-minded" was to become a feature of the newly emerging IRA. The proclamation of an Irish Republic in 1949 forced the IRA to move away from confrontation with the southern government and focus its energies entirely on undermining the Northern Ireland state.

The fact that the rearming of the IRA depended almost entirely on arms raids on British military installation in the north of Ireland and mainland Britain tells a lot of the weakened and ineffective role that Clan na Gael were to play in what would become known as "Operation Harvest" or more commonly as the "Border Campaign"[212]. A noteworthy exception to the Clan's direct military contribution was what would become known as the "Harrison Network". George Harrison was a veteran member of the IRA who had immigrated to the U.S. in 1938. Harrison would go on to join the U.S. Army and fight in WW2 on behalf on his newly adopted home. Harrison never forgot his homeland or the Republican struggle. Harrison became an active member of Clan na Gael sometime after leaving the army at the end of WW2. From the 1950s Harrison's contacts with the IRA deepened. It is very possible that Harrison's military background and possible contact with Irish American sympathizers within the U.S. military who would turn a blind eye to missing weapons was seen as a major asset. Clan na Gael's leadership would almost certainly have been aware of Harrison's actions and where possible would have facilitated smuggling operations with its extensive connections amongst port worker's unions. However, a certain distance would have been maintained in order to argue a plausible deniability should the entire operation be exposed to the FBI. Harrison's gunrunning career would last into the 1980s. Although never

212   Flynn, Barry. Soldiers of Folly. The Collins Press. Cork. 2009. P. 14-22.

fully established he seems to have been the main gunrunning contact point between Clan an Gael for the IRA[213].

During the IRA campaign that was to last from 1956-62 Clan na Gael's role was to be almost entirely confined to fundraising efforts in the U.S. through what it would call the "Freedom Fighter Fund". During this time period McCarthyism was rampant in the U.S. with any association with leftist organizations such as Labor Unions coming under deep scrutiny and suspicion. As stated earlier there was a significant overlap in membership between Clan na Gael and the Transport Workers Union in New York. Michael Quill, a leading figure within Clan na Gael, would eventually appear in front of the House of Un-American Activities Committee and forced to answer questions relating to his ties with the Communist Party[214]. With the Cold War heating up from the late 1940s onward any organization carrying the label "anti-imperialist", "anti-colonial" or in any way hostile to U.S. foreign allies immediately came under the radar of McCarthyism and the FBI under the ever vigilant and fervent anti-communist, J. Edgar Hoover.

Quill's notoriety as being on the left of the Labor movement in the U.S. put him under pressure to reassess his, and very likely the Clan's, re-lationship with the Communist Party and other far-left organizations in the U.S. over their possible ties and connections to Soviet influence and infiltration. Quill split with the Communist Party in 1949 purging many Communist Party members from the Union. Despite these measures his continued relationship with Clan na Gael and his growing support for the burgeoning Civil Rights movement in the 1950s kept him constantly on the radar of McCarthyism and the FBI and as a result Clan na Gael also. Such a claustrophobic and hostile political atmosphere with close state monitoring left very little room for maneuver for Clan na Gael during the IRA campaign of the late 1950s and early 60s. Such activity that did exist was relatively low-level propaganda efforts with fundraising that was equally ineffective.

213　Boyne, Sean. Gunrunners – The Covert Arms Trail to Ireland. The O'Brien Press. Dublin. 2006. P. 89-94.

214　Whittemore, L.H. The Man Who Ran the Subways. Holt, Reinehart and Winston. New York. 1968. P. 88-90.

The IRA campaign came to its almost inevitable end in 26 February 1962. The entire military campaign was marred by a romantic nationalist ideal that grossly oversimplified the obstacles the IRA faced in ending British rule in Northern Ireland. The tactics used were almost identical to that used during the War of Independence with the use of Flying Columns which attacked Police barracks and carried out a sabotage campaign against internal economic and transport targets such as bridges and railway lines. What was fundamentally different this time round was that the IRA operated within a mostly hostile Protestant community which did not offer safe havens and who were openly fundamentally opposed to the IRA campaign. Protestant loyalists, who were the majority community in Northern Ireland, remained steadfastly loyal to British rule and rallied in support of the RUC and B-Specials becoming the eyes and ears of the state security apparatus. Also, in most cases the IRA were poorly armed and trained in comparison to their adversaries. On an organizational level many IRA columns operated virtually independent of central control. IRA activity was also not evenly spread throughout Northern Ireland because of Protestant hostility and as a result often geographically limited to small areas where they received limited support. Sinn Fein, the political wing of the IRA, failed to build any political momentum on events. Part of the IRA and Sinn Fein failure can be attributed to very poor financial support which is a prime indicator on just how much Clan na Gael were struggling in the U.S. in their fundraising efforts.

The end of the campaign came with an IRA statement which stated – "The leadership of the Resistance Movement has ordered the termination of the Campaign of Resistance to British occupation launched on 12 December 1956. Instructions issued to Volunteers of the Active Service Units and of local Units in the occupied area have now been carried out. All arms and other material have been dumped and all full-time active service volunteers have been withdrawn...Foremost among the factors motivating this course of action has been the attitude of the general public whose minds have been deliberately distracted from the supreme issue facing the Irish people – the unity and freedom of Ireland. The Irish resistance movement renews its pledge of eternal hostility to the British Forces of Occupation in Ireland. It calls on the Irish people for increased support and looks forward with confidence – in co-operation with the other branches of the Republican Movement – to a period of consolidation, expansion and preparation for the final and victorious phase of the struggle for the full freedom of Ireland".

Operation Harvest of 1956-62 and its major failings was very well summed up by noted Irish journalist Eamon Mallie in his well-regarded book "The Provisional IRA" when he described the campaign as a – "Classic manifestation of the physical force tradition. All the energies of the participants had gone into military preparations, and almost no thought had been devoted to the political consequences of their actions. The insurgents had promised in their declaration of war "A new Ireland, upright and free" without offering the people of Ireland to whom they were constantly appealing, the slightest idea of what that state would be like".

The criticism put forward by Mallie can be applied to Clan na Gael in an even more critical manner. The IRA's disastrous campaign brought a lot of internal soul searching in the aftermath which was marked by a distinctive ideological drift to the left. The thinking behind this shift was that the only way forward was not through militarism buy through the working-class unity of both Protestants and Catholics. This left Clan na Gael in the extremely isolated position of fending off accusations in the U.S. of having communist leanings and now supporting a revolutionary movement in Ireland drifting potentially into the arms of world communism. The internal discussions and soul searching within the IRA was not reflected within Clan na Gael who remained steadfast in the traditional right leaning armed tradition of Irish Republicanism. While many within the IRA were coming face to face with the reality of a majority of Protestant loyalists in Northern Ireland and the monumental impediment this posed to ending partition the Clan's geographical and psychological distance meant they never had to face up to this obstacle. This political inflexibility and narrow political vision was a continuation of what Joseph McGarrity's leadership had started and a rejection of the John Devoy's ability to politically adapt to changing circumstances[215].

The years 1962-68 were not years of complete inactivity for Clan na Gael. Thanks to declassified FBI files from the time period we get an

---

215   Flynn, Barry. Soldiers of Folly. The Collins Press. Cork. 2009. P. 195-204.

insight into a movement struggling to stay relevant by remaining active in attempting to keep the issue of partition alive as a topic relevant to Irish America and to a much lesser extent American foreign policy in general.

At the end of 1963 Clan na Gael held their annual national convention. The Clan reasserted support for the IRA while at the same time conceding ever more authority to the organization. Resolutions were passed giving the IRA full control over financial support for the families of prisoners which previously had come directly from the Clan. The FBI seemingly had inside observers who afterward recommended that Clan na Gael register under the Foreign Agency Registration Act. The act stated that agents representing a foreign power in a political capacity had to disclose their relationship with the foreign power with information about related activities and finances[216]. Considering that this act was in place since 1938 it is quite remarkable that it took almost twenty-five years for the law to be applied to Clan na Gael who were an organization that hardly made a secret of their support of the IRA. The move by the U.S. government showed how far the role and political influence of Clan na Gael had declined as well as the growing Anglo-American relationship in the midst of the Cold War. It would also be safe to assume that pressure from the British Consulate also played a role during the period in making the final decision.

The continued drive to rebuild from the embers of the disastrous Border campaign was marked on 12 November 1963, with the visit of leading IRA commander Cathal Gould to Philadelphia to commemorate the contribution of the Irish Brigade who fought in the American Civil War. The event had the double benefit of reasserting Clan loyalty to the United States and at the same time acting as a moment of protest against British rule. The following is how it was reported by the Philadelphia Enquirer –

> "The Irish Republican Army kicked off a new organization drive here Monday in paying homage to the famed Irish Brigade that fought in the Civil War battle 100 years ago. But the activity was greeted officially with silence from the U.S. State Department and unofficially with behind the scenes protests. The reason is the Irish Republican Army is a revolutionary group. It is outlawed in Ireland.

216   Date: 04-18-2008. Classified by 60324 UC BAW/STF/TH. Declassified on: 25X 3.3(1) 04-18-2033

Undaunted, the group, headed by Cathal Goulding, a Dublin house painter, presented to Gettysburg Mayor William Weaver a replica of the Civil War Irish Brigade flag – a green banner with a golden harp emblazoned on it. "I'm here to organize Irish societies and Clan na Gael to aid the fight to free Ireland", Goulding declared. Gettysburg is the first of the communities he plans to visit in the next five months".

Goulding's visit, the 95th anniversary of Clan na Gael, as well as other events seems overall to have had a positive effect on the movement which is in itself somewhat remarkable so soon after the failed Border Campaign of the previous year. According to the Irish World newspaper based in New York – "The Clan is building constantly in the Philadelphia area, its membership has increased over 200 per cent in the past year. No doubt the dynamic activity of the American Committee for the Release of Irish Political Prisoners had a great deal to do with this upsurge. Reports from the major cities indicate that they too are gaining new strength".

In February of 1964, as a result of being registered as a foreign entity and a drift to the left by the IRA back in Ireland the Clan leadership seems to have made the decision to continue reasserting its American nationalist credentials when Secretary Michael O'Brien called for a national boycott of all British goods because of the country's continued trade with communist nations who were enemies of the U.S. Although the call had little effect it was a public statement of Clan allegiance to the U.S. and the country's national interest and security.

The 95th anniversary of the founding of Clan na Gale on 14 March 1964, gave the organization the opportunity to come together to celebrate achievements and to look at what direction the movement was heading. It became very clear that the event was a reassertion of American loyalty as the poem "The Worrying of the Green" written for the event indicates. In the poem we also see a deep sense of victimhood and a feeling of almost betrayal by the U.S. toward the cause of Irish nationalism –

The Worrying of the Green

Oh Paddy dear and did you hear The news that's going round,

The Clan na Gael is under wraps, In good old New York town.

No more the F.B.I shall seek The Nazi of the Red,

It concentrates on Irish now, Whose blood was freely shed.

In every war for freedom's cause, From Concord to Berlin;

Yet to strike a blow to free their own, Is now a grievous sin.

They are following the Fenians, While Commies wander free;

They're harassing conscientious men, While England plies the sea,

And ships her goods to Castro, Who sits right at our door.

We ask Lord Home to end the trade, He smirks and sends him more.

So guard the lamb, my minions, And let the lion roam;

You save a little patch of grass, But who protects the home[217]?

The strategy of trying to turn American public opinion against Britain had little overall effect. In more than one F.B.I internal memo from the time period references are made of an informant. Just how high ranking this person was and if there was more than one is uncertain. The F.B.I show a detailed insight into fundraising, the distribution of money raised as well as contacts between the IRA and Clan na Gael. The visit of Cathal Goulding and his tour of the U.S., is well documented. Despite F.B.I and British consulate concerns that Goulding was organizing aimed toward future operations as opposed to anything of an immediate nature. The period is also marked by pickets outside British consulates and intensive letter writing campaign of protest to the British consulate as well as leading Democratic party figures such as Aldai Stevenson[218].

By 1965 Clan na Gael activities were primarily confined to propaganda efforts involving public commemoration ceremonies, speeches and letter writing campaigns. By the F.B.I's own admission the organization posed little threat in terms of national security. However, events in Ireland in the next few years would accelerate Clan activity as Northern Ireland petered on the edge of a violent explosion.

The IRA in Northern Ireland in the years 1962-68 verged on the spectrum of irrelevant to almost non-existent. The failed Border Campaign and

217   Date:04-17-2008 BY 60324 UC BAW/STF/TH
218   Date: 04-18-2008 BY 60324 UC BAW.STF.TH

the drift of many IRA members to the left of Irish Republican ideology left the organization adrift in a sea of irrelevancy for most northern Catholics. A new and younger generation looked for a political alternative that provided a way out of the sectarian quagmire they found themselves in and also a way to move on from the violent past that was such a hallmark of recent Irish history.

Two advances, one in the area of media, the other a large-scale political movement unrelated to Ireland in the U.S., were to have profound effects on Northern Ireland. The advent and growing popularity of the television meant that more people than ever had access to TV and images from around the world brought events into people's living rooms. One international event that was paid particular attention to by the Catholic youth of Northern Ireland as well as socialists, communists and left leaning IRA members was the burgeoning civil rights movement in the United States.

The sight of African Americans and liberal white supporters marching in demand of the right to vote, the end to racial discrimination and Jim Crow laws ignited a younger generation of native Catholic activism into emulating the inspiring images they were seeing on their TV screens and reporting they we're seeing from British and Irish news media on events in the U.S. The creation of the Northern Ireland Civil Rights Association in 1967 brought under its umbrella a wide spectrum of political activists from a minority of old IRA veterans of the Border Campaign, Communists, Socialists, Anarchists, Labor Unions, Trotskyites, the Catholic Church and Student organizations. At no time was the IRA ever to play any central or significant role in the overall Civil rights movement. The objective for the majority of activists was to bring about reform of the Northern Ireland state, not its destruction.

Just like the Civil Rights movement in the U.S. civil rights activists in the north of Ireland emulated the tactics and strategy of bringing attention to discrimination by carrying out high profile marches, protests and sit-ins. Instead of seeing this new organization for what it was, a movement for reform, the Loyalist government in Stormont saw it as nothing less than an IRA inspired conspiracy to overthrow the Northern state. The response very much mirrored that of such individuals as "Bull" Connor in the U.S. with mass arrests and the savage beatings of protestors. The most notorious such incident was when the RUC joined forces with loyalist protestors and attacked a civil rights march at Burntollet Bridge in January, 1969. The images of police joining with sectarian protestors was sent around the country and the world and ignited mass protests. The impact of these developments on the IRA and Clan na Gael in the U.S. was to have momentous consequences[219].

219   Purdie, Bob. Politics in the Streets – The origins of the civil rights movement in Northern Ireland. The Blackstaff press. Belfast. 1990. P. 121-157.

CHAPTER 27

Clan na Gael and the Northern Ireland Conflict

As Ireland commenced down the road of a long and agonizing twenty-eight years of conflict Clan na Gael found itself in a dilemma not totally dissimilar to that of the 1930s. The IRA was in a weak political and military position at the start of what would become known as the Troubles. More consequential, however, was the distinct drift of the Republican movement in Ireland toward Marxist ideology in the years after the end of the failed Border Campaign. Considering the domestic situation in the U.S. with the heightened Cold War tensions as well as the ongoing war in Vietnam against communist forces the Clan was put in a very precarious position. The situation was made distinctly more clear and easier when a major split occurred within the IRA and Sinn Fein in 1969.

The split was as much a result of a generational difference as it was ideological. A new and younger generation of Irish Republicans had become increasingly radicalized during the course of the late 1960s and the failure of the civil rights movement and the vicious and violent state response pushed many toward reverting back to the traditional armed Republicanism. The older ranks of the IRA maintained that progress could only made through working class grass root political activism and pointed to the failures of earlier armed campaigns. The IRA leadership at this point began to be seriously undermined by brutal sectarian rioting which saw thousands of Catholics burned out of their homes, often with the assistance of local RUC. Soon murals began to appear on walls in places like west Belfast saying such things as "I.R.A – I Ran Away". Many in vulnerable Catholic communities who felt under siege both from a sectarian and hostile police force and violent loyalist mobs, often working hand in hand, were crying out for help. In December of 1969 the IRA and Sinn Fein split into what would become known as the Official IRA who would maintain its Marxist ideology and at times be dragged into violent conflict and the new Provisional IRA which carried on the traditional credo of Republican armed resistance to British rule. It would be the Provisional movement that Clan na Gael would now gravitate toward in giving its support to in the emerging bloody years ahead[220]. The new Provisional movement was also quick to acknowledge the importance of Clan na Gael and very soon made contact through Sean MacStiofain, a leading figure in the newly formed movement. Ideologically both movements were inseparable.

The early years of the Troubles was introduced to an Irish American audience primarily through images on a TV screen and written articles in newspapers. It is fair to say that many were caught off guard completely and had little understanding of the complicated nature of Northern Irish society. Clan na Gael's propaganda efforts sought to exploit the knowledge gap by portraying the conflict as a continuation of the Irish struggle against British imperial rule. The fact that the majority of people in the north of Ireland were Protestant and loyal to the British monarchy was conveniently left out of the discussion. To have done otherwise would have complicated the messaging and propaganda efforts.

During this tumultuous time period another organization was created that would go on to compete with Clan na Gael and overshadow it somewhat in the public imagination as the Provisional IRA and Sinn Fein's main fundraising organization in the United States. The Northern Ireland Aid Committee was formed in 1969 by old IRA veteran Michael Flannery. Although NORAID would always deny being a fundraising body for the Provisional IRA it was widely believed by both British and U.S. intelligence that NORAID was involved in gunrunning operations from the U.S. as well as sending money directly to the Provisional movement in Ireland. Although NORAID has been given a lot of attention as an organization that played a leading role in financing the Provisional IRA leading Irish investigative journalist and IRA historian, Ed Maloney, has argued that it was Clan na Gael that was the leading financier or the new movement[221]. Maloney's insight and research contradicts FBI conclusions that NORAID was the main fundraising body for the Provisional movement.

---

220   Coogan, Pat, Tim. The IRA. London. Harper/Collins publisher. 1995. P. 365-385.
221   Available online <http://www.nuzhound.com/articles/mal10-41.htm>

What is one then to make of the contradictory findings? While the FBI could point to financial records and money transfers made by NORAID to Ireland and compare it to that of Clan na Gael this can be a misleading measurement. Clan na Gael had a long record of smuggling in funds illegally and undetected into Ireland without leaving any electronic or paper trail. Maloney also had significant contacts within the Provisional IRA in Ireland that would have corroborated the importance of the financing efforts of Clan na Gael in the early formation, survival and later expansion of the movement from the early 1970s onward.

When looked at in this light the Clan played an important role in the early emergence and development of the new fledgling Provisional movement without whose direct financial input and very likely gunrunning operations, may have struggled to have gotten a foothold against the rival Official IRA as well as not having the means to launch the violent and relatively effective military campaign against the British state in the years ahead.

Clan na Gael had a number of advantages over other emerging Irish American organizations at the beginning of the Northern Ireland conflict. Despite its diminished membership since the heydays of early twentieth century it still maintained its organizational framework in most of the major urban centers where Irish American communities were concentrated[222]. The Clan had also developed into a movement that moved away from far-left political leanings and associations becoming a more "patriotic" and right leaning movement at a time when transnational revolutionary movements were under deep suspicion of communist leanings in the U.S. It's messaging of portraying the emerging Northern Irish conflict as simply a continuation of the overall struggle for independence started in 1916 was a safe, familiar and simple message that tapped into less visible but still present Anglophobia within the broader Irish American community. As seen from declassified FBI reports from the time period extensive monitoring of NORAID in some ways took the heat off Clan na Gael who reports show

---

222 Dumbrell, John. 2018. The United States and the Northern Irish Conflict, 1969-1994: From Indifference to Intervention. Irish Studies in International Affairs. P. 112.

low level political activity and propaganda efforts. It may well have been a case that the older and much more experienced revolutionary movement was more adept at keeping below the radar and keeping its activities more secretive compared to its upstart rival, NORAID.

The early 1970s were to be the most violent years in the history of the Northern Irish conflict with IRA bombings and shootings almost daily and with equally violent loyalist retaliations through groups such as the Ulster Volunteer Force and the larger Ulster Defense Association who received regular intelligence leaks from the RUC and Ulster Defense Regiment on political targets within the IRA and Sinn Fein. In 1969 the British army was introduced on to the streets of Northern Ireland and at the beginning it was used as little more than an instrument of the Stormont government in attempting to quell the growing IRA insurgency. Two major events were to have major propaganda benefits to Clan na Gael's propaganda and fundraising efforts in the U.S. The first was the disastrous British introduction of Internment and the second was the event known as Bloody Sunday.

The loyalist and sectarian government in Stormont was on the verge of collapse as it was facing what was virtually a full-scale rebellion. In August 1971 the British government introduced imprisonment without trial which eliminated any legal protections and rights previously guaranteed to all British citizens. What would become known as Operation Demetrius involved a massive military operation that arrested hundreds of mostly Irish Catholics. Almost no Protestants were arrested although almost half the violence was perpetrated by Loyalist paramilitary groups. Also, much of the information used by British military intelligence in drawing their list of those to be arrested was outdated and resulted in many former and older IRA members being interned as well as peaceful political activists. Clan na Gael was at the forefront of the Irish American media in immediately pouncing upon what would be a major tactical error by the British government. As internees were released stories of torture began to be seen in media reports adding fury and rage to the protests on the streets and to the IRA campaign[223].

---

223   Bishop, Patrick; Mallie, Eamonn. The Provisional IRA. London. Heinemann. 1987. P. 144-147.

The highest profile incident of a bloody period came in 1972 when the British Army shot dead thirteen unarmed protestors in Derry in an event known as Bloody Sunday. The event was to prove a massive propaganda coup for Clan na Gael as it was for the Provisional IRA back in Ireland. The event increased not only the exposure of the conflict but also support for the Irish republican cause. The widespread condemnation of the massacre in mainstream American media validated Clan na Gael's message for many within the Irish American community. One example was an article from the St. Louis Globe-Democrat.

"The British government must stand before the court of world opinion as guilty of massacre in Northern Ireland, or at very least plead failure to maintain law and order in the tragic enclave it pretends to rule.... Sunday's bloody slaughter in Londonderry, in which 13 unarmed civilians were slain by British paratroopers, is inexcusable. Disciplined soldiers do not run amok with automatic weapons, mowing down little children because a few bullies on the fringe of a crown have thrown rocks .... Mistakenly, the English have abandoned all concept of law. They have rounded up and detained hundreds of people without charge.... When will the British learn that Ireland should be one country – with justice for all[224]."

As the 1970s progressed chapters of the Clan which were previously all but defunct re- emerged with an energized propaganda and fundraising campaign. One such case was in Toledo, Ohio. Dr Seamus Metress revitalized the local Clan na Gael branch and organized demonstrations against British officials throughout the Midwest. Metress further expanded his efforts beyond the political arena by establishing cultural awareness forums. The local branch of the Clan was also at the forefront in pressuring the Toledo media to include the Irish Republican perspective in its media reports on events in Ireland. The Toledo example was to be repeated in many cities throughout the U.S.

At the beginning of the northern conflict what became known as the "Harrison Network" was also reactivated. The network for gunrunning was last active during the failed Border Campaign of 1956-62. As

---

224   Wilson, J., Andrew. Irish America and the Ulster Conflict, 1968-1995. The Blackstaff Press. Belfast. 1995.P. 62-63.

stated earlier the connection between Clan na Gael and the Harrison network while never formally established seems likely to have existed at some level considering Harrison's own membership of the organization. The importance of this arms smuggling operation was highlighted by the fact that leading Provisional IRA figure Daithi O Conaill came to New York to meet with George Harrison and his close colleague Tom Falvey. The first guns successfully smuggled was a small shipment of just forty weapons, mainly handguns. With this operation completed successfully later in 1971 the Harrison Network managed to successfully smuggle the first armalites which increased the Provisional IRA's ability to engage the British army on the ground. It is estimated that Harrison managed from 1973 to supply approximately 200 to 300 firearms a year to the Provisional IRA. In 1979 things went wrong for the network when a major arms shipment was intercepted arriving through Dublin[225].

The Harrison Network came to an end with the arrest of George Harrison and a number of his associates in 1981. During the course of a high-profile trial all men were acquitted, to the embarrassment of the FBI. Despite the acquittals it was the end of the extraordinary gunrunning career of Harrison and his fellow gunrunners. Despite the end of the network in 1981 Harrison was the single most important source of weapons for the Provisional IRA during its formative years of the 1970s. One estimate suggests Harrison sent over a million rounds of ammunition and a total of 2,500 weapons to the Provisional IRA in Ireland[226]. Without this contribution to would be hard to see the IRA having the military ability to challenge the British military in Northern Ireland in the way that it did and raising the violence to the level that would eventually bring down the Stormont parliament in 1972. The role of Clan na Gael was never revealed by Harrison and his associates or discovered by the FBI. It is hard to believe, however, that over years of a sophisticated gunrunning operation that would have required close cooperation with dock workers, certain other port authorities, storage for weapons while awaiting transit and funds required to buy

---

225   Boyne, Sean. Gunrunners – The Covert Arms Trail to Ireland the O'Brien Press. Dublin. 2006. P. 96-98.

226   Maloney, Ed. A Secret History of the IRA. W.W Norton & Co. New York. 2003. P. 16.

weapons that Harrison and his associates would not have used the already well-established network of supporters and finance provided by Clan na Gael, who, as already stated, Harrison was a long-time member of.

Besides the re-emergence of militant Irish-American nationalism in the form of organizations such as Clan na Gael other more moderate voices were beginning to emerge during the course of the 1970s. These moderate voices would challenge and later overcome the more violent forms of nationalism emanating from within Irish-American communities. John Hume, leader of the Social Democratic and Labor Party (S.D.L.P) and the main voice of moderate constitutional Irish nationalism in Northern Ireland began to make contacts with what became known as "The Four Horseman" – Democratic House Speaker Thomas P. "Tip" O'Neill, Senator Ted Kennedy, Governor Hugh Carey and Senator Daniel Patrick Moynihan. All four men were established figures within the Democratic Party with strong connections to the Irish American community. Irish Taoiseach Liam Cosgrave and President Gerald Ford announced a joint communique appealing to those within the Irish American community to end their financial and political support for the violent IRA campaign in Ireland.

The efforts of moderate Irish American nationalists were certainly helped with the images of the bloody and violent consequences of the Provisional IRA's campaign on the streets of Northern Ireland as well as their expanded bombing campaign in mainland Britain on American TV screens and newspaper publications. House Speaker O'Neill also sought to portray a tough image and in 1979 advocated and supported an amendment banning the American sale of arms to the RUC. What O'Neill was essentially doing was sending a message to Irish America that the constitutional path to intervening in the Northern Ireland conflict could have practical effects on the ground[227]. The general effect of the rise in moderate Irish American nationalism in the U.S. was to see a decrease in support for groups such as Clan na Gael while in Ireland the British we're beginning to come to grips with the Provisional IRA military campaign which began to

227 Cooper, James. 2017. "The situation over there really bothers me": Ronald Reagan and the Northern Ireland Conflict. Irish Historical Studies. Vol. 41, No. 159. P. Available online <https://ray.yorksj.ac.uk/id/eprint/3833/1/Reagan%20 and%20Northern%20Ireland%20edit%20JC.pdf>

see a slackening off by the late 1970s. The election of hardline right-wing British Prime Minister Margaret Thatcher in 1979 and her promise to destroy the IRA was seen by some in the British and Northern Ireland political establishment as the potential end of the Republican armed campaign.

The decade of the 1980s would begin with two major events, one on the domestic political front in the U.S. and the other in Ireland that would define the entire conflict in Northern Ireland from the point of view of Clan Na Gael for the rest of the decade and even into the 1990s. The election of Ronald Reagan in 1980, similar to the Thatcher victory in Britain, marked a sharp right turn on the political spectrum within the U.S. and the strengthening of the Anglo- American relationship to a level not seen since Roosevelt and Churchill during World War 2. There was not just a strong political relationship and common Cold War vision but also a personal rapport between Reagan and Thatcher not commonly seen on the international stage.

The international developments and strengthening of Anglo-American relation boded ill for more militant Irish American organizations such as Clan na Gael. The situation became even more threatening with the formation of the Friends of Ireland which was made up of among others leading Irish American Congressional figures such as Ted Kennedy and "Tip" O'Neill. Although leading Democrats would talk up the cause of a peaceful solution to the Northern Ireland conflict the Republican Party, particularly Reagan, began to see the conflict more as part of global terrorism as opposed to historically unresolved national issues.

"Peace cannot be at the barrel of a terrorist's gun. Americans should question closely any appeal for funds from groups involved in the conflict to make sure that contributions do not end up in the hands of gun-runners. Further, as terrorists of either side are apprehended and jailed, extradition procedures should not be relaxed on the grounds these are political prisoners. Terrorism is just that and must not be allowed to be condoned or excused".

Reagan's approach to the Northern Ireland conflict was essentially in step with Thatcher's hardline approach in defining the IRA armed campaign in Northern Ireland and mainland Britain as simply a terrorist/criminal campaign with no political legitimacy. The United States would become increasingly difficult for Clan na Gael to propagate its militant message, fund raise and to even attempt gunrunning operations. Under Reagan Clan na Gael and other groups such as NORAID would come under increasing FBI scrutiny. It was at this time as the IRA campaign in Ireland and Britain began to falter that the situation in prisons over the political status of IRA prisoners became explosive and opened a new window of opportunity for Clan na Gael.

From almost the beginning the of conflict authorities in Northern Ireland recognized IRA prisoners as having political status. This in essence meant that the IRA was allowed to have its own recognized command structure within the prison system, kept separate from common prisoners and were also allowed to wear their own clothes. Since 1975 the British government has been toying with the idea of removing political status but never implemented the plan for fear of the potential backlash that it would trigger. Thatcher had no such hesitations and was more than willing to attempt to break the IRA within the prisons further undermining their legitimacy and strengthening the seeming progress being made by British security forces on the streets.

The IRA tactic of using hunger strikes as a political weapon was one that not only went back generations in the history of Irish Republicanism but one that had a deep resonance within broader Irish culture. This was a fact never fully realized or appreciated by many previous British governments and even less so by Thatcher's government in 1981. Hunger strikes had a history in Ireland dating back to pre-Christian times, when those who lacked power protested against the more powerful by fasting in order to call attention to an injustice. The power, and thus, the responsibility, to end the fast rested on the wrongdoer. In the twentieth century the use of hunger strikes began to take on wider political significance in the struggle against British rule in Ireland. Such early examples were Thomas Ashe who died on hunger strike in 1917 after been forced fed by British prison authorities and Mayor of Cork City, Terence MacSwiney, who died on hunger strike at the height of the Irish War of Independence after seventy-four days on protest.

Father James Healy, who monitors hunger strikes worldwide attempted to sum up the uniqueness of the of the 1981 hunger strike when he said –

"A hunger strike is an interaction between two parties. What is so distinctive when this interaction is between the Irish and British? Perhaps it is a combination of great determination in both parties, mutual incomprehension, fear and distrust, and in each an unshakable conviction that any death which occurs will be the responsibility of the other party. In the Irishman there is also likely to be the conviction that he is showing great love in laying down his life for his friends. From reading a great deal about hunger strikers I am convinced that any suggestion that they are taking, rather than giving, their lives would sound absurd to them, a plain mistake".

Irish poet, William Butler Yeats summed up the Irish attitude to the use of hunger strikes in his work "The King's Threshold" when he said –

"King: .... He had chosen death. Refusing to eat or drink, that he may bring Disgrace upon me; for there is a custom, that if a man Be wronged, or think that he is wronged, and starve Upon another man's threshold till he die, The common people, for all time to come, Will raise a heavy cry against that threshold, Even though it be the King's"[228].

When the hunger strike commenced neither the British nor U.S. governments were fully prepared for the consequences of what was about to occur. On the part of the British government it was perceived as little more than a desperate attempt by the IRA to revitalize a campaign that was losing momentum. No one in the political establishment of Northern Ireland or mainland Britain seemed to have understood the historical, social and political context in which the hunger strikes were taking place. The assassination of Thatcher's top advisor, Airy Neave, in March of 1979 by a Republican splinter group known as the Irish National Liberation Army, would have added to her belligerent and confrontational attitude toward Irish Republicanism. Considering the long history of the Anglo-Irish conflict this is somewhat remarkable, however, if looked at through the lens of the Thatcher government's campaign of politically delegitimizing Irish Republican demands and constantly referring to them as "gangsters" and "godfathers of crime" it was perhaps inevitable that events unfolded as they did.

228   Beresford, David. Ten Men Dead. Harper/Collins Publishers. London. 1994. P. 9-43.

In protest to having to wear prison uniforms and losing political status IRA prisoners went "On the blanket" which meant refusing to wear the assigned prison garb and instead covering themselves with a prison blanket. On 27 October 1980, IRA prisoners began their first hunger strike under the prison leadership of Bobby Sands. This was soon called off when it looked like concessions from the British government might be forthcoming. When these negotiations failed a second and much more momentous hunger strike began in January of 1981. During the course of this momentous hunger strike Bobby Sands was put forward as a parliamentary candidate for the vacant seat of Fermanagh and South Tyrone. Unbelievably, and to the consternation of the loyalist community in Northern Ireland and horror of the Thatcher government in London, Sands won the election. Hopes of any compromise being reached as a result of Sands election was soon dashed as Thatcher became more entrenched in her position of no compromise with prisoner demands. Bobby Sands died on 5 May and was to be followed by nine more hunger strikers in the weeks and months that followed before the strike eventually ended.

IRA prisoner demands were eventually conceded but by that time violence erupted on the streets and the Republican armed campaign was reinvigorated with an influx of new recruits, money, arms and a massive international publicity campaign which brought huge propaganda gains[229]. No country outside of Ireland and Britain saw the impact of the hunger strikes than the U.S. For Clan na Gael it offered the opportunity of re-establishing itself at the forefront of militant Irish American nationalism ahead of NORAID and to challenge the increasingly successful messaging of moderate Irish American nationalists through organizations such as the Friends of Ireland.

Moderate Irish American nationalists tried to preempt what they saw would be a huge upsurge in support of the IRA during and in the aftermath of the hunger strikes. On 6 May 1981, leading members of the Friends of Ireland sent a telegram condemning Thatcher's intransigence and urged increased flexibility in bringing to and end the crisis. Thatcher's cold response

229   Beresford, David. Ten Men Dead. Harper/Collins Publishers. London. 1994. P. 83-358.

laid all responsibility for the crisis at the door of the IRA. There would be no room for negotiation. No exact figures are available as to Clan na Gael fundraising during this period but it can be assumed it followed the same trajectory as that of NORAID. From January to July 1981 NORAID took in a total of over $250,000. During the week of Bobby Sands death, a total of $20,000 was collected by NORAID's Bronx branch alone[230]. More than 100,000 attended the funeral of Bobby Sands. Just two years later the head of NORAID, Michael Flannery was chosen as Grand Marshall for the Saint Patrick's Day Parade in New York which brought protest from both the Irish government and moderate Irish American groups such as the Friends of Ireland[231]. Thatcher, instead of destroying the IRA, had reinvigorated the Republican movement and created widespread support that would sustain its campaign right up until the Good Friday Agreement of 1998.

In the early 1980s Clan na Gael was seemingly riding the crest of a political wave. This reached its pinochle with what was called The Irish People Tours which began in August of 1983. Although NORAID organized the tour in order to build on the emotional outpouring of the hunger strikes and to counteract U.S. and British anti-Republican efforts they also invited other groups including Clan na Gael. The tour would involve leading members of NORAID, Clan na Gael and the Ancient Order of Hibernians among others travelling to Northern Ireland under the guidance of Sinn Fein where they would visit Republican communities in IRA strongholds such as Crossmaglen, West Belfast and of significance to Clan na Gael leaders, Carrickmore, birthplace of Joseph McGarrity. Although publicly stated as a "fact finding mission" the entire exercise was little more than a propaganda exercise with NORAID receiving a large amount of the publicity compared to Clan na Gael. Although heavily criticized by constitutional nationalists in Northern Ireland and moderate Irish groups in the U.S. the tour largely had the effect of a successful publicity campaign

---

230   Wilson, J., Andrew. Irish America and the Ulster Conflict, 1968-1995. The Blackstaff Press. 1995. Belfast. P. 194-195.

231   Brundage, David. Irish Nationalists in America – The Politics of Exile, 1798-1998. Oxford University Press. New York. 2016. P. 206.

highlighting the importance of Irish American groups such as Clan na Gael in sustaining the IRA campaign[232].

By the mid to late 1980s things had started to go wrong for Clan na Gael. According to FBI reports from the time period division and factionalism began to become more prominent within the movement. Much of this was related to what was happening within the Republican movement back in Ireland. Prior to the hunger strikes of 1981 the political wing of the IRA, Sinn Fein, was little more than a mouthpiece and public defender for the IRA armed campaign. During and in the aftermath of the hunger strikes Sinn Fein experienced significant electoral successes. Not only did Bobby Sands win a parliamentary seat while on hunger strike but Gerry Adams, President of Sinn Fein, won the seat for West Belfast in 1983. What evolved out of these political successes was significant debate within the Republican movement about developing a greater political strategy outside of the IRA armed campaign. Important Sinn Fein political strategist, Danny Morrison stared at the 1981 Ard Feis – "Who here really believes we can really win the war through the ballot box? But will anyone here object if with the ballot paper in this hand and an Armalite in the other, we take power in Ireland?". What was to develop was a new strategy referred simply as the Armalite and Ballot Box strategy where Sinn Fein and the IRA would carry out simultaneous political and armed campaign operating in parallel toward achieving the same goal of a united Ireland. It would mark the beginning of a change in relationship between both wings of the movement and the emergence of Sinn Fein as the dominant partner.

The growing emphasis on grass root political action was further highlighted in 1985 when a motion was put forward at the Sinn Fein Ard Feis to allow elected members to end abstentionism and take their seats in the Dail, while still refusing to take seats in the British parliament. Although the motion was narrowly defeated it was reintroduced again in 1986 and was given the full support of the IRA. Although the motion succeeded by a two-third majority about twenty delegates walked out in protest to eventually form a new party they would call Republican Sinn Fein. The

232   Wilson, J., Andrew. *Irish America and the Ulster Conflict, 1968-1995*. Belfast. The Blackstaff Press. 1995. P. 216-217.

events of 1985 and 1986 was another major step in the growing dominance of Sinn Fein and the greater subservience of the IRA to its political wishes and strategy.

Events in Ireland were to have profound consequences for Clan na Gael in the U.S. As stated earlier ever since Joseph McGarrity essentially took over control of Clan na Gael in the aftermath of the death of John Devoy the organization had developed in the following decades as one of the most hardline, militant and uncompromising of all the Irish republican organizations in both Ireland and the U.S. According to FBI reports the middle to late 1980s saw a dramatic fall off in Clan membership to approximately 150 members. The organization was also "riven with conflict, suspicion and intense disharmony". This internal confusion was almost certainly the result of disagreement over the political direction the IRA was taking back in Ireland. For many members even the hint of greater involvement in constitutional politics spelt betrayal to the supreme cause of the armed campaign against British occupation.

Is it clear from FBI reports from the period that they had a highly placed informant within Clan na Gael with their constant reference to a "good source of reliability". Another insight which is very revealing in was the FBI's comparison to how Clan na Gael distributed its funds compared to that of NORAID. According to the FBI while NORAID collected more in fundraising than the Clan and distributed it between the IRA and Sinn Fein the Clan's resources went 100 per cent toward funding the armed campaign. This was just another example of the Clan's political vision and why it struggled to come to terms with the evolving Sinn Fein strategy back in Ireland. For Clan na Gael the ballot box was a weakening and distraction from the primary task that involved the Armalite[233]. Despite the internal tensions within Clan na Gael as long as the armed campaign continued in Ireland it would continue its support for the IRA and to a much lesser extend its political wing, Sinn Fein. Suspicion and hostility

233   Smyth, Ted. 2020. Irish American organizations and the Northern Ireland Conflict in the 1980s: Heightened Political Agency and Ethnic Vitality. Journal of American Ethnic History, Vol. 39, No. 2. P. 51.

toward constitutional Republicanism ran deep as did anything that remotely resembled compromise of the ultimate goal of a United Ireland.

As the Northern Ireland conflict entered the 1990s political conditions in the U.S. for Clan na Gael began to deteriorate further as moderate Irish American nationalists gained political ground. The election of Democratic President Bill Clinton in 1993 was to prove a major turning point. Also, in Ireland Sinn Fein's growing influence and political dominance over the IRA increased further. The IRA's armed campaign had reached a stalemate and the continued conflict meant that Sinn Fein had reached a metaphorical glass ceiling in relation to further electoral success. With no possibility of further political gains with a continued IRA campaign voices within Sinn Fein began to look for an alternative political path outside of violence.

As a Democratic President Clinton came immediately under the influence of the influential Friends of Ireland. Other conditions also began to favor a more influential role for moderate Irish American nationalists. The end of the Cold War and the collapse of the Soviet Union in the early 1990s meant a lessening in importance of the Anglo-American relationship. As a result of common membership of the European Union Anglo-Irish relations began to improve to the point of increased cooperation and more open dialog as to the future of Northern Ireland which previously was dismissed by the British political establishment as a purely internal matter.

Being less hampered by Anglo-American political considerations Clinton's approach to the Northern Ireland conflict was a complete break with his predecessors. Unlike previous administrations Clinton openly recognized and acknowledged Sinn Fein's political legitimacy and role in any future political settlement. To entice and assist Adams and the political wing of the Republican movement in Ireland into the arena of constitutional politics Gerry Adams, President of Sinn Fein, was granted a visa to visit the U.S. Clan na Gael was needless to say delighted at the opportunity of a huge propaganda coup that a visit by the President of Sinn Fein would bring. While groups like Clan na Gael aspired to a political outcome resulting in a British withdrawal from Northern Ireland, moderate Irish American nationalists limited their aspirations to including Sinn Fein and the IRA in a new political arrangement within Northern Ireland that contained a vague and undefined hope of a united Ireland at some distant point in time. The granting of the visa to Gerry Adams is seen by many today as the starting point of the peace process that come to full fruition in 1998 and end well short of the Clan's aspirations of a united Ireland.

The British response to the Clinton's legitimizing of Sinn Fein and the IRA on the world political stage was furious to say the least. Despite this Clinton was on the crest of a political wave being a newly elected President and fairly popular through his eight years in office. The brief forty-eight-hour visit by Adams was an unmitigated propaganda success as he appeared on numerous prime time talk shows expressing the aims and ambitions of Irish Republicanism. Adams was far from the image his detractors tried to portray. Instead of the "Terrorist fanatic" Adams came across as more of a professorial intellectual who was soft spoken and personally appealing in many ways. In the aftermath of the visit Sinn Fein's hand was strengthened considerably and they were able to negotiate the IRA into a ceasefire in 1994.

Although the 1994 IRA ceasefire lasted a little more than seventeen months and ended due to what were hardline demands by the British government and Unionist political establishment the political path of the Republican movement in Ireland was set. In the years between 1994 and the final peace settlement known as the Good Friday Agreement Clan na Gael was little more than a distant and almost irrelevant observer. The formal visit of Bill Clinton to Northern Ireland and his personal influence is pushing both Irish Republicans and northern Unionists to a peace settlement was another crucial step in pushing both parties toward compromise and a negotiated peace settlement. A further visit to Dublin saw an estimated 80,000 people greet the U.S. President's visit.

Despite verbal jousting, threats, disagreements, internal fractures within both Unionism and Republicanism a final peace agreement was reached and signed on 10 April 1998. The agreement established a power sharing executive in Belfast where power was divided between Unionists and nationalists. Sinn Fein would become the second largest party in the new Assembly with the Democratic Unionist Party being the largest. It became clear from the early stages of negotiations that a united Ireland, at least in the short to medium term, was never going to be a realistic objective as long as the majority Protestant community in the north of Ireland wanted to remain part of Britain. Despite substantial devolved power and local authority the new political arrangement left Northern Ireland within the United Kingdom even though the Republic of Ireland now had an increased say in the region[234]. In a war weary Irish society, particularly the working-class Republican and loyalist communities who bore the brunt of the violence, many started to veer toward political compromise. Inevitably this would lead to splits within Irish Republicanism in Ireland. Clan na Gael would be no exception to the age old fault lines of revolutionary violence and constitutional politics within Irish nationalism.

When word of the terms of the Good Friday Agreement began to become public knowledge Clan na Gael was shaken to its core. Intense and heated debate within the organization over the Good Friday Agreement brought about a split and the formation of what would turn out to be two separate organizations. What would become known to insiders as Provisional Clan na Gael remained loyal to the Sinn Fein and IRA leadership in Ireland. According to experts the only Clan districts that could be relied on as solidly loyal was New York and Pittsburg. Other Clan na Gael strongholds in cities such as Philadelphia and Chicago came out as solidly anti-Agreement or were riven with internal splits.

The wing that split entirely from the Clan became known unofficially as Republican Clan na Gael which aligned itself with Republican Sinn Fein in Ireland and other militant dissident groups such as the 32 County Sovereignty Committee and its newly formed armed wing, the Real IRA. According to a dissident Clan member during this time "we have a lot of people here who have spent most of their lives working for the movement. Those of us who are breaking away are very distressed at what is going on. We feel that the Good Friday Agreement is possibly the worst settlement in all of Irish history". The split that took in the U.S. place was identical to that taking place in Ireland and was one which formed a long historical pattern as militant Irish Republicanism followed the long and often agonizing path down the road to constitutional politics. The frustration by

234 Cooper, James. The Politics of Diplomacy – U.S. Presidents and the Northern Ireland Conflict, 1967-1998. Edinburgh University Press. Edinburgh. 2017. P. 195-234.

Clan na Gael dissidents was best summed up by the earlier mentioned Clan member, "There is no merit to it. We are not hawks, we are not seeking war. Clan na Gael survives very well in peace as in war. But the way things are lining up it is unacceptable to our constitution, out oath and our tradition. Quite honestly we don't see how it is possible for people to sit there (in the Assembly), take a big British check and continue to fight for Irish freedom. It does not seem to make sense".

The central concern for Sinn Fein and the Provisional IRA back in Ireland was that funds would not make its way into the coffers of the newly formed dissident groups and threaten the tentative peace agreement. It was decided that IRA and Sinn Fein veteran, Joe Cahill, would deliver a strong warning to dissident Clan members in the U.S. In a communication Cahill said "If districts didn't give the money then they couldn't call themselves Clan na Gael". The insinuation was that Clan branches collecting money that did not go directly to Sinn Fein in Ireland were fundraising under false pretenses. Officially speaking dissident Clan na Gael members were not formally allied to any particular anti-agreement body in Ireland. However, dissident told unhappy members to donate directly themselves to one of three organizations – Republican Sinn Fein, the 32 County Sovereignty Committee and National Graves Associations[235].

In Ireland dissident Irish Republicanism took an early and severe setback when a bomb attack in the town of Omagh went disastrously wrong and ended up killing 29 innocent bystanders and injuring almost 300 others. Although dissident groups such as the Real IRA and Continuity IRA continued a limited and sporadic armed campaign their activities petered out in the decade that followed due largely to failed bomb attacks which were more often than not foiled due in heightened and effective intelligence both from the British and Irish governments who worked in closer cooperation since the Good Friday Agreement. Although the funding for these organizations come primarily from smuggling of alcohol, cigarettes and fuel they still received funding from the U.S. and dissident Clan members among others. The political wings of dissident Irish Republicanism in Ireland such as Republican Sinn Fein and the 32 County Sovereignty

235   Available online <http://www.nuzhound.com/articles/mal10-41.htm>

Committee continue to exist in the political wilderness with very little political support.

In sharp contrast to the increased marginalization of dissident Irish Republicanism Provisional Sinn Fein has gone on to become a major political force in both Northern Ireland and the Irish Republic. In the 2020 election in the Republic of Ireland Sinn Fein made historic gains becoming the largest party by popular vote and joint largest by Dail seats won alongside Fianna Fail. In the 2019 elections in Northern Ireland Sinn Fein won almost 23 per cent of the popular vote and maintained its position as the second largest party in the Northern Ireland Assembly behind the Democratic Unionist Party[236]. On both fronts Sinn Fein's political strategy seems vindicated in the eyes of the vast majority of Irish Republicans.

Britain's withdrawal from the European Union in January 2021 has increased the possibility of a medium to long term unification of the island of Ireland. In extremely difficult and volatile Brexit negotiations the British government conceded Northern Ireland remaining economically within the EU trading block and what is known as a "soft border" with the Irish Republic being maintained. Essentially the island of Ireland exists today as a single economic unit within the EU. The basis for the agreement was to maintain the Good Friday Agreement and the continued economic prosperity of all those living both north and south in Ireland. A "hard border" would have hit the Irish economy very hard indeed. The majority of Northern Irish voters voted to stay in the EU but were outvoted by an English populist nationalist vote that were essentially willing to sacrifice Northern Irish Protestants in order to get a deal. The sense of betrayal within the Unionist community was palpable leaving some to consider a future within a possible united Ireland and viewing the EU as much as part of their future as being British[237]. Economic considerations have rapidly caught up with nationalist sentiment and connections to the British monarchy both during Brexit negotiations and particularly in its aftermath.

---

236 Available online <https://www.bbc.com/news/election/2019/results/northern_ireland>

237 Available online <https://www.theguardian.com/commentisfree/2020/feb/01/unionists-northern-ireland-brexit-backfired-uk-government-nationalists>

Conclusion

The overall growth and development of Clan na Gael from its foundation in 1867 up until 1916 differed markedly from its sister organizations in Ireland. Up until almost the beginning of the Irish War of Independence Clan na Gael was the dominant organization, especially during long time periods when Republicanism in Ireland struggled for any meaningful relevancy or role. During critical times it was the Clan that pushed for political alliances with the Irish Land League and Home Rule Movement which kept the issue of separatism at least part of the overall political discussion even it was not at the forefront.

The unique environment under which Clan na Gael developed and evolved as compared to its counterparts in Ireland gave it a huge advantage for much of its history in terms of being geographically and politically out of reach from repressive British and later Irish government actions. The Clan's political environment brought it into close contact with other global anti-colonial revolutionary movements giving the organization a more global perspective on the issue of Irish independence and later Irish unification.

The split of 1920 and the following ascension of Joseph McGarrity to the leadership of the Clan changed from being an independent voice and organization within Irish American nationalism to one of serving a mere subsidiary role to the IRA in Ireland. In essence Clan na Gael veered away from being a uniquely Irish American nationalism movement to one of simply being a support organization for the IRA based in the U.S.

Almost from the moment of Joseph McGarrity's death in 1940 the fortunes of Clan na Gael mirrored almost exactly that of the IRA in Ireland with numerous low points and a resurgence during the period of the Troubles ending in 1998. The division within Irish Republicanism following the Good Friday Agreement was again replicated within Clan na Gael leaving it essentially divided into two organizations with certain branches supporting the peace agreement and others supporting dissident groups opposed to the deal.

For nearly all of its history revolutionary violence was the central tenet for Clan na Gael. Political philosopher Hannah Arendt once stated that political theory "can only deal with the justification of political violence because this justification constitutes its political limitations; if instead it arrives at a glorification of violence as such, it is no longer political but anti-political". The point being made by Arendt is that violence must always be subordinate to a justifiable political end that it is intended to serve. The dissident elements within Clan na Gael today seem totally to have fallen into the trap of violence for violence sake and losing the vision of the political end goal. This ingrained belief in revolutionary violence is perhaps inevitable when one considers that not only is the Clan the oldest Irish revolutionary movement in existence today but from the 1880s up until the Northern Ireland conflict ending only in 1998 the organization was involved either in a leading or supporting role in every violent campaign for Irish independence and unification. Even today elements within the Clan support dissident elements of the former IRA.

In considering the present plight and future prospects of Clan na Gael one may consider the following passage from Samiel Beckett's "The Unnamable" comes to mind –

> Perhaps they have carried me to the threshold of my story, which would surprise me, if it opens, it will be I, it will be the silence, where I am, I don't know, I'll never know. In the silence you don't know, you must go on, I can't go on, I'll go on.

Bibliography

Bardon, Jonathan. A History of Ulster. The Blackstaff Press. Belfast. 2005. P. 466-552. Available online <https://journals.openedition.org/etudesirlandaises/2348>

Baron, Harold. 1957. Anti-Imperialism and the Democrats. Science & Society. No. 3, P. 222-239.

Beames, Michael. Peasants and Power – The Whiteboy Movement and their Control in Pre-famine Ireland.

Belchem, John. The Past and Present Society. Nationalism, Republicanism and Exile: Irish Emigrants and the Revolutions of 1848. No. 146. 1995. P. 103-135.

Bell, Bowyer. The Secret Army – The IRA. Routledge. London. 2017. P. 166.

Beresford, David. Ten Men Dead. Harper/Collins Publishers. London. 1994. P. 9-43.

Beresford, David. Ten Men Dead. Harper/Collins Publishers. London. 1994. P. 83-358.

Bernstein, Judah. 2017. "The two finest nations in the world": American Zionists and Irish Nationalism, 1897-1922. Journal of American Ethnic History. Vol. 36, No. 3. P. 5-37.

Bishop, Patrick; Mallie, Eamonn. The Provisional IRA. London. Heinemann. 1987. P. 144-147.

Bornemann, Sara Bethany, "Political activism and resistance in Irish America: The Clan na Gael 1912-1916. 2018. Electronic Thesis and Dissertation. Paper 2940. Retrieved from <https//ir.library.louisville.edu/etd/2940>

Bornemann, Sara Bethany. "Political activism and resistance in Irish America: The Clan na Gael 1912-1916. 2018. Electronic Thesis and Dissertation. Paper 2940. Retrieved from <https//ir.library.louisville.edu/etd/2940>. 100. Inglis, Brian. Roger Casement. Penguin Books. London. 1973. P. 19-151.

Boyne, Sean. Gunrunners – The Covert Arms Trail to Ireland. The O'Brien Press. Dublin. 2006. P. 89-94.

Boyne, Sean. Gunrunners – The Covert Arms Trail to Ireland the O'Brien Press. Dublin. 2006. P. 96-98.

Breen, Dan. My Fight for Irish Freedom. Anvil Books. Tralee. 1975. P. 38-59.

Browne, N, Thomas. The Review of Politics. The Origins and Character of Irish-American Nationalism. Vol. 18, No. 3, July, 1956. P. 327–358.

Brundage, David. Irish Nationalists in America – The Politics of Exile, 1798-1998. Oxford University Press. New York. 2016. P. 88-99.

Brundage, David. Irish Nationalists in America – The Politics of Exile, 1798-1998. Oxford University Press. New York. 2016. P. 129-132.

Brundage, David. Irish Nationalists in America – The Politics of Exile, 1798-1998. Oxford University Press. New York. 2016. P. 206.

Caulfield, Max. The Easter Rebellion. Gill & MacMillan. Dublin. 1995. P. 1-264.

Chicago. 2015. O'Brien, Gillian. Blood Runs Green – The Murder That Transfixed Gilded Age Chicago. University of Chicago Press.

Christ, Fran. 2013. Former Resident of the Mount, Kilcock, Ran Secret Missions for Clan-na-Gael and IRB. Kildare History Journal. Available online <http://www.kildare.ie/library/ehistory/2013/02/>

Clark, Dennis. Erin's Heirs – Irish Bonds of Community. University Press of Kentucky. 1991. Lexington. P. 144-156.

Clarke, Thomas. Glimpses of an Irish Felon's Prison Life. Maunsel and Roberts. Dublin. 1922.

Cole, J.A. Prince of Spies – Henri Le Caron. Faber and Faber publishers. London. 1984.

Connell, E. A., Joseph. 2006. John Redmond's Woodenbridge Speech. History Ireland. Vol. 22 (Issue 5).

Connell, Joseph. 2012. Thomas Clarke returns to Dublin. History Ireland. Vol. 20 (Issue 1).

MacAtasney, Gerard. Sean MacDiarmada. Drumlin Publications. Manorhamiltion. 2004. P. 43.

Connell, Joseph. 2013. Founding of the Irish Volunteers. History Ireland. Vol. 21 (Issue 6).

Coogan, Pat, Tim. De Valera – Long Fellow, Long Shadow. Arrow Books. London. 1995. P. 1-124.

Coogan, Pat, Tim. De Valera – Long Fellow, Long Shadow. Arrow Books. London. 1995. P. 522-526. 196.

Coogan, Pat, Tim. De Valera – Long Fellow, Long Shadow. Arrow Books. London. 1995. P. 486-490.

Coogan, Pat, Tim. Michael Collins. Arrow Books. London. P. 3-157.

Coogan, Pat, Tim. The IRA. Harper/Collins Publisher. London. 1995. P. 5.

Coogan, Pat, Tim. The IRA. London. Harper/Collins publisher. 1995. P. 211.

Coogan, Pat, Tim. The IRA. Harper/Collins Publisher. London. 1995. P. 212-214.

Coogan, Pat, Tim. The IRA. London. Harper/Collins Publisher. 1995. P. 365-385. Available online <http://www.nuzhound.com/articles/mal10-41.htm>

Cooper, James. The Politics of Diplomacy – U.S. Presidents and the Northern Ireland Conflict, 1967-1998. Edinburgh University Press. Edinburgh. 2017. P. 195-234. Available online <http://www.nuzhound.com/articles/mal10-41.htm>

Available online <https://www.bbc.com/news/election/2019/results/northern_ireland>

Available online <https://www.theguardian.com/commentisfree/2020/feb/01/unionists-northern-ireland-brexit-backfired-uk-government-nationalists>

Cooper, James. 2017. "The situation over there really bothers me": Ronald Reagan and the Northern Ireland Conflict. Irish Historical Studies. Vol. 41, No. 159. Available online <https://ray.yorksj.ac.uk/id/eprint/3833/1/Reagan%20and%20Northern%20Ireland%20edit%20JC.pdf>

Cronin, Sean. The McGarrity Papers. Anvil Books. Tralee. 1972. P. 81-82.

Cronin, Sean. The McGarrity Papers. Anvil Books. Tralee. 1972. P. 130-136.

Cronin, Sean. The McGarrity Papers. Anvil Books. Tralee. 1972. P. 156-158.

Cronin, Sean. The McGarrity Papers. Anvil Books. Tralee. 1972. P. 162.

Cronin, Sean. The McGarrity Papers. Anvil Books. Tralee. 1972. P. 165.

Cuddy, Edward. 1981. The Irish Question and the Revival of Anti-Catholicism in the 1920s. The Catholic Historical Review, Vol. 67, No. 2, P. 236-255.

David, Troy. 2006. Eamon De Valera's Political Education: The American Tour of 1919-20. New Hibernia Review. Vol. 10, No. 1. P. 71.

David, Troy. 2006. Eamon De Valera's Political Education: The American Tour of 1919-20. New Hibernia Review. Vol. 10, No. 1. P. 73.

Davis, Troy. Eamon De Valera's Political Education: The American Tour of 1919-20. New Hibernia Review. Vol. 10, No. 1. P. 72.

Davis, Troy. 2014. Irish Americans and the Treaty: The View from the Irish Free State. New Hibernia Review. Vol. 18, No. 2. P. 85-90.

Davis, Troy. 2014. Irish Americans and the Treaty: The View from the Irish Free State. New Hibernia Review. Vol. 18, No. 2. P. 91.

Devoy, John. Recollections of an Irish Rebel. Irish University Press. Shannon. 1969. P. 392-393.

Doerries, Reinhard. Prelude to the Easter Rising. Frank Cass. London. 2000. P. 1-25.

Donnelly, James. Captain Rock. The University of Wisconsin Press. Madison. 2009.

Doorley, Michael. Irish-American Diaspora Nationalism – The Friends of Irish Freedom, 1916-1935. Four Courts Press. Dublin. 2005. P. 81-82.

Doorley, Michael. Irish-American Diaspora Nationalism – The Friends of Irish Freedom, 1916-1935. Four Courts Press. Dublin. 2005. P. 96-99.

Doorley, Michael. Irish-American Diaspora Nationalism – The Friends of Irish Freedom, 1916-1935. Four Courts Press. Dublin. 2005. P. 116-117.

Doorley, Michael. Irish-American Diaspora Nationalism – The Friends of Irish Freedom, 1916-1935. Four Courts Press. Dublin. 2005. P. 128-130.

Doorley, Michael. Irish-American Diaspora Nationalism – The Friends of Irish Freedom, 1916-1935. Four Courts Press. Dublin. 2005. P. 131-133.

Dorney, John. Irish Clans in the Sixteenth century. The Irish Story. 2017. Available online <https://www.theirishstory.com/2017/08/15/irish-clans-in-the-sixteenth-century/#.Xy1azIhKjIV>

Douglas, Delia, Shanon. 2015. The Rise and Fall of the Friends of Irish Freedom: How America Shaped Irish American Nationalism in the Twentieth Century. History PHD. Union College. Schenectady. P. 38-56.

Douglas, Delia, Shanon. 2015. The Rise and Fall of the Friends of Irish Freedom: How America Shaped Irish American Nationalism in the Twentieth Century. History PHD. Union College. Schenectady. P. 57-58.

Douglas, Delia, Shanon. 2015. The Rise and Fall of the Friends of Irish Freedom: How America Shaped Irish American Nationalism in the Twentieth Century. History PHD. Union College. Schenectady. P. 59-62.

Douglas, Delia, Shanon. 2015. The Rise and Fall of the Friends of Irish Freedom: How America Shaped Irish American Nationalism in the Twentieth Century. History PHD. Union College. Schenectady. P. 72-73.

Douglas, Delia, Shanon. 2015. The Rise and Fall of the Friends of Irish Freedom: How America Shaped Irish American Nationalism in the Twentieth Century. History PHD. Union College. Schenectady. P. 75-76.

Douglas, Delia, Shanon. 2015. The Rise and Fall of the Friends of Irish Freedom: How America Shaped Irish American Nationalism in the Twentieth Century. History PHD. Union College. Schenectady. P. 79-81.

Doyle, David. 1968. American Catholics, Racism and Imperialism: A Select Study of Responses to the Issues as Involved in American Expansion, 1890-1905. Marquette University. Master's Thesis.

Duff, John. 1968. The Versailles Treaty and the Irish-Americans. The Journey of American History. Vol. 55, No. 3. P. 583.

Duff, John. 1968. The Versailles Treaty and the Irish-Americans. The Journey of American History. Vol. 55, No. 3. P. 592-597.

Dumbrell, John. 2018. The United States and the Northern Irish Conflict, 1969-1994: From Indifference to Intervention. Irish Studies in International Affairs. P. 112.

Falon, Donal. 16 Lives – John MacBride. The O'Brien Press. Dublin. 2015. P. 18-41.

Falon, Donal. 16 Lives – John MacBride. The O'Brien Press. Dublin. 2015. P. 22.

Falon, Donal. 16 Lives – John MacBride. The O'Brien Press. Dublin. 2015. P. 29-30.

Falon, Donal. 16 Lives – John MacBride. Dublin. The O'Brien Press. 2015. P. 61-64.

Flynn, Barry. Soldiers of Folly. The Collins Press. Cork. 2009. P. 14-22.

Flynn, Barry. Soldiers of Folly. The Collins Press. Cork. 2009. P. 195-204.

Date: 04-18-2008. Classified by 60324 UC BAW/STF/TH. Declassified on: 25X 3.3(1) 04-18-2033. Date:04-17-2008 BY 60324 UC BAW/STF/TH. Date: 04-18-2008 BY 60324 UC BAW.STF.TH

Freeman, Joshua. In Transit – The Transport Workers Union in New York City, 1933-1966. Oxford University Press. New York. 1989. P. 28-29.

Freeman, Joshua. In Transit – The Transport Workers Union in New York City, 1933-1966. Oxford University Press. New York. 1989. P. 39-45.

Freeman, Joshua. In Transit – The Transport Workers Union in New York City, 1933-1966. Oxford University Press. New York. 1989. P. 55.

Freeman, Joshua. In Transit – The Transport Workers Union in New York City, 1933-1966. Oxford University Press. New York. 1989. P. 56-57.

Funchion, Michael. Chicago's Irish Nationalists, 1881-1890. Loyola University. Chicago.

Funchion, Michael. Chicago's Irish Nationalists 1881-1890. Loyola University. Chicago. 1973. P. 51.

Funchion, Michael. Chicago's Irish Nationalists, 1881-1890. Loyola University. Chicago. 1973. P. 52.

Funchion, Michael. Chicago's Irish Nationalists, 1881-1890. Loyola University. Chicago. 1973. P. 116-171.

Gantt, Jonathan. 2006. Irish-American Terrorism and Anglo-American Relations, 1881-1885. The Journal of the Gilded Age and Progressive Era. Vol. 3, No. 4.

Goldstone, Lawrence. Going Deep – John Philip Holland and the Invention of the Attack Submarine. Pegasus Books. New York. 2017.

Golway, Terry. Irish Rebel – John Devoy and America's Fight for Ireland's Freedom. St. Martin's Griffin. New York. 1999. P. 1-41.

Golway, Terry. Irish Rebel – John Devoy and America's Fight for Ireland's Freedom. St. Martin's Griffin, New York. 1998. P. 112-113.

Golway, Terry. Irish Rebel – John Devoy and America's Fight for Ireland's Freedom. St. Martin's Griffin. New York. 1998. P. 120.

Golway, Terry. Irish Rebel – John Devoy and America's Fight for Ireland's Freedom. St. Martin's Griffin. New York. 1999. P. 186-188.

Hanley, Brian. The IRA – 1926-1936. Four Courts Press. Dublin. 2002. P. 167.

Hanley, Brian. The IRA – 1926-1936. Four Courts Press. Dublin. 2002. P. 169-170.

Hanley, Brian. 2005. "Oh here's to Adolph Hitler"? The IRA and the Nazis. History Ireland. Vol. 13 (Issue 3).

Hannigan, Dave. De Valera in America. 2010. Palgrave Macmillan. New York. P. 1-41.

Heckscher, August. Woodrow Wilson. Maxwell MacMillan International. New York. 1991. P. 76.

Heckscher, August. Woodrow Wilson. Maxwell MacMillan International. New York. 1991. P. 136-253.

Herlihy, Jim. Peter Golden – The Voice of Ireland. Peter Golden Commemoration Committee. Cork. 1994. P. 49-52.

Herlihy, Jim. Peter Golden – The Voice of Ireland. Peter Golden Commemoration Committee. Cork. 1994. P. 66.

Herlihy, Ronnie. 2009. Jerome Collins. History Ireland. Vol. 17 (Issue 4).

Hernon, Joseph. Celts, Catholics and Copperheads. Ohio State University Press. 1968. P. 11-59.

Hopkinson, Michael. 1993. Woodrow Wilson and the Irish Question. Studia Hibernica. No. 27. P. 89-92.

Hopkinson, Michael. 1993. Woodrow Wilson and the Irish Question. Studia Hibernica. No. 27. P. 106-107.

Hopkirk, Peter. The Great Game: The Struggle for Empire in Central Asia. Kodansha International. Tokyo. 1992.

Ingham, R., George. Irish Rebel, American Patriot. CreateSpace Independent Publishing Platform. 2014. P. 221-237.

Inglis, Brian. Roger Casement. Penguin Books. London. 1973. P. 263-264.

Isacsson, Alfred. Always Faithful – The New York Carmelites, the Irish People and Their Freedom Movement. Vestigium Press. New York. 2004. P. 8.

Janis, Ely. A Greater Ireland – The Land League and Transatlantic Nationalism in Gilded Age America, University of Wisconsin Press. 2015. P. 17-50.

Kee, Robert. The Green Flag – A History of Irish Nationalism. Penguin Books. London. 2000. P. 168-169.

Kee, Robert. The Green Flag – A History of Irish Nationalism. Penguin Books. London. 2000. P. 299-311.

Kee, Robert. The Green Flag – A History of Irish Nationalism. Penguin Books. London. 2000. P. 358.

Kee, Robert. The Green Flag – A History of Irish Nationalism. Penguin Books. London. 2000. P. 367-368.

Kee, Robert. Ireland, a History. Weidenfeld and Nicolson. London. 1980.

Kelly, Augustine, Joseph. The Labor Philosophy of Michael J. Quill. 1967. Master's Thesis. Loyola University Chicago. P. 3-4. Available online <https://core.ac.uk/download/pdf/48603736.pdf>

Kenna, Shane. Jeremiah O'Donovan Rossa. Merrion Press. Sallins. 2015. P. 239.

Kenna, Shane. Jeremiah O'Donovan Rossa. Merrion Press. Sallins. 2015. P. 240-241.

Kenna, Shane. Jeremiah O'Donovan Rossa. Merrion Press. Sallins. 2015. P. 247-252.

Kenna, Shane. War in the Shadows – The Irish-American Fenians who bombed Victorian Britain. Merrion Press. Sallins. 2013.

Kenna, Shane. War in the Shadows – The Irish-American Fenians who bombed Victorian Britain. Merrion Press. Sallins. 2014.

Keyes, Michael. 2009. Money and Nationalist Politics in Nineteenth Century Ireland; From O'Connell to Parnell. History PHD. National University of Ireland. Maynooth.

Lado, Dal, Enrico; Healy, Roisin; Barry, Gearoid. 2018. 1916 in a Global Context – An Anti-Imperial Moment. London. Routledge. P. 3-4.
Available online <https://www.opendemocracy.net/en/opendemocracyuk/easter-rising-and-soviet-union-untold-chapter-in-ireland-s-great-rebellion/>
Available online <https://www.rbth.com/history/326719-1917-bolshevik-revolution-ireland> Available online <http://theconversation.com/the-easter-rising-100-years-on-how-the-irish-revolution-fired-up-american-politics-58586>
Available online <https://www.anphoblacht.com/contents/26525> 116. Available online <https://newrepublic.com/article/132042/irish-rebellion-resonated-harlem> 117.
Lynch, Timothy. "A Kindred and Congenial Element": Irish-American Nationalism's Embrace of Republican Rhetoric. Vol. 13, No. 2, 2009. University of St. Thomas (Center of Irish Studies).
Lyons, F.S.L. Charles Stewart Parnell. Oxford University Press. New York. 1977.
Funchion, Michael. Chicago's Irish Nationalists, 1881-1890. Loyola University. Chicago. 1973. P. 51-52.
Maloney, Ed. A Secret History of the IRA. W.W Norton & Co. New York. 2003. P. 16.
McCracken, P., Donal. MacBride's Brigade. Four Court's Press. Dublin. 1999. P. 22-25.
McCracken, Donal. Forgotten Protest. Ulster Historical Foundation. Belfast. 2003. P. 49-52.
McGee, Owen. The IRB – The Irish Republican Brotherhood from the Land League to Sinn Fein. Four Court Press. Bodmin. 2007. P. 279-83.
McGee, Owen. The IRB – The Irish Republican Brotherhood from the Land League to Sinn Fein. Four Court Press. Bodmin. 2007. P. 307.
McGee, Owen. 2008. Originator of the New Departure. History Ireland. Vol. 16 (Issue 6).
McKenna, Joseph. The IRA Bombing Campaign against Britain, 1939-1940. McFarland & Company. Jefferson. 2016. P. 20.
McKenna, Joseph. The IRA Bombing Campaign Against Britain, 1939-1940. McFarland & Company. Jefferson. 2016. P. 82.
Available Online <https://www.bbc.com/news/world-12848272>
McKenna, Joseph. The IRA Bombing Campaign Against Britain, 1939-1940. McFarland & Company. Jefferson. 2016. P. 92.
McKenna, Joseph. The IRA Bombing Campaign Against Britain, 1939-1940. McFarland & Company. Jefferson. 2016. P. 99-129.
McKenna, Joseph. The IRA Bombing Campaign Against Britain, 1939-1940. McFarland & Company. Jefferson. 2016. P. 138-143.

McMahon, Richard. 2016. Irish Chicagoans, Nationalism, and the Commemoration of Rebellion in 1898. Eire-Ireland, Vol. 51. P. 218-242.

Meleady, Dermot. John Redmond. Irish Academic Press. Sallins. 2014. P. 179-182.

Milano, Kenneth. The Philadelphia Nativist Riots. History Press. Charleston. 2013.

Mitchell, Brian. 1996. The Ordinance Survey Memoirs; a Source for Emigration in the 1830s. History Ireland. Vol. 4 (Issue 4).

Moran, Farrell, Sean. Patrick Pearse and the Politics of Redemption. The Catholic University of America Press. Washington D.C. 1997. P. 71-75.

Mulcrone, Michael. 1993. The World War 1 Censorship of the Irish American Press. History PHD. University of. Washington. P. 19-20.

Mulcrone, Michael. 1993. The World War 1 Censorship of the Irish American Press. History PHD. University of. Washington. P. 62-63.

Mulcrone, Michael. 1993. The World War 1 Censorship of the Irish American Press. History PHD. University of. Washington. P. 119-121.

Mulcrone, Michael. 1993. The World War 1 Censorship of the Irish American Press. History PHD. University of. Washington. P. 298-300.

Mulcrone, Michael. 1993. The World War 1 Censorship of the Irish American Press. History PHD. University of. Washington. P. 317-319.

Murphy, F., Angela. Immigration and Ethnic History Society. Daniel O'Connell and the "American Eagle" in 1845: Diplomacy, Nativism, and the Collapse of America's first Irish Nationalist Movement. Vol. 26, No. 2, 2007. P. 3-26.

Murphy, Paul. World War One and the Origin of Civil Liberties in the United States. W.W Norton & Company. New York. 1979. P. 74-199.

Nelson, Bruce. Irish Nationalists and the Making of the Irish Race. Princeton University Press. Princeton. 2012. P. 16.

Ni Bhroimeil, Una. 2003. Building Irish Identity in America. Four Court Press. Dublin.

Ni Bhroimeil, Una. 2004. The South African War, Empire and the Irish World, 1899-1902. Retrieved from <https://dspace.mic.ul.ie/bitstream/handle/10395/1528/N%C3%AD%20Bhroim%C3%A9il%2c%C3%9A.%282004%29%20%27The%20South%20African%20War%2c%20empire%20and%20the%20Irish%20World%2c%201899-1902%27%20%28Book%20Chapter%29.pdf?sequence=2&isAllowed=y>

Noer, Thomas. Britain, Boer and Yankee. The Kent State University Press. Kent. 1978. P. 69-71.

O'Brien, Gillian. 2015. "A diabolical murder": Clan-na-Gael, Chicago and the murder of Dr. Cronin. History Ireland. Vol. 23 (Issue 3).

O'Brien, Gillian. Blood Runs Green – The Murder That Transfixed Gilded Age Chicago. University of Chicago Press. Chicago. 2015. P. 204-207.

O'Donoghue, David. The Devil's Deal – The IRA, Nazi Germany, and the Double Life of Jim O'Donovan. New Island publishers, Dublin. 2010. P. 112.

O'Grady, Joseph. 1963. Irish-Americans, Woodrow Wilson and Self-Determination. American Catholic Historical Society. Vol. 73, No. 3. P. 159-163.

Osborne, David. 2013. The Terrorist Cell: An Historical and Evolutionary Study of Irish Terrorist Cells, 1881-1896. PHD Thesis. Massey University. <https://mro.massey.ac.nz/bitstream/handle/10179/5761/02_whole.pdf>

Pakenham, Thomas. The Boer War. Avon Books. New York. P. 3-116.

Plowman, Erin, Matthew. 2003. Irish Republicans and the Indi-German Conspiracy of World War 1. New Hibernia Review, Vol. 7, No. 3, P. 80-95.

Pollard, H.B.C. The Secret Societies of Ireland. The Irish Historical Press. Kilkenny, 1998.

Pollard, H.B.C. The Secret Societies of Ireland. The Irish Historical Press. Kilkenny. 1998. P. 57.

Potter, Gary. 2014. Woodrow Wilson, The Great War and Our World Today. Available online <http://catholicism.org/woodrow-wilson-the-great-war-and-our-world-today.html>

Prince, E., Carl. Society for Historians of the Early American Republic. The Great "Riot Year": Jacksonian Democracy and Patterns of Violence in 1834. Vol. 5, No. 1, 1985. P. 1-19.

Purdie, Bob. Politics in the Streets – The Origins of the Civil Rights Movement in Northern Ireland. The Blackstaff Press. Belfast. 1990. P. 121-157.

Rogers, Silas, James; O'Brien, J., Matthew. After the Flood – Irish America, 1945-1960. Irish Academic Press. Dublin. 2009. P. 38-49.

Rowland, Thomas. 1995. The American Catholic Press and the Easter Rebellion. The Catholic Historical Review. Vol. 81, No. 1.

Schmuhl, Robert. Ireland's Exiled Children – America and the Easter Rising. Oxford University Press. Oxford. 2016. P. 119-140.

Sheehy-Skeffington, Francis. Michael Davitt. MacGibbon & Kee. London. 1967. P. 26-81.

Sim, David. American Nineteenth Century History. Filibusters, Fenians, and Contested Neutrality: The Irish Question in U.S. Diplomacy, 1848-1871. Vol. 12, No. 3, September, 2011. P. 265-287.

Smith, M.L.R. Fighting for Ireland – The Military strategy of the Irish Republican Movement. Routledge. London. 1997. P. 63.

Smyth, Ted. 2020. Irish American organizations and the Northern Ireland Conflict in the 1980s: Heightened Political Agency and Ethnic Vitality. Journal of American Ethnic History. Vol. 39, No. 2, P. 51.

Stevens, Kenneth. Border Diplomacy – The Caroline and McLeod Affairs in Anglo-American-Canadian Relations, 1837-1842. University of Alabama Press. Tuscaloosa. 1989.

Stevens, Peter. The Voyage of the Catalpa. Carroll and Graf Publishers. New York. 2002.

Strauss, Charles. 2008. God Save the Boer: Irish American Catholics and the South African War, 1899-1902. U.S. Catholic Historian, Vol. 26. P. 1-9.

Tarpey, Marie. 1971. Joseph McGarrity, Fighter for Irish Freedom. Studia Hibernica. No. 11, P. 164-180.

Tarpey, Veronica, Marie. The Role of Joseph McGarrity in the Struggle for Irish Independence. Arno press. New York. 1976. P. 212-213.

Tarpey, Veronica, Marie. The Role of Joseph McGarrity in the Struggle for Irish Independence. Arno press. New York. 1976. P. 216-266-268.

Tarpey, Veronica, Marie. The Role of Joseph McGarrity in the Struggle for Irish Independence. Arno press. New York. 1976. P. 305.

Tarpey, Veronica, Marie. The Role of Joseph McGarrity in the Struggle for Irish Independence. Arno press. New York. 1976. P. 308-313.

Tarpey, Veronica, Marie. The Role of Joseph McGarrity in the Struggle for Irish Independence. Arno press. New York. 1976. P. 328-330.

Tarpey, Veronica, Marie. The Role of Joseph McGarrity in the Struggle for Irish Independence. Arno press. New York. 1976. P. 331-334.

Tarpey, Veronica, Marie. The Role of Joseph McGarrity in the Struggle for Irish Independence. Arno press. New York. 1976. P. 338.

Tarpey, Veronica, Marie. The Role of Joseph McGarrity in the Struggle for Irish Independence. Arno press. New York. 1976. P. 337-340.

Taylor, Alan. The Civil War of 1812. Alfred A. Knopf. New York. 2010. P. 75-101.

Townsend, Charles. The Republic – The Fight for Irish Independence. Penguin Books. London 2013. P. 6-14.

Townsend, Charles. The Republic – The Fight for Irish Independence. Penguin Books. London. 2013. P. 32-78.

Townsend, Charles. The Republic – The Fight for Irish Independence. Penguin Books. London. 2013. P. 111-221.

Tully, Day, John. Ireland and Irish Americans, 1932-1945. Irish Academic Press. Dublin. 2010. P. 134-40.

Tumulty, Joseph. Woodrow Wilson as I knew him. Doubleday, Page and Company. 1921. P. 75.

Ward, Alan. 1974. Lloyd George and the 1918 Conscription Crisis. The Historical Journal. Cambridge University Press. Vol. 17, March. Available online <https://www.irishtimes.com/culture/heritage/fintan-o-toole-the-1918-election-was-an-amazing-moment-for-ireland-1.3719853> 131.

Whittemore, L.H. The Man Who Ran the Subways. Holt, Reinehart and Winston. New York. 1968. P. 88-90.

Wilk, Gavin. Transatlantic Defiance – The Militant Irish Republican Movement in America, 1923-45. Manchester University Press. Manchester. 2014. P. 13-15.

Wilk, Gavin. Transatlantic Defiance – The Militant Irish Republican Movement in America, 1923-45. Manchester University Press. Manchester. 2014. P. 32.

Wilk, Gavin. Transatlantic Defiance – The Militant Irish Republican Movement in America, 1923-45. Manchester University Press. Manchester. 2014. P. 34-35.

Wilk, Gavin. Transatlantic Defiance – The Militant Irish Republican Movement in America, 1923-45. Manchester University Press. Manchester. 2014. P. 37-70.

Wilk, Gavin. Transatlantic Defiance – The Militant Irish Republican Movement in America, 1923-45. Manchester University Press. Manchester. 2014. P. 124-126.

Wilk, Gavin. Transatlantic Defiance – The Militant Irish Republican Movement in America, 1923-45. Manchester University Press. Manchester. 2014. P. 127-129.

Wilk, Gavin. Transatlantic Defiance – The Militant Irish Republican Movement in America, 1923-45. Manchester University Press. Manchester. 2014. P. 162-166.

Wilk, Gavin. Transatlantic Defiance – The Militant Irish Republican Movement in America, 1923-45. Manchester University Press. Manchester. 2014. P. 174-176.

Wilk, Gavin. Transatlantic Defiance – The Militant Irish Republican Movement in America, 1923-45. Manchester University Press. Manchester. 2014. P. 176-181.

Wilson, David A. United Irishmen, United States. Cornell University. Ithaca. 1998.

Wilson, J., Andrew. Irish America and the Ulster Conflict, 1968-1995. Belfast. The Blackstaff Press. 1995. P. 62-63.

Wilson, J., Andrew. Irish America and the Ulster Conflict, 1968-1995. Belfast. The Blackstaff Press. 1995. P. 194-195.

Wilson, J., Andrew. Irish America and the Ulster Conflict, 1968-1995. Belfast. The Blackstaff Press. 1995. P. 216-217.

Wipf, Jacob. Clan na Gael and the Decline of Irish American Nationalism, 1900-1921. School of Historical, Philosophical and Religious Studies. Arizona State University. Tempe. Available online <https://online.norwich.edu/academic-programs/resources/isolationism-and-us-foreign-policy-after-world-war-i>

Wolfensberger, Don. 2007, March 12. Woodrow Wilson, Congress and Anti-Immigrant Sentiment in America. An Introductory Essay by Don Wolfensberger for the Congress Project Seminar "Congress and the Immigration Dilemma: Is a Solution in Sight?" Woodrow Wilson International Centre for Scholars. Retrieved from <https://www.wilsoncenter.org/sites/default/files/immigration-essay-intro.pdf>

Younger, Calton. Ireland's Civil War. London. 1986. P. 50-420.

Printed in Great Britain
by Amazon